D1071312

K. STANISLAVSKY
1863-1963

MAN AND ACTOR

STANISLAVSKY AND THE WORLD THEATRE

STANISLAVSKY'S LETTERS

PROGRESS PUBLISHERS · MOSCOW

This book is a translation of the Russian centennial collection, *Stanislavsky*, compiled by Sergei Melik-Zakharov and Shoel Bogatyrev (Iskustvo Publishers, Moscow, 1963), and of materials compiled by Nikolai Solntsev.

TRANSLATED FROM THE RUSSIAN BY
VIC SCHNEIERSON

DESIGNED BY
I. FOMINA

CONTENTS

STANISLAVSKY'S LETTERS

INTRODUCTION

A great man whose creative genius has enriched mankind for centuries to come was born a hundred years ago, January 17, 1863.

I maintain that an appreciation of Konstantin Stanislavsky solely as a man of the theatre would be tantamount to a lack of appreciation of his prodigious accomplishments in provinces other than the stage. It is not my intention, in this introduction, to dwell upon the substance of his teaching, but I will not hesitate to say that to reduce it to mere stage technique is to rob it of its significance. Stanislavsky's teaching cannot be properly understood if divorced from his philosophy of life, his world outlook and his sense of the poetic.

Some day scholars will probably put their finger on the deep-going scientific sense in his discoveries. But today we speak of him – such as we remember him – as of a great actor and leader. He was, indeed, a peerless actor, a peerless stage director, and a great maker of actors.

I had the good fortune of associating with him twelve years long at the Moscow Art Theatre. I met him first when I was cast in his revival of Griboyedov's *Wit Works Woe.* He rehearsed me for the part of Chatsky in a production he had staged earlier, and in which he himself played Famusov. Yet, frequently, the director and instructor in him, the teacher who watched his pupil with an exacting and penetrating eye, emerged from beneath the elaborate Famusov make-up. The *Wit Works Woe* experience was followed by a wonderful period: Stanislavsky set to work on a new production, *Le Mariage de Figaro.*

To Alexander Golovin,* the scene painter he had invited to design the sets, Stanislavsky said he should "show Spain as

* *Alexander Golovin* (1863-1930) – prominent Soviet scene painter. People's Artiste of the R.S.F.S.R.

a Frenchman sees it". This startling instruction reveals much of Stanislavsky's idea of realistic art. It reveals how far removed he was from naturalism, from mere photography of the environment.

Stanislavsky created new worlds for every one of his productions, worlds with their own rules, their own points of view, their own human relationships. But all of them were his own, Stanislavsky's worlds, worlds that reaffirmed his deep faith in the human race, in its immense creative powers that would some day better the troublesome state of affairs on earth.

Stanislavsky was a resourceful man. Yet he made but one prime demand in his teaching, his messages to the actor, stage director and scene designer: no matter what the circumstances, be yourself!

Golovin, too, who was to "show Spain as a Frenchman sees it", was to be himself, to be Man and Artist in the finest sense of these two words.

Stanislavsky did not treat stagecraft in terms of mere performing. For him stagecraft was creation. This should be borne home most emphatically, because it would go against the Stanislavsky spirit if we accepted his creative recommendations, his so-called system, simply as an elementary guide to craftsmanship. He did not develop his system to entrammel the actor with rules of histrionic conduct, with "do's" and "dont's" of stage behaviour. He meant his system to mould, augment and liberate man's creative powers, to make man their master.

I say this, because all too often Konstantin Stanislavsky and his conception of theatrical emotion are understood too directly, or altogether wrongly. Has not Stanislavsky said time and again that emotion by itself did not make art?

I see an actress on the stage. She weeps. Her feelings are indubitably sincere. I see it clearly. But I am not moved. Stanislavsky used to say the actor should generate "five minutes of genuine temperament and distribute it evenly over the part". What he meant were theatrical emotions, emotions distinct somehow from the real emotions of life. Stanislavsky's theatrical emotions materialise from the actor's living his part on the boards, and living a part is, above all, thinking, behaving, speaking and doing as if (oh, that magic "as if"!) the actions of the play were unfolding here and now, as if all the conflicts, the encounters with people and circumstances, with nature and history, were occurring for the first time. It is here and now that the character appraises, thinks and does. If the actor accomplishes this "here and now", he will find that he is not alone, that the audience is with him, that the audience, too, is living the part, that the emotions generated by the events and twists of the play seize the audience as they do himself, the actor.

What Stanislavsky was after was theatrical impersonation. Be yourself in every part you play, he pleaded, but be different in every part. Your environment is different, your life story is different, and, hence, your mentality, your sense of values and your conduct. What he implied was not an abstract mentality, but a specific one, an individual mentality, the mentality of the character you play, fashioned by his background, his past, by what he, Stanislavsky, usually referred to as the "yesterday". This "yesterday" is the character's time, his epoch, his environment, his social relationships and associations. It is the story of his life, his tastes, interests and inclinations, his culture, his habits, or, to put it briefly, all the effects and trappings that he brings with him to the stage.

All too often it is simply an actor wearing the outward shell of his part that comes on the stage from the wings. He wears a fake moustache or beard, and someone's suit, he affects someone's voice and someone's carefully rehearsed gestures. He adopts another man's behaviour, another man's character and habits, but does not transform himself into that other man.

Here is how Stanislavsky described it. Picture to yourself, he said, that you have met two old friends. One of them has grown older, is carelessly dressed, has grown a beard and put on eye-glasses. His appearance has changed so much that you do not recognise him. The other does not seem to have changed at all. At most, he has grown a bit older. But when the first, the bearded one, opens his mouth to speak, you espy the same old friend, all his old habits, tastes and interests, the same man you knew for years. You get the impression that time has stopped its march. The clock seems to have turned back. You realise that the man has not changed in the least. His changed appearance, his living "make-up", is no more than a meaningless shell.

Then you speak to the other old friend, the one whose appearance has not changed. As you speak to him, you realise with a jolt that he is no longer the same, that he is a stranger, that he has drifted away, that his outlook has changed, that something new and different governs his life.

This applies equally to the stage. You see the actor make his appearance before the footlights and do not recognise him at first. He looks a total stranger. But in a flash you are disappointed: he is an actor you know, a man with the same old uninspiring world, the same uninspiring manner of speaking, without a background, devoid of genuine emotions, a blank, a fraud, but playing a different role.

Then another actor comes on the stage. You know him at once – by his features, his voice, his idiosyncrasies. He looks the same. He is the same, but at once so different! As the play proceeds, he startles you with novel qualities and facets. You hurry to his dressing-room between the acts and see the man you knew before the curtain rose – the same, but at once so different, different to the marrow of his bones. He is a man with a different biography, with different inclinations, interests, thoughts and a different mentality.

To achieve this artistic effect, the actor must cultivate his part within himself. To make his point, Stanislavsky liked to compare the inception and development of an artificial flower with that of a real one. When a craftsman patterns his flower, he cuts out its petals, attaches them to the calyx, and fits the calyx on a stem. Yet his flower is dead. The life of a real flower does not begin with the petals, not with the "result". The "result", or blossom, develops in the process of maturation, and the first grain (that is probably where Stanislavsky got his expression, "the grain of the role") has no external points of resemblance to the blossom-to-be. Neither do the first sprouts hold any resemblance to the flower, not even the bud. It is not until the blossom gets sufficient sun and moisture, not until it develops gradually, naturally and organically that it becomes a flower.

It is for this organic development of a part that Stanislavsky appealed to us. I write "appealed" instead of "taught" quite deliberately. Art is not "taught". One can learn oneself, one can learn life. One can learn the processes that shape it, and hence shape one's creative endeavours, because the two are homogeneous.

The greatness of Stanislavsky's system lies in his finding the connection between the organic creative process and the organic process of life in the biography of the character. Yet so many wrong and harmful things are done in this sphere. Must one really invent a biography for one's character on the strength of some general conclusions or, worse still, without taxing one's imagination about the director's or dramatist's intentions? That is not so. One need not invent a kind of literary biography for one's character, for more likely than not it will have no relation to what one, the actor, is going to play. It would be much like an extra sum done by a hard-trying pupil after lessons – a biography made up after rehearsals. At subsequent rehearsals the text, or lines, would remain inanimate and strange.

To play a part well, according to Stanislavsky, is to make every line of it your own. Once you accomplish this, you will find yourself performing every action in a certain way and in no other, performing it of necessity to suit the circumstances, and, likewise, speaking of necessity in a certain way and in no other. Stanislavsky called that "justifying the role", that is, making every element of it a necessity.

He also called it "penetrating a role". Very aptly, too, for nothing could define the creative work done on a part by the actor more clearly. When speaking of the logic of behaviour, the logic of a character's mentality, the logic of his emotions, I mean just this "penetrated" creative logic, not frigid logic detached from the imagination, not logic built on a deliberate use of literary experience.

It is the whole of the actor that participates in the theatrical imagination. It is not only his brain that does the imagining. His body imagines as well. It transforms itself, as it were, as it enters a part creatively. It is not only the actor's vocal apparatus that relates the biography of a character, but the whole of him. The actor's stage behaviour, his bearing, should be organic in that very sense.

Many basic elements of Stanislavsky's creative method may appear unclear at the first reading. Stanislavsky himself said his method could not be grasped but in the act of practising. "In our trade," he used to say, "to understand means to know how."

You may learn to lift weights from a written instruction. It will tell you how far you must spread your feet, how you must lift the bar at a specific instant, how you must rest it on your chest, pause, then push it above your head. But you will never lift the bar until you start training, develop your muscles and grasp the substance of the prescribed movements through practice, until you obtain the organic appreciation that a certain set of movements is essential for it. Conversely, it is by lifting weights and mastering the requisite movements that you will at once develop your strength.

The same is true of the exercises prescribed by Stanislavsky. I might add that the very process of rehearsing is a kind of intermittent, continuously resumed exercise. The actor who labours to master the technique of penetrating his part gains strength. He magnifies his artistic scope by his enthusiastic concentration on the creative process, for, as Stanislavsky observed, "there is no true creation without enthusiastic concentration".

My references are to the actor, but no actor ever exists alone on the stage, just as no man ever exists in solitude. He is one of a multitude, the multitude that surrounds him. Hence, to grasp one's part, or one's place in life, one must know and understand life, know and understand one's place in that multitude.

The theatre, said Stanislavsky, is collective creation. Whenever a theatre is merely a group of individuals, each preoccupied with himself, each thinking the actor's art is an individual process of creation – whenever a theatre is no more than a collection of individuals – the most precious, most fascinating, most enthralling element of theatrical art will escape it. It will never produce integral collective art, hence no "atmosphere", as we say, which weaves the very music, the poetry of the theatre, the "something" that binds all the members of a company, creating the vibrant, life-giving climate for the play to develop in.

Stanislavsky's ethics, his uncompromising demand for rigorous discipline prompted by the wish of controlling every element of a performance, derive from his belief that the creative atmosphere of the rehearsals, an atmosphere of contagious enthusiasm, mutual respect and supreme dedication, the spiritual and creative abandonment of every member of the cast, the purity of human relations, are all essential for the consummation of high-minded art.

It is in the context of this consummate art that we should approach Stanislavsky's injunction to be yourself. To be yourself does not imply placing yourself before all else. It does not imply doing everything by yourself, or for yourself. Egoism and self-admiration are not at all signs of true existence. Generosity of spirit, kindness, sincerity, trust, genuinely noble conduct, selfless devotion – those, said Stanislavsky, are the attributes of a true actor, the conditions that help to put the conflict between the whole and the individual out of the way.

Stanislavsky's ethics are often misinterpreted. Many think him an old fogey and fanatic. But that is untrue. He was never a bigot, never a narrow-minded scholastic and ascetic. He preached a pagan love of life. He relished the sun, he was avid in whatever he did, he loved freedom, he loved fun, and said:

"Art is never forced. You can't order art about."

If he was ever incensed or irritated by people whose indifference interfered with the creative process (were it but indifference!), this was because he cherished it, because he guarded it from dissolution. He always said it was infinitely harder to create than to destroy. And he himself was a great creator before all else, moved by faith in the infinity of human ability, the endlessness of man's creative powers.

That was the source of his aversion to evil, enmity, egoism and injustice. That was why he loathed the law of the jungle, the philosophy of "man is to man a wolf".

"No," his heart cried out, "man is to man a brother! All people are people first; irrespective of the colour of their skin, they feel grief and joy equally."

To him genuine, profoundly human art transcended geographical and political boundaries. It erased them. He used to say that art proffered humankind the olive branch of peace, and repeated after Pushkin, the great Russian poet, that genius and evil were incompatible.

To sum up, Man, as defined by Stanislavsky, is his elaborate inner world outwardly expressed by the organic unity of the mental and physical. Man is a logic of actions, thoughts and desires, of a distinctly personal perception of reality.

Developing continuously through the collisions of his individual logic and the surrounding reality, as seen by the dramatist and director, man's inner world is subject to the laws governing the genre and the style.

"Clever", "angry", "suspicious", or "good" even, are general, assumed, unprecise definitions productive of *clichés,* of no more than approximate depictions. All too often they stand in for the one and only unrepeatable characteristic which is far too big to fit into them.

Just as in life, it is the complex and unusual that creates interest on the stage. And Stanislavsky the mentor led the actor unfailingly along the most entrancing, difficult path, the unique, subordinating the solution of every individual part to the general – the system of interconnections defining the philosophical and poetical substance of the play.

There is the example of Vakhtangov. He was that kind of man – unrepeatable, unique, seemingly at odds with Stanislavsky's practices, yet always genuinely and truly his pupil (because those who seize unimaginatively upon Stanislavsky's past really betray him). From this standpoint, Meyerhold, and Bertolt Brecht even, are inconceivable without the influence exercised on them by Stanislavsky.

It is tragically too little, perhaps tragically inaccurate, what I have said here about Konstantin Stanislavsky. But I hope that whatever I have said will show that for Stanislavsky the theatre was something greater than a spectacle, that it was an immense, inspired force, strong enough to transform reality.

That is what a stage director should be – always himself, in all plays, no matter how different in genre and style, in all his searching for the truths and regularities, the forms and the music implicit in the play and the dramatic genre, and in the style.

To be sure, in his struggle for the revival of art, Stanislavsky really struggled for the revival of mankind. The theatre was to him no more than a battlefield. He regarded his life's work as part of the great battle in behalf of light, against darkness, waged before him by the great Russian writers and by all those artists of the Universe who believed in the inexhaustible capacity of the human spirit.

This is why his name is inscribed today in the history of Russian culture, Soviet culture, world culture, beside those of Pushkin, Gogol, Dostoyevsky, Tolstoi, Chekhov and Gorky. For as their immediate successor in the grand struggle for humanism, he took from them their firm belief that the theatre is a potent enough force to transform life.

Stanislavsky believed, and I say so not simply on the strength of his printed statements, for I heard him speak it – Stanislavsky believed that some day mankind would forget the meaning of the word "war". He was convinced that the law of the jungle, the law of rivalry and competition that roused beastly instincts, would give place in human relations to the lofty law of goodness and beauty. Many people today will think these things to be axioms, and axioms that may to some, indeed, appear unsophisticated and provincial. But in Stanislavsky's mind they burned brightly, fanned by inextinguishable conviction, and it is this conviction which he willed as his prime gift to all his disciples.

What good is there in the petty and vainglorious art of posing and play-acting if it does not yield the genuine pleasure of high-minded perception?

You may have noticed that I spell Man with a capital letter, for that is how the word sounded when Stanislavsky spoke it.

Art and the theatre are a service to the people. This is what propelled Stanislavsky, for he was deeply convinced in their truth, in their right to exist. He wanted them to be greater today than they were the day before, and greater tomorrow than they were today.

Those were not mere words. Not for Stanislavsky. They were the greatness of the human spirit in the man himself.

"Life of the human spirit" is how Stanislavsky described the object and purpose of his art, an art he never viewed as a personal possession.

Stanislavsky had an amazingly accurate sense of time and succession, a sense of vital, spiritual and historical connection with his forerunners. He looked back with a prophetic eye on mankind's past, and probed its future. Sober, dependable, earthly, he was capable of the loftiest flights of thought. He upheld the motive power of the creative process and the great power art wielded over humans. He upheld the right and duty of art to bring people together by the laws of their physical and spiritual beauty.

"Everything must be beautiful in a man – his face, his clothes, his soul and his mind."* This line from Chekhov, spoken by Astrov, Stanislavsky's most inspired role, expresses one of the most essential features of Stanislavsky himself, his love of freedom and goodness to people. Art is the greatest enemy of evil, crime, violence and, hence, the greatest

* Anton Chekhov, *Uncle Vanya,* Act II.

enemy of war. It is therefore only natural that mankind celebrates Stanislavsky's 100th birthday with an accent on Stanislavsky's yearning for world peace.

I want to say over and over again that Stanislavsky was not a dreamer. He had a keen and sensitive perception of the hardships of daily life, which degrade the soul and whittle away faith. He knew the depressing force of popular grief, poverty, human weakness, of the inexorable doom that marked some people, the unhealing wounds of mortal partings. He was an ordinary, very human human being. He knew that all men are brothers and that nothing human is foreign to man. But he believed! And it is in the name of his belief, his faith, that we have "no now" and are always on the move "from yesterday to tomorrow", that each one of us is destined to impart direction to this movement – it is in the name of this faith of his that his friends, men and women who think as he did, have been assembled here in this book.

See how many they are, how different they are, how seemingly inimical, but united today by his genius, the genius of the great Stanislavsky!

Yuri Zavadsky

People's Artiste of the U.S.S.R.

MAN AND ACTOR

K. S. Stanislavsky and Maxim Gorky backstage at the Moscow Art Theatre after the first showing of *Armoured Train 14-69* by V. Ivanov, 1928

MAXIM GORKY

I admire you. You are a prodigy – yes, but your heart is a mirror! How deftly you snatch from life its smiles, the sad and kind smiles of its stern face!...

From a letter to Konstantin Stanislavsky
Late December 1900-early January 1901

Your "observations" are very valuable to me! I swear it! You are a discerning artist in that province as well. Some day, when I come to Moscow, I'll steal a day of your time just to talk to you. There is a surfeit of something stable, something so full of love in your heart. I adore people who love life! I say this often.

Thank you for your "observations". If it does not discommode you, keep noting them down, will you? I shall be sincerely grateful for them...

From a letter to Stanislavsky
*and Maria Lilina**
Late 1901-early 1902

I'd like to see you, great rebel, to speak to you, to pass on a few ideas – to stoke some combustibles into your flaming heart, whose fire it has always been my pleasure to admire, and which I shall always admire. I shall admire it always, to my dying day, no matter what you happen to do, my dear sir!

From a letter to Stanislavsky
Late 1910

Very happy to have seen you, and deeply grateful that you have introduced me to the workings of your tireless and beautiful mind. I wish you health and vigour from the bottom of my heart, and believe deeply that your excellent undertakings will be valuable...

From a letter to Stanislavsky
March 14-17 1911

The bearers of this letter represent a group of workers who want to found in Moscow their own, workers' theatre... I know, dear Konstantin Sergeyevich, that, a good Russian, you are sure to be elated over this longing of the masses for art, I know that you have striven to arouse this longing.

Here it is – roused and assuming forms of its own. I am sure you will not refuse to help it materialise.

No other man, I am sure, could benefit it more than you, and none is more able to give it a firmer foundation. So I beg you to devote some of your attention, your heart and intelligence, to this worthy cause...

From a letter to Stanislavsky
1912

* *Maria Lilina* (1866-1943) – distinguished Art Theatre actress, People's Artiste of the R.S.F.S.R., Stanislavsky's wife.

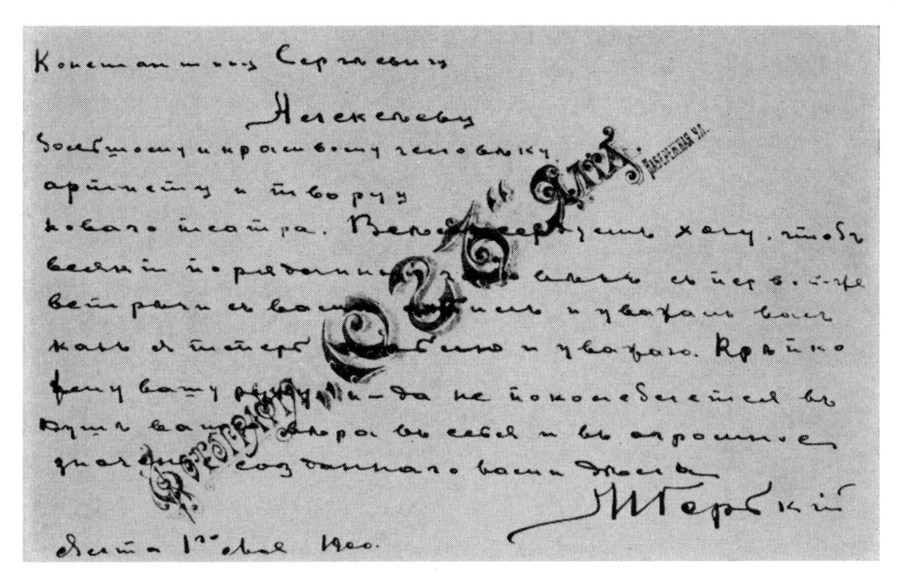

To Konstantin Sergeyevich Alexeyev, a big and beautiful creature, artist and creator of the new theatre. I wish with all my heart that the moment he meets you every decent person should love and respect you as I now love and respect you. I shake your hand firmly, and may your faith in yourself and the immense importance of what you are doing never falter.

Maxim Gorky

Yalta, May 1, 1900

Dear Konstantin Sergeyevich, my meeting you has left a clear, resonant and reassuring impression. When I see people like you, my faith in my country's future grows stronger, and my love for it greater. Do not take this as a compliment. Need I make compliments to you? I know you have more than enough of them.

I tenderly love your beautiful and living soul . . .

Keep well, dear man, be happy and do your good work, so useful to all.

You in Russia, and we here, will all live and work with joy and love for our country, albeit along different paths and in different ways. If anyone of us errs, we shall censure each other, but will keep our respect. Isn't that so?

...Keep well! Usually people write: Cheer up, have faith in life and in man's creative powers. But you do not need to be told that, and that is so good, so gratifying.

Shaking your hand sincerely, smiling joyfully from ear to ear...

From a letter to Stanislavsky
April 1911

Dear Konstantin Sergeyevich,

You are a recognised and great reformer of theatrical art.

You and Nemirovich-Danchenko have created a model theatre, one of the biggest achievements of Russian artistic culture. The edifying influence of your theatre is evident and recognised throughout the world. That is an immense and incontestable service. It is known to everybody, and perhaps I should not have mentioned it.

But there is something in your activities, something concealed backstage, which I prize most highly, and admire: how sensitive and great a man you are in discovering talent, and how skilful a diamond cutter you are tending and training it!

You have built up a prodigious army of amazingly gifted performers. Many of them, who follow your trail, have also become teachers of stagecraft. They have trained, and keep on training, fresh groups of excellent performers. That is a part of your work, whose cultural impact does not seem to have as yet been fully appraised. And if you need the gratitude of the Soviet Union, it should be conferred upon you most of all for this, your unseen and, of course, most difficult work of training the world's best masters of theatrical art. A magnificent and subtle actor, you have proved once more by this work how rich and inexhaustible is the creative energy of our country.

In one of my articles I described the Soviet land as happy. A correspondent remarked at once that this must have been a "slip of the pen". No, it was not. Happiness has its source in hatred for unhappiness, in a physiological aversion to all things that warp and cripple human beings, in an intrinsic and organic rejection of all that complains, groans, and yearns

K. S. Stanislavsky, A. M. Gorky and M. P. Lilina

for a petty kind of well-being, battered more and more by the hurricanes of history.

Konstantin Sergeyevich, we live in a happy land, where all conditions are being rapidly furnished for material and spiritual enrichment, for the free development of the powers, abilities and talents of its people.

Only those who, poor in spirit, see nothing but our growing pains and are ready to sell their souls for a humble philistine welfare, do not feel happy to live and work in this land.

Dear Konstantin Sergeyevich, you have done amazingly much, and will still do much in your field for the happiness of our people, the growth of its spiritual beauty and strength. I take off my hat to you most respectfully, my beauty of a man, great actor and prodigious worker, the mentor of actors.

I embrace you heartily,

M. Gorky

Letter to Stanislavsky on his 70th birthday, January 10, 1933

Konstantin Stanislavsky and Anatoly Lunacharsky in Uzkoye Sanatorium near Moscow. 1931

ANATOLY LUNACHARSKY

Stanislavsky, the Theatre and the Revolution

Whenever I spoke with Stanislavsky, it gave me pleasure to look at his calm, confident, understanding face, illumined by an inner light, and from time to time by a seemingly embarrassed smile. I liked looking at the figure of this man, which showed his substance with such rare clarity. Indeed, no matter where Stanislavsky entered, be it a crowded gathering in, say, a hall where few people knew him, he at once attracted everybody's attention, and questions were asked who that magnificent silver-haired old man might be.

Stanislavsky's appearance accorded with his own principle – from the inner to the outer. Externally, Stanislavsky was in most profound harmony with the excellent fabric of his consciousness and mentality.

I see him smiling his somewhat embarrassed smile, saying these momentous words:

"Anatoly Vasilyevich, I am not in the least at odds with the Revolution. I realise perfectly that it contains much of the sacred and deep. I feel excellently what lofty ideas and tense emotions it induces. But what we are afraid of is that this music of the new world will take a long time finding expression in the artistic word, in artistic dramaturgy. At least, we have seen nothing of the sort so far, and if we, the theatre, are furnished with imperfect, tongue-tied, dry and artificial material, then, no matter how well it may be tied up with the lofty ideas of the Revolution, we shall be unable to use it and impart to the theatre the ring it should have: we shall be unable as a theatre, as artists, to serve the Revolution, to be its mouthpiece, and shall debase ourselves, our art, because musicians who have had a certain schooling, who have achieved a high degree of musical culture, cannot be made to play school music, immature and lifeless. Pushkin described the way *Freischütz* may be performed by timid schoolgirls, but that, I think, is only half the trouble. It would be a real pity if masters had to perform, not *Freischütz,* but semi-literate attempts at reflecting most important living developments."

To be sure, one cannot reproduce a passage spoken ten years earlier with complete fidelity. But I vouch for the complete fidelity of its purport, and for most of the expressions I have here quoted.

I sensed the deep-felt sincerity of this great artist. I sensed his confusion: suppose he rejected the revolutionary repertoire – then truly still very childish – and would be told his magnificent theatre, his excellent instrument, built by him with so much ardour, was useless if it could not live up to its purpose after the Revolution, after a new world had come into being and begun to develop, that it could only turn the disks of the past like an old, albeit splendid, barrel-organ. Suppose he compromised and said, "Let's have what you've written, we'll try to play it." What would come of it? The imperfect play would ring false to everybody, and the theatre would be the most likely to be blamed for it. People would say that the old hands, the Mohicans of a receding culture, were unable, or still worse, perhaps, unwilling to give the proper ring to the new ideas. His old friends – and this meant

Stanislavsky in 1916

a great deal to Stanislavsky – those people of highly refined demands and a deeply artistic conscience, would say: what's happened to the Art Theatre? What it is doing now is not real art.

* * *

Vikenty Veresayev* read us his play. This, too, was a long time ago. The play was neither good nor bad, but in any case, it was written with the degree of skill you would expect in an author of repute, a genuine man of letters. The reading was followed by a discussion. Stanislavsky was among the speakers. Big, monumental even, with his silver-streaked head of a sage and his embarrassed smile – a smile that did not at all indicate timidity or indecision and was rather the expression of the politeness of a giant speaking to his fellow-men – he said:

"What I like, Vikenty Vikentyevich, is that your play is alive, that the people in it are alive, and that what they say is alive too. Acting on very excellent motives, an author may sometimes wish to make a good point. Important ideas infest his mind, and in the final analysis he compounds a kind of laboratory-made chemical, an apoponax. Some perfumes, you know, smell of live flowers – lilac, or acacia. But there is also this apoponax. I have no idea what that means. But I don't like its smell."

When Stanislavsky was saying this he probably, most certainly even, did not realise how close he came to Marx's ideas of the theatre. For it was Marx, and Engels too, in their well-known letters to Lassalle about his play, who censured none other than Schiller (let us never forget that great playwright) for "apoponaxing", to use Stanislavsky's expression. They compared him to Shakespeare, since Shakespeare's fabric is alive throughout, and this vitality, this most profound dialectical truthfulness of Shakespeare's plays seemed to them an articulate and faithful reflection of class relations in the period concerned, a faithful expression by individual characters of the class substance.

Shakespeare did not know these terms. He was not interested in this side of things. But since he was an artist and a dialectician, since he

* *Vikenty Veresayev* (1867-1945) – well-known Soviet author.

took from life and turned what he took into something still more alive than life itself, he laid his paints on thickly, he produced dramaturgy which Marx and Engels appreciated and declared a model for the theatre of the future.

But speaking of the theatre of the future, uncertain that a dramaturgy entirely satisfactory would arise in Germany, Engels said it should contain the Shakespearean wealth of colour, coupled with a deeply scientific analysis of the social phenomena it undertook to depict. Engels wanted the playwright to be a Marxist, a revolutionary, but at once an artist. The one does not have to interfere with the other. On the contrary, it should on all accounts help the other in really normal conditions. But these normal conditions arise when the proletarian revolution has won politically, and even then they do not come at once, but gradually, as we have seen very well by our own example.

* * *

What was Stanislavsky after in his theatre, the very spirit of which he shaped so gradually, just as his system evolved gradually, or, more precisely, what was his conception of the theatre, of its substance and its purposes?

To be sure, Stanislavsky's theatre was a theatre of hard times. One would think that a theatre of hard times should itself be insipid and pale, unable to rise above the decades that anteceded and followed these hard times.

However, that is not always so. And it was not so in Stanislavsky's case.

The times before the end of the 1880s were glorious times for Russian literature. That is not to be gainsaid, because from the forties to the end of the eighties the Left wing – the revolutionary, *narodnik,* sacrificial and militant advocates of Russia's development along the American path, to use Lenin's phrase – was developing powerfully, though painfully.

The existence of this wing strongly affected the sentiments of the intelligentsia, and through it, through the educated public, it affected literature, all the arts, and the theatre. In the final analysis, it was in just this atmosphere that the people of the theatre developed, such as Shchepkin, Mochalov,

Sadovsky and his great company, etc.* True, for reasons of censorship, the theatre reflected the revolutionary ferment less than literature did, but the impelling motive for art as a whole, in the general, the main, was to serve the people, or, to use the terminology of the times, to serve one's ideas.

The defeat of the *narodnik* revolution in the eighties and, coupled with it, the Prussian way of Russia's growth, created new conditions for the arts, induced by the powerful development of capitalism, which I have just called hard times.

The *narodnik* movement spent itself on trifles, on the preaching of little deeds. It drifted towards the startling emergence of Tolstoism, and frequently to complete and utter pessimism. It was practically impossible to serve one's ideals. To harbour them without serving, was shameful. To abandon them was painful and also shameful.

In the meantime, an immense market appeared for the intelligentsia. Capitalists of the European type, and the wealthy intelligentsia they had created, clamoured for the refined Western arts in all their forms and varieties. Characters with a penchant for creative work saw a substantial market open to them. The aesthetic demand for a formal order increased considerably. But what could the content of this new art be like? The reader may think it would extol capitalism as such, or proclaim the need to turn coat, to play up to the idols of autocracy and similar monstrous ideas?

No, a closer examination of the art of the nineties, and of the turn of the century, reveals little or none of these elements.

Very soon a new and decisive revolution, not a *narodnik* revolution any more, but a proletarian one, began to stir on the Left wing, and a unique kind of formalism was proclaimed on the Right. It was not a formalism of *pure* form. In the case of the finest people of the time it was a harrowing, often a self-sacrificing search. Life, in effect, was bleak. There were no ethical luminaries of any kind. And the intelligentsia, which had only recently lived so intensive an ideological life, went to great pains to fill

* *Mikhail Shchepkin* (1788-1863), *Pavel Mochalov* (1800-1848), *Prov Sadovsky* (1818-1872) – famous Russian actors.

this life with a new content. In response to the new market demand, it created many vivid, sublime, vibrant works, learning easily, often with a touch of genius, from the West-European bourgeois culture, brilliantly decadent at the time. It also tried to overhaul its former ideals, replacing the day of retribution and truth with a metaphysical day in other worlds, somewhere higher up, above the grey skies of reality. The search for beauty as such, the very conception and idea of "beauty", were understood to be expiatory, a great departure from the thraldom of the little things of life.

Russian decadence, for example, was unquestionably a special type of romanticism, and from that point of view, as Plekhanov noted rightly, it testified to the conflict between artist and reality, but it was a conflict that was rather passive than revolutionary, agonising on the one hand, and one that found consolation, on the other – a very gilded, a honeyed consolation – precisely in the world of beauty.

The most sparkling materialisation of that search, its most valuable progeny, was the Art Theatre. And in the realm of theatrical art Konstantin Stanislavsky, scion of a capitalist family who escaped to the camp of the intellectuals, was the greatest representative of that period in the development of the intelligentsia.

Just one truth reigns over all his searching, over his prescience, over his mature appreciation of the purpose of the theatre. It is that art is sacred, the theatre a high-minded institution, and artistic creation a labour of love and sacrifice.

The bleaker the environment, and the more the darkness of capitalist growth was accentuated at the outset of the new social movement, so to speak, by the shudders of the foetus in the womb of this society, the more desperately the most discerning people, those, however, to whom the paths of revolution were ruled out, clung to just these aesthetic and ethical protests against reality.

What formal excellence and true-to-lifeness does Stanislavsky exact of a play for it to be produced by the Art Theatre?

Let us take a closer look at that.

* * *

Was Stanislavsky a realist? Did he really want his theatre to be *true to life,* in terms of an extraordinary resemblance to reality?

Yes, in a way this was so. Striving to reflect life realistically, he demanded the reproduction of various details and made an unusually sensitive and intense effort to re-create reality as it is. But he noticed very soon – he could not help noticing it with a companion like Anton Chekhov – that life as a whole cannot be reproduced in a novel, or drama, or the theatre. It is reproduced in a manner described by Treplev in *The Sea-Gull* in his reference to Trigorin: "He makes the neck of a bottle on the dam glisten in the moonlight, and all of the moon-lit night arises before you."

This is why Stanislavsky soon abandoned realism of the Meiningen type to adopt an unusually subtle impressionism which, so to speak, conveyed the very essence, the aroma of life in the aspect which the production sought to catch.

But did Stanislavsky stop there? No. Not only did he produce historical plays (there is no break with realism in this field as yet); he also produced symbolical plays, such as Henrik Ibsen's and the later Gerhart Hauptmann's (*Lonely Lives*), in which, quite beyond question, life was very strongly and thoroughly accentuated from the standpoint of definitive ideas. He went even further. He produced Maurice Maeterlinck's tales, and the same Hauptmann's *Sunken Bell,* that is, plays which were obviously fantastic.

To sum up, the *true-to-lifeness* sought by Stanislavsky did not at all boil down to an immediate and direct likeness of life. It seems to me that Stanislavsky's demands on the playwright are best defined thus: Konstantin Sergeyevich required that the literary material offered to his theatre should be *significant and expressive.*

Once the dramatic material was in itself significant and once it was artistically expressive in the sense that its literary expressiveness could easily be coupled with theatrical expressiveness, Stanislavsky was prepared to place his delightful instrument at its service.

This is how Stanislavsky reasoned or felt: the ultimate purpose of art is to rouse the general public (the popular theatre) by a psychological medium, the medium of many many nights, to a state of lofty emotion, a fruitful emotion that makes the heart more exacting, strong, sensitive, genuinely human. This meant that Stanislavsky knew, or at least felt, how this public should be relieved of the disgusts of their every-day existence, the existence that Chekhov, a close companion of Stanislavsky's, ridiculed so caustically.

It took a special kind of theatrical art to achieve this purpose. The theatre-goer had to feel how deeply emotion gripped the company, how sincere the company was in whatever it did. Hence the most profound *seriousness* of art, hence the devotion to its every detail, hence the synthesis of all details in an over-all picture – bringing it home to the spectator that the theatre is not merely entertaining, but also edifying in the finest sense of that word. Education is all too often associated with sickeningly dull lecturing, which is quite useless, especially at the theatre. But genuine education (which is always at once self-education), what Goethe called "Bildung", is a source of deep pleasure. It is a pleasure that does not dissipate our strength, but rather concentrates it and gives it purpose.

* * *

But does all this exempt Stanislavsky and his theatre from the rebuke that his theatre was eclectic? I will be told that I defended it against the charge of hidebound realism, of attachment to "veterans" and "idols", but that by so doing I imputed eclecticism. Well, the theatre was incontestably eclectic.

It produced Russian and foreign classics. An immense place in it was devoted to Chekhov. It relished playing Gorky. It played historical and fantastic plays. Essentially, it gave new fabric to each production. Stanislavsky seemed to say to the dramatists of all times, not only his own – bring me those big plays of yours, your sadness and your joy, the images you moulded from painstaking observation; bring them here in the systems, the plays, you thought best suited to express your experience. My theatre and I will see to it that the fire you have put into your work will really illumine and warm the minds and hearts of hundreds of thousands of people, perhaps of millions. We shall find the right theatrical body for your literary text. We, the creators of this body, shall be very flexible. We shall ponder what you give, we shall do what you bid, we shall not impose anything of our own. Since we have found your play deserving to be presented on the boards of our theatre, we shall present it with utmost artistic integrity. It will be our task to make the production convey with the greatest vigour of theatrical expression in its scenes, movements, intonations and rhythms, the treasured message of your artistic work.

Strictly speaking, it is eclecticism that produced Stanislavsky's superlative orchestra. Which orchestra are we going to value more highly? The one whose conductor says: I play everything up to and including Brahms, for everything after Brahms is trash, or the one whose conductor says: we play nothing but our national music; or who says something just as warped, or yet the one whose conductor says – my orchestra does not play bad music, but we shall submit all music of a certain level of conception and perfection of form, whatever this conception and form may be, to the judgement of our hearers as it should be submitted in the voice appropriate to its character.

It is just that sort of unique, flexible orchestra, just that sort of artistically translucent orchestra, the sort of orchestra that is not dominated by the score, that conveys its true message, its true characteristic existence, that we cherish most.

It was that sort of orchestra that Stanislavsky created in his theatre.

* * *

This was a great service. It lay in the fact that Stanislavsky availed himself of the hard times to create a theatre that was, I daresay, the loudest and most beautiful voice heard in those times. His service lay in the fact that he made this voice not only forceful and beautiful, but that he endowed it with an infinite range of modulations, that he made it flexible enough to express the social conceptions that reached its magnificent membrane through the dramatists.

In Stanislavsky's case, eclecticism was of help. It enabled him to employ his instrument in a great variety of ways. But let us be frank; the Art Theatre, and the theatrical art of Stanislavsky and of the splendid performers he had raised were not old wineskins, and were not old wineskins to us either. They were *new wineskins,* but there was no *new wine* to pour into them. Classics will always be classics. No Shakespeare can address the new times as their own son could address them.

What about the moderns?

Of the new dramatists associated with the Art Theatre we can single out Chekhov and Gorky. But Chekhov was himself a writer of the hard times. He, too, was one of those great progenies of the hard times who cursed them, and demonstrated the frightening leer of these hard times in the magic mirror of art; he, too, was one of those who yearned to overcome them.

But *how* to overcome them, *where* to go, what haven to travel to, and how to find the roads leading to this haven – that was something Chekhov did not know himself.

This is why the theatre, too, could no more than present vicious people, the foul reptiles of the authoritarian quagmire, on the one hand, and fine people, on the other, people whom you pitied, people you wept with.

The theatre and Chekhov stood guard over the beautiful minds and hearts against sordid reality, and this defence was their only form of attack. Mind you, we are grateful for it. But if that was new wine, it was still very, very weak.

Gorky's wine was a little stronger. The Gorky of that day was no longer a progeny of the hard times. He was much more the progeny of Russia's then imminent future. He was one of the sprouts of that future. He was warmed by the rays of the rising sun. He will develop with that future. But neither the intrinsic degree of his maturity of the time, nor the theatrical conditions, permitted of producing plays that were really and truly stormy petrels.

One *could* discern the cries of the stormy petrel not only in Gorky, but in Chekhov too, in the plays produced by the Art Theatre, provided one had a very keen ear, for these cries were very much muffled. This is why the Art Theatre became the supreme institution for the protection of cultural, ethical and artistic treasures. The Art Theatre sang in a velvet voice, with untold grace, to Russia, and mainly to its intelligentsia, ballads that life, in substance, was beautiful, that there was hope, that at least one route of escape lay in the realisation of man's inner beauty. Do not surrender to the sordid, this ballad said. *Sursum corda.**

But these same hard times left the imprint on the Art Theatre of something akin to hostility to the *active spirit,* a mistrust of noisy martial music, a mistrust of slogans, appeals and directives. The Art Theatre was no "wild duck" of the Ibsen type, but in a way it was a swan, a singing swan, although in its swan song we did not hear only of the end, albeit a beautiful end, but also the message of a lofty life even on this foul earth. Yet it was a swan all the same, one that had lost the knack of flying. The wings of the Art Theatre were the wings of a dream. It did not have wings that would slash the air and propel it through the whirlwinds and clouds, oblivious of distant thunderclaps, to reach the watershed out in front at any cost – that was something the Art Theatre could not do, or at least was not inclined to do.

* * *

Came the Revolution and set the theatre that very task. The Revolution said to it:

"Theatre, I need you. I need you, but not to sit back in comfortable armchairs in a magnificent hall and enjoy a performance after my labours and my battles. I need you, but not merely to laugh merrily and relax. I need you as a helper, a beacon, a counsellor. I want to see my friends and enemies on your stage. I want to see them in retrospect, in the present, and in the future, in their development and in their proper order. I want to see them at first hand. I want to know them by your methods as well. And not just to know them. Through you, I want to grow fond of some of the things that surround me, and to learn to hate others – not more avidly either, for I am generally avid – but more clearly. I want you to sing the praises of my feats and sacrifices. I want you to reveal my errors, my defects and my scars, and I want you to do it truthfully, for I do not fear the truth. I want you to do all this with all the magic resources at your disposal, not clinging to any pigmy schools and any hidebound pigmy rules.

* Lift up your hearts (Lat.), i.e., chins up! A versicle found in all ancient liturgies, an incitement to courage.

Stanislavsky in 1933

Photograph, concentrate, stylise, use your imagination – employ all the colours of your palette, all the instruments of your big orchestra, and help me know and feel the world, know and feel myself. I thirst for knowledge, I thirst to know my own feelings. I need an intensive inner life, so that my labour on earth, my battle for happiness, should be more fruitful."

Some theatres shrank back in fright. Others wagged their tails, and said: "Always prepared." New theatres burgeoned. In haste, they attuned new instruments to the new music, and some did it wrongly, while others came close to the tasks of the Revolution. The Art Theatre and its brilliant leaders gave ear to these appeals thoughtfully and cautiously.

They wondered whether they could be translated into stage music. Perhaps they were crude? Perhaps too journalistic? Perhaps one-sided? Was there possibly a sect behind the Revolution? What was a *class*? Why a class, rather than the *humanity* that they believed to be serving?

The Revolution, for its part, was just as suspicious of Stanislavsky and his theatre. Was it bourgeois, or too aesthetically intellectual? Was it perhaps a theatre of pathetic sobs and beautiful tears of weakness? Was it perhaps a theatre of indulgence, one that degalvanised? It had been a succour in the hard times. But did we need a consoler? What sort of a consoler was it, with its soft voice, its graceful manners and perfumed silk handkerchief, with which it wiped the tears of a harrowed soul in the dusk of morning? Would it come with us to tend the wounds of the revolutionary fighters? Could this magnificently perfumed and elegantly theatrical handkerchief be a banner, if only a very small banner, of our struggle?

Revolutionary playwriting developed very slowly. This was unavoidable. Just as slowly, the theatre, a delicate aesthetical instrument, advanced to meet the requirements of the new times. It searched, and searching it clung to its pivot, to its basic faith in its mission of joining the new construction or adding new *motifs* to its symphony. For long, it succeeded only in part.

Perhaps it was the drama, *Days of the Turbins*,* that helped it. It was a drama of restrained, if you like even arch, surrenderism. The playwright surrendered, but he demanded a blanket amnesty and the recognition that

* *Days of the Turbins* – a play by Mikhail Bulgakov, the well-known Soviet dramatist. Produced by the Art Theatre in 1926.

the fighters gone astray, the fighters on the other side of the barricades, were noble in heart.

Many people rebuked the theatre for this play. The Party subtly discerned the positive aspects of it. There were two such aspects – first, after all was said and done, it was a surrender by the standards of the times, and one that meant a lot; second, it was a play Stanislavsky's theatre accepted without any artistic reservations, a play distinctly modern, dealing with revolutionary realities.

The theatre interpreted it superbly. The mass scenes and the diverse types of the troubled times in the Ukraine were breath-takingly vivid. Since then most playwrights who followed the revolutionary lead and were really eager to clothe their ideas in an artistic garb, longed to have Stanislavsky and his craftsmen pick the theatrical costumes for their literary flesh. *The Armoured Train** was, in its climaxes, something of a historical cultural event.

The actors of the Art Theatre were moved to tears when they played the scene with the captured American.

The theatre, too, was moved deeply. I was in a box with a young playwright, a radical. He wept. He wept and thought, even at that time, "how lucky I am to see such wonderful masters of the stage embody their artistic ideas".

Everybody realised that as an instrument, an orchestra, the Art Theatre had by no means lived out its time, that this new "wineskin" created by Stanislavsky's startling sincerity, his high-minded faith in art, his exacting approach to himself and the theatre, was not outdated at all. Everybody realised that if this wineskin had until then contained various soft drinks and weak wine, this only meant that there had been no red revolutionary grapes, that there had been no full-blooded wine yet of renovated life, forceful human activity driving for the greatest of ideals, expressed in a new repertoire.

Had Stanislavsky at last received what he wanted? Not quite. Not entirely. Let us not delude ourselves. Let not success turn our heads.

* *The Armoured Train 14-69* – a play by Vsevolod Ivanov produced by the Art Theatre in 1927.

Someone told me an excellent anecdote, and I hope it is true. Speaking to a leader of our Party, one playwright, rebuked for the scarcity of good plays, replied:

"There's nothing we can do about it if we aren't Shakespeare."

The leader is said to have replied (how good if he did):

"Why aren't you Shakespeare? That is your fault. Isn't our epoch much higher than Shakespeare's? So why should it not have a theatrical voice still more powerful than Shakespeare's?"

Believe me, we shall have our Shakespeares. We shall have them for sure. They may come somewhat later, but they are certain to come.

On this day, the seventieth birthday of Konstantin Stanislavsky and the fiftieth anniversary of his rich artistic career, known throughout the world, enthusiastically acclaimed in dozens of countries, and so vast in our history, on this day I wish most of all that he should arrive at the full, undivided conviction that the wonderful instrument he has wrought with supreme patience, with deep reverence – that this instrument had been built really (though he may not have been conscious of it) to be an instrument of a great revolution, the onset of the world revolution.

The revolutionary playwrights must put their shoulders to it. The theatre must put its shoulder to it as well. After all, the instrument will have to be retuned, and quite substantially, to play the new music. Function alters the organs. The Art Theatre may adopt the new music, but the new music, too, must transform the Art Theatre. The final consonance of the theatrical legacy of the pre-revolutionary decade and that of the already matured artistic periods of the Revolution, will no doubt come for Konstantin Stanislavsky, because Kachalov* was quite right when he said in his fetching article about his elder friend that Stanislavsky's beautiful soul is just twenty-two and hasn't a single grey hair.

It will be a series of revolutionary productions, artistically filled to the brim, that will crown his head with a radiant wreath. It will beyond question – no matter what happens – be placed on the head of Stanislavsky the creator, that will even then be without a single grey hair.

* See *Notes*, p. 284.

K. S. Stanislavsky and V. I. Nemirovich-Danchenko, 1928

VLADIMIR NEMIROVICH-DANCHENKO

Fragments from "Of the Past"

Stanislavsky always had a picturesque figure. He was very tall, superbly built, with vigorous gait and seemingly effortless plastic movements. But, in effect, this apparent and attractive naturalness was attained by great effort. He told us that he practised his movements before a mirror for hours on end, year after year. At thirty-three his hair was all grey, but his thick moustache and dense eyebrows were black. This always caught the eye, especially because of his height.

There was nothing specifically actorish about him, and that was fine. There was no dramatic coating, no intonations borrowed from the stage – something that always clung to the Russian actor and never failed to please people of bad taste . . .

. . . Naturally, I do not remember how we began our conversation.* Since it had been my initiative, I probably told him of all my theatrical disappointments, and of my dream to create a theatre with a new purpose. I probably suggested that we begin building such a theatre, and recruit our company from among the best of the amateurs of his art group and the most gifted of my own pupils.

It was as though he had been expecting someone to come to him one day, as I did, and say all the words he himself had long since rehearsed. Our conversation developed at once with extraordinary sincerity. The general tenor of it was seized upon without hesitation. We had a lot to talk about. There was no aspect of the old theatre that either of us did not ruthlessly pick to pieces. We interrupted each other in our eagerness to overwhelm the other fellow in the number of venomous darts. But what was still more important, there was no aspect in the elaborate theatrical organism for which we did not have a ready-made positive plan – reforms, reorganisations, and total revolution even.

The most wonderful thing about this conversation was that we never once stooped to argue. In spite of its surfeit of subject matter, and the immense detail, we had nothing to argue about. Our programmes either merged or supplemented each other, and never conflicted. In some things he was more modern, and went farther than I, and easily entranced me. In others, he willingly conceded my point.

Our faith in each other mounted irrepressibly. Mind you, we did not at all seek to please each other, as people do when, setting out on a common cause, they first bargain over their own part in it. Our conversation boiled down to our determining, discussing and asserting the new laws of the theatre, and it was after these were spelled out that our own role in it came out.

Stanislavsky and I smoked continuously (subsequently, both of us succeeded in breaking the habit). We could not bear it any longer in the private room of the Slavyansky Bazar – we had had our breakfast there, our coffee,

* Vladimir Nemirovich-Danchenko tells here of his rendezvous with Stanislavsky at Slavyansky Bazar, a Moscow restaurant, on June 21, 1897. This "momentous rendez-vous", as Stanislavsky described it, conceived the Moscow Art Theatre.

and our dinner. So Konstantin Sergeyevich suggested that we go to his *dacha*, and that I stay the night there.

It was the private country-house of the Alexeyevs.* We reached it after a forty-minute train ride from one of the city railway stations through magnificent forests of ancient luxuriant giant firs and pines, and then some three versts in a four-wheeled victoria. The *dacha* was called Lyubimovka – a modest-looking house, but durable, like all things of the merchant class – the furniture, crockery, and linen all of "quality". Beside the small two-storey villa was a theatrical pavilion where the Alexeyevs put on their home performances. One of Konstantin Sergeyevich's sisters, Anna Sergeyevna, developed into a very good amateur actress.

Konstantin Sergeyevich was a good host. A year later, when full-scale rehearsing was in progress some five versts from Lyubimovka for the soon-to-open Art Theatre, I stayed there for something like a fortnight. And a few years later Chekhov spent the summer there, deliberating upon his *Cherry Orchard* and indulging himself in his favourite occupation – "angling in the little river with a historic name, Klyazma".

The *dacha* stood in a superb pine wood. By the way, a word about this wood. It was when Konstantin Sergeyevich was producing one of our famous productions, Maeterlinck's *Blue Bird*. At one of the first dress rehearsals, to which I was invited as a critic (just as I always invited Stanislavsky to the first dress rehearsals of my own productions), I attacked the scene painter. "Your pines are just like your poplars," I said. Stanislavsky rallied to his defence: "Has anyone ever seen a pine? You have to go to the south of Italy to see one."

"My dear Konstantin Sergeyevich, your *dacha,* where you spent the summers of your youth and childhood, stands in a pine wood."

"Is that true?" he was stunned by this revelation.

Here is another episode of the same order.

He was working on Maeterlinck's *The Blind.* Came the dress rehearsal. The moon halted a moment as it rose before us on the horizon, then swam on slowly leftwards. I objected to this arbitrary cosmography. But at first

* Alexeyev is Stanislavsky's real surname.

Konstantin Sergeyevich refused to countenance my objections, because it was very difficult technically to propel the moon on its natural parabola.

This is a very noteworthy point for an appreciation of Stanislavsky as stage director. He was never in the least interested in nature. He created it such as he wanted it in his theatrical imagination. He was inclined to brand all raptures over nature as sentimentality. Yet, surprisingly, this did not prevent him from creating an exciting morning in *The Cherry Orchard*, the wind and rain in *Uncle Vanya*, the summer twilight in *The Cherry Orchard*, etc.

En route from the Slavyansky Bazar we naturally kept on talking.

In Lyubimovka Konstantin Sergeyevich marshalled pen and paper. In this, our first meeting, he revealed one of the very distinct features of tenacity: a love for detail, an urge to thrash things out to the finish, to note them down, even to put them on record. All his associates knew this, no matter who they were – the electrician, stage hand or actor. He did not trust his own memory, nor that of others.

"Put it in writing," he would say.

"What for? I won't forget."

"That won't do," he would retort, trying to mitigate his insistence with a smile. "I don't trust you."

"But I assure you," the reply would come, "I have an excellent memory."

"I don't believe you. I don't believe you. And I advise you – don't trust your memory. Put it down in writing."

A good memory is of paramount importance to an actor. Different theatre people have different memories. Stanislavsky always had an amazing visual memory – for things, for detail, for gestures. But for a long time he had a very bad memory for words. Jokes made the rounds about his confusing words in life and on the boards. The striking thing is that for many years he even thought this was no defect for an actor. Ultimately, he found some way of memorising. In the revival of *Wit Works Woe*, for example, he, as Famusov, never misquoted. Much more, none of the Chatskys, Repetilovs and Skalozubs could match his clarity and lightness of speech and rhyme.

It stands to reason that later things followed a slightly different course, and in many cases a very different course from what we noted down during our first conversation. I have said above that we had ready-made positive prescriptions for all, even the most trifling points of theatrical organisation. But in fact we ran into an endless number of surprises. And what devastating surprises they were! To be sure, it was very good that we did not know everything and did not anticipate everything. Because if we had anticipated everything, we would probably never have ventured on our cause. The important thing was that we were obsessed. It was only to ourselves and to each other that we appeared "in our right minds and firmly conscious". In fact, however, we were "in tantrums". There was never a doubt in our mind that we were strong enough, and capable enough to succeed. We felt we could do anything in the world. We thought we knew everything, that we knew what had to be done, and how it had to be done.

We went over his pupils, and mine, and picked out the best. We described everyone of them to each other. Admittedly, being their teachers, we were more or less enamoured of our pupils, and doubtlessly overrated them. Whenever, by chance, we compared them with actors of the Maly Theatre, Stanislavsky was more audacious than I. Captivated by the freshness of a gifted actor, and his being untainted by theatrical *clichés,* he was as yet indifferent to the stagecraft of the veteran players. Their *clichés* made him underrate their personalities. I remember, for one, that we asked ourselves whether Luzhsky, an amateur from Stanislavsky's group who had played many parts by then and had a good theatrical background, but had not as yet created a single striking artistic image – whether he or Konstantin Rybakov, a prominent Maly Theatre actor, one of its principals, was the more attractive.

"Luzhsky, beyond question," Stanislavsky replied promptly.

There was a dual intolerance in what he said. First, intolerance of everything known as "Maly Theatre traditions". Rybakov had been raised on these traditions. His stage personality was knitted of them. A pupil of Fedotova, an imitator of Samarin,* he had absorbed their art with all its charms and vices – its sentimentality and its conservatism. And he served

* *Glikeria Fedotova* (1846-1925) and *Ivan Samarin* (1817-1885) – famous Maly Theatre actors.

this art strikingly with all his fine theatrical ability. He was a typical bearer of "tradition". Under this head we did not mean only the substance, but more often the forms, ossified through repetition. It was "tradition" that blocked the way to the novel and fresh, and it was against it that our dreams were aimed.

Poised for the voyage in pursuit of new mirages, we would never conquer the theatrical habits of such an actor. They had become second nature with him. He could never be converted to the new faith. But the main thing: he would never reconcile himself to our discipline and would *never submit to the dictatorship of the producer-director . . .*

. . . How great was Stanislavsky's vanity?

Often I asked myself this question when I discerned satisfaction, which pleased him, or annoyance, which displeased him, or yet marked restraint, a sentiment he did not want to reveal, behind the rise and fall of his low, always warm, somewhat hoarse voice.

All too many undertakings perfectly equipped for realisation fell apart before my eyes due to the vanity of the actors.

But there was this passage in our conversation. We were discussing the repertoire. Before opening a theatre for daily performances we had to have a few ready plays. The American and French system of presenting the same play every night so long as it attracted the public, was unknown to the Russian theatre. Nor would it ever catch on, for it was too suggestive of artisanship. We went over the productions already put on by Stanislavsky's group. We assessed them from the standpoint of our future theatre. The two biggest, *Othello* and *Uriel Acosta*, cropped up in the course of our discussion. I did not conceal my doubts. In spite of their outward merits, I questioned the performance of the leading character.* The undertaking we were about to launch was too much in earnest to suffer indulgence. Our conversation came to a razor-sharp psychological crisis.

Yet Stanislavsky did not say a word in his own defence. Submissively, he let me decide whether or not he was good in tragic parts. In the long run, we did not include *Othello* and *Uriel* in our repertoire.

* Meaning Stanislavsky, who played the leads in these plays, put on by the Art and Literature Society, to which Nemirovich-Danchenko here refers as Stanislavsky's art group.

It is quite safe to say that no actor of prominence would ever be capable of so selfless a gesture.

Was I to conclude from this one fact that the autocratic stage director will know how to submit to the discipline he framed for others? Would he make the sacrifices he required from others?

Naturally, I was never so naïve as to think that a prominent man of the theatre is devoid of all vanity. But like every other emotion, the force of vanity could either be constructive or destructive. Under its impact the artist may be spurred to produce the best that is in him. But everybody knows, too, to what foul acts this passion may drive a man. This evidently depends on some other features of a man's character.

At long last, a series of minor remarks created the impression in me that no matter what vanity Stanislavsky possessed – whether the vanity of an actor wishing to be a second Lensky,* for he was deeply enamoured of Lensky in his youth, or a second Ernesto Rossi or Ernst Possart, the European tragedians of whom he liked to speak and whom he obviously liked for their imposing monumentality; or whether the vanity of a stage director who wished to be a Russian Chronegk, the director of the famous Meiningen Hoftheater, for Stanislavsky kept citing examples of the brilliant receptions which Chronegk held to display his monarchic directorial power – his minor remarks wrought the impression in me that he had superb taste and supreme tact, and I acquired the confidence that our dream of the undertaking as a whole would overwhelm the sources of that dream.

Then, suddenly, came an entirely unexpected development. It was at the close of our conversation, during our morning coffee, that I said:

"There is one thing we have to settle – we must always say the truth, the whole truth, to each other."

I expected a curt affirmative after all the things we had settled. Something like, "that stands to reason", or, "we have already begun to do so". I was therefore deeply startled when Konstantin Sergeyevich leaned back in his armchair, fixed his gaze, that seemed to have paled, on me, and said:

"That is something I cannot do."

* *Alexander Lensky* (1897-1908) – distinguished actor of the Maly Theatre.

I did not grasp his meaning at once, and replied:

"Believe me, I won't mind the least bit."

"You have misunderstood me," he said. "I'm the one who'll mind. I cannot bear to hear the whole truth, I – – –."

This was just as startlingly sincere and simple as it was startlingly in conflict with all that had gone before. I tried to compromise:

"There is always a way," I said, "of saying the truth without hurting one's feelings . . ."

Down the many years of our association, time and time again, I recalled his confession. At times I thought it was prophetic. But also inaccurate. I could often say very cruel things to Konstantin Sergeyevich, and he took them pluckily, like a man. At other times, he grew excited, suffered, or, worse still, revolted against a truth much less important.

Stanislavsky was a complex and ardent character. He unfolded before us over the years. Many things in him were unfathomable because of his staggering extremes. Stereotype formulas, formulas in black and white, were never adequate to describe him.

For years, his ardent and loyal admirers called him "big baby", but that did not say much, in the final count, and was not profound enough.

During our first encounter we were both moved by an urgent desire to get to like each other. There was little room left in it for a level-headed analysis. Most likely, he, too, wondered about my character. He confessed even that for well over a year he had "toyed with the idea" of dealing with me . . .

Two bears will never get along if they live in one den. We wondered about it, smiling trustingly at each other, boldly, without subterfuge. How, we asked, should we divide our rights and duties. In the field of administration this could be done with relative ease. Stanislavsky was to devote himself largely to acting, and hence, though he retained the rights and duties to delve into all affairs, the bulk of them would fall to me. We decided that I should be what a juristic "association" would call the managing director.

But apart from that, and most of all, we were both full-fledged directors and teachers in our own groups. We were both accustomed to do our will, and taught our pupils in this spirit. Furthermore, we were both convinced that this was as it should be. As far as directing was concerned, Stanislavsky was more experienced and had by then devised novelties in his *mises en scène,* in moulding his stage characters and in his popular scenes – something I could not but acknowledge.

We were bound to feel like two bears in one den when it came to shaping the intrinsic theatrical lines of a production. But Konstantin Sergeyevich had a cut-to-measure solution for this difficult problem. He suggested that we divide the artistic realm in two – the literary part and the theatrical. Both of us would handle the production as a whole, assisting and criticising each other.

We would see later how this worked technically. In any case, we were to have equal rights in the artistic realm, but in every dispute and in every crucial issue he would possess veto powers in theatrical matters and I in literary matters.

It boiled down to his having the final say as concerned the *form,* and I as concerned *content.*

It was not a very wise solution, and I am sure both of us suspected that. We would soon learn that form cannot be divorced from content and that by insisting on some psychological detail or literary image, I would be likely to strike squarely at their theatrical expression, that is, at the form. Conversely, by insisting on some form he had found and fancied, Stanislavsky would be likely to repugn against my literary interpretation.

It was this, indeed, that later became the most explosive terrain in our relations.

Yet that wonderful morning both of us seized eagerly upon the artificial demarcation, for we were keen on putting all obstacles out of the way. Both of us were fascinated and overcome by the edifice, so enormous and precious, that we had ornamented within and without, infecting each other since two o'clock of the day before with our temperaments, our rapturous dreams and the imminence of their realisation.

Each of us was sincerely and recklessly willing to make sacrifices and concessions, just so the fire that was raging within us would not be quenched.

That winter Stanislavsky had produced his finest play, Hauptmann's *Sunken Bell,** while my pupils had performed the unheard-of feat of preparing six plays for their final examination.

Stanislavsky sensed keenly that Hauptmann was a writer of "our" mentality.

Incidentally, Chekhov was very fond of Hauptmann, and did not like Ibsen.

The dress rehearsal of *The Sunken Bell* at once revealed all the fine qualities and basic defects of Stanislavsky's group. The staging was strikingly rich in imagination; it was novel and inventive. Every inch of the tiny club stage was exploited with astounding dexterity. There were hills, cliffs and precipices in place of the usual flat theatrical platform. The lighting and sound effects, and, most particularly, the pauses, evoked a gamut of new scenic accomplishments. The round dances, the inhuman cries and voices, the nocturnal hooting of birds, mysterious shadows and spots, the wood goblin and the elfs – all this filled the stage with a very entertaining faery spirit.

This was the most forceful feature of the production, but there were also the colours and drawings, the settings, costumes, and other things theatrical, all created by genuine artists.

Last but not least, the figures of the actors were original, characteristic and free from stereotype.

The picturesque side of *The Sunken Bell* was forceful to the extreme, and, indeed, seemingly one could not wish for anything better in the first two acts. But as the performance proceeded, its basic defect came to the surface. The inner lines were not firm. The psychological springs were unclear, perverted even. From this derived the instability of the dramaturgical pivot. The production reaffirmed my opinion of the Stanislavsky of that period. His directorial *pallette* had a vast range of external colours. Yet he did not use them as intrinsic necessity required, but rather followed the whims of a temperament that rebelled against stereotype, no matter what.

* Presented on January 27, 1898, by the Art and Literature Society.

This was true for quite a few years. It seemed to me sometimes that he attached unusually little importance to the spoken word, to psychology.

I remember that even in the fifth or sixth year of the Art Theatre, during a heated discussion – one of those seemingly turbid and perplexing, but extremely useful arguments that usually broke out between us after rehearsals, when everybody had gone and the stage hands were preparing the stage and hall for the evening performance, while the two of us migrated from one still unoccupied corner to the next – I spoke to him thus:

"You are a remarkably good stage director, but so far only for melodrama or comedy, for vividly theatrical plays, ones that do not bind you either psychologically or textually. You adapt every play you tackle to your own taste. Sometimes you succeed in merging with it, and the result is then superb. But often, after the first two acts, the author, provided he is a big poet or playwright, takes his revenge for the neglect you show of his most profound and most important intrinsic movements. This is why your production starts rolling down in the third act."

Stanislavsky, too, says so of himself in *My Life in Art* quite mercilessly and that is probably why he let me handle the "content", while reserving the form for himself. But it is so much easier to *épater* the public with the picturesque, so in a way Stanislavsky was right. In any case, the production was a big success, and the public at the dress rehearsal was very timorous: I left at 1.30 a.m., when two big acts were still unplayed. One more trait of his revealed itself: his immense perseverance – which was perhaps the most tangible of his qualities – now as a display of his strong will, now of his stubborn artistic whim, was coupled with a total absence of any sense of time and space. While on stage, he felt every inch clearly, but off stage he confessed frankly that he could not picture 50 *sagenes*,* or 300. Neither did he know the difference between a quarter of an hour and an hour and a half. There was a rehearsal of *Shylock* which I persuaded him to stop at half past four in the morning, when Act III had not yet begun, because, between scenes, Konstantin Sergeyevich had been telling the actor how to use his sword and how to bow.

* A linear measurement.

By our agreement he had the theatrical veto. When staging *The Sea-Gull* he overlooked the facets that should have captured his imagination. The characters seemed half-baked to him, their emotions unspectacular, the lines too simple, and the images devoid of meat and bone.

I had to deal with a director who knew how to achieve breath-taking scenic effects with the settings, costumes, actors and the rest of the theatrical property. He had excellent taste in the device of colours, a taste cultivated in museums and in contacts with artists. But he concentrated this explosive charge of his soul merely on stunning the audience, on novelty and originality, which, to be sure, was unusual in itself, and I faced the challenge of rousing his interest in the lyricism of everyday life.

I had to channel his imagination from the fantastic or historical, that source of spectacular plots, to the ordinary day-to-day environment filled with the most ordinary day-to-day emotions . . .

There was one beautiful day when neither he nor I had rehearsals, when nothing distracted us, and we spoke Chekhov from morning until late at night. More precisely, I did the talking. He listened, and scribbled something in his notebook. I walked up and down, squatted once in a while, then walked again, groping for more convincing words whenever I saw by the strain in his eyes that what I had said escaped his attention. I supplemented words with gestures, repetitions, and inflections of my voice. And he listened to me with an open heart, trustingly.

Alexeyev had always lived in Moscow. He was a Moscow factory owner, and had an incisive knowledge of the merchant class. Then he began associating with the stage world, the Moscow stage world. He knew the classical repertoire and the best Russian and European actors. Whenever he went abroad, he studied theatrical art, frequented the museums and, as a stage director should, "ransacked" them for his theatrical needs. But he did not know the immensity of the Russian provincial intelligentsia and semi-intelligentsia, the multimillion stratum of Russian life that provided the prototypes for Chekhov's writing. Their sentiments, tears, discontents and quarrels, all that patterned provincial life, were foreign to him.

What was worse, he did not feel the overwhelming charm of the writer's lyricism, the lyricism that enveloped this Chekhov setting.

Out there, among those broad far-flung groups of intellectuals, among people yearning for a better life, people bogged down in petty day-to-day affairs, people who lived by inertia, yet could not reconcile themselves to the coarseness of life, who suffered from injustice and tended hope lovingly in the secluded and pure nooks of their heart – there Chekhov was loved, there he was kin, an intimate kin. Nor was he welcome there as an abstract poet, but as a man who walked and lived among us, a man like ourselves, not a whit taller than we, on the face of it, a man who liked what we liked, who smiled and laughed as we, who was not always deeper than we, just more sharp-sighted and possessed of the great gift of perceiving our sins and our dreams . . .

Two or three weeks later Alexeyev began sending me the *mise en scène* act by act from the village. It was audacious, unusual for the ordinary public, and very life-like. To be sure, Stanislavsky did not grasp Chekhov's lyricism, but his theatrical imagination prompted him to pick out the most suitable bits from real life. He sensed the dullness of a day in the country manor, the near-hysterical irritability of the characters, the scenes of arrival and departure, and the autumn evening, and showed a knack for filling the acts with suitable things and characteristic details.

This excellent use of things was one of the bigger elements of director Stanislavsky's theatrical innovation. Not only did they occupy the audience, helping to create the right mood. They were useful much more to the actor, for one of the greatest troubles of the old theatre was that the actor was left to his own ends, all of him, as though removed from time and space. This directorial trait of Alexeyev's happened to conform with Chekhov's type of writing. It lacked the fragrance of the author's charm as yet, and there was still the tinge of pure naturalism about these things, a tinge of Zolaism and even of the *Théâtre Antoine* of Paris, or the Reinhardt theatre of Berlin, both already contaminated with naturalism. On our stage it was being done for the first time – a match and a lit cigarette in the darkness, the face powder in Arkadina's pocket, and Sorin's blanket in *The Sea-Gull*, the comb, the cuff-links, the washing of hands, drinking water in gulps, etc., etc. The actor's attention was to be focused on these things, then his speech would also be more natural. Later on, no more than seven or eight years later, a reaction would set in, and he would be opposed to these very things. But at the time, Stanislavsky urged their use, and was even extravagant in his employment of everyday colour. He would go to extremes, but since a copy of the play also passed through my hands, I could throw out whatever seemed excessive or too audacious.

A year later, in *Uncle Vanya,* he would still have the actor cover his head against the mosquitoes, and accentuate the chirring of the cricket behind the stove. Theatre critics would fulminate against the Art Theatre for these mosquitoes and crickets. Chekhov himself would say half seriously:

"The next play I write will contain the remark that the setting is in a country with no mosquitoes, crickets and other insects to interfere with people talking."

But in the meantime all these things were of great help.

The pauses were another important aspect of theatrical novelty. In this, too, lay a kind of unconscious kinship with Chekhov, who always had two or three pauses on every page.

Today, pauses are taken for granted, but at that time they were relatively new, used in the old theatre only as spectacular exceptions. They diverted the actors from the classic, continuous "literary" stream typical of the old theatre. The *mise en scène* of *The Sea-Gull* groped for the most meaningful and necessary pauses; they allowed the preceding emotion to settle, or paved the way for the outburst of a new emotion, or gave vent to long emotion-packed silences.

They were not dead, but rather active pauses, pauses that accentuated emotions or pauses marked by sounds accentuating moods – a factory or locomotive whistle, the cry of a bird or the melancholy hoot of an owl, the rattle of a passing carriage, the sound of distant music, etc. As the years went by these pauses became so much a part of the Art Theatre that they developed into a "stereotype", often fatiguing, even annoying. But at that time they were new and delightful. It was not easy to accomplish these pauses. Stanislavsky looked for them doggedly, his search was complex, not only external but also psychological, and sought harmony between the emotions of the characters and their environment.

I stressed frequently that Chekhov makes his characters indivisible from nature, from the weather, from the surrounding outer world.

Last but not least, the third element of Stanislavsky's directorial novelty was the artist – not a scene painter, but a true artist. A big part in the theatrical "miracle" due to occur was played by Simov – flesh of the flesh of Russian realistic art, of the school of the so-called *Peredvizhniki* – Repin, Levitan, Vasnetsov, Surikov, Polenov, etc.

The Three Sisters was the finest production of the Art Theatre, thanks to the superb ensemble and Stanislavsky's *mise en scène.*

I recall that one of the performances of Ibsen's *Dr. Stockman* – whom Stanislavsky played with consummate skill – coincided with a stormy and bloody political demonstration outside Kazan Cathedral.* One would think the young people would have no time for the theatre in the evening, because many of them participated in the demonstration. Many of their comrades were wounded, beaten, taken to hospital or arrested. The general mood was galvanised by politics. Yet in the evening the top galleries of the theatre were crowded as always. Young men and women, still flushed from their physical exertions, would not miss an Art Theatre performance, excited and hungry though they were. I remember a young girl, fervent, passionate, saying:

"The play is far removed from us in its political make-up. One would think we ought to hiss. But there is so much truth in it, and Stanislavsky urges us so hotly to be true to ourselves that it is at once a holiday for us and just as important a 'cause' as the demonstration outside the Kazan Cathedral."

From Letters and Articles

... My "merger" with you is especially valuable, because I see that you have the qualities of an artist *par excellence,* which I lack. I am fairly keen-sighted when it comes to the content and its significance for the modern audience, but in the matter of form I am inclined to stereotype, although

* Nemirovich-Danchenko refers to the Art Theatre's guest performances in Petrograd in 1901. It was a time of student unrest, which was brutally suppressed by the tsarist police.

I react sensitively to originality: that is a terrain in which I lack your imagination and craftsmanship. I think, therefore, that plays which I shall fancy for their content and you for the scope they give to your creative imagination will be our best . . .

From a letter to Stanislavsky
June 21, 1898

. . . In your person we possess the most upright, the most straightforward and the most convinced man of the stage . . . The success of our cause rests *solely on our association and closeness.* I can *do nothing* without you. You can do without me, but far less than with me. I have told you this time and again, and that is the way I feel . . .

From a letter to Stanislavsky
(1898-1900)

. . . I want to tell you that there is scarcely another person who appreciates as much as I your generosity, your honesty in work, untainted by triviality, your tact in treating the most sensitive feelings of the people you work with. Throughout this month you have often reminded me about the finest days of our association, the association that produced out theatre and all its finer sides . . .

From a letter to Stanislavsky
(1900-01)

. . . Who can I compare Konstantin Sergeyevich with in respect to myself? Just with someone *very close* to me. If it were my mother, or my brother who were so ill, it would have concerned me less, depressed me less than Konstantin Sergeyevich's illness. In spite of everything, the most important threads of my soul and life are intertwined with his. Surely, this is the reason why so many estrangements cropped up between us – because the most important things I lived by are all in him. Our association has long since developed from a mechanical one to much more than one of kinship. I have been my brother's brother and my mother's son for 50 years. But has there ever been so much spiritual closeness between us for even a year as there has been between Konstantin Sergeyevich and myself in the past ten years? In my life and soul he is myself. That is not comparable to anybody. No common yardsticks of friendship, affection and sympathy are applicable to us. We may not cry over each other, we may be hostile now and then, but the bonds that bind us only God and death can sever. Aye, not even death.

From a letter to Maria Lilina
September 5, 1910

... Yesterday I was in a state of absolute amazement over the difference between what you predicted about *The Three Sisters*, and what I saw. I have been ruminating over it to this hour, that is, even through the night ...

It was one of the most magnificent performances our theatre has ever given.

To begin with, I saw an exceptionally lively bond arise between the stage and the auditorium. The audience reacted to every trifle, the least little trifle even.

Furthermore – especially so this time, I must admit – all the performers, all without exception (you, perhaps, less than the others) were so *vibrant* as they rarely are. But the main thing I want to say, and why I am writing you this letter, is that the performance was the *ideal* of what, in my opinion, your so-called system aspires to.

That is what made me ruminate since last night! Either I am absolutely confused over your system, or (I beg you to heed me) you yourself are so absorbed in the *ways and means* that you have lost the *goal*. Make sure you are not changing the role of prophet for that of high priest. Perhaps the ways and means of finding God have made you forget God himself, because you are preoccupied entirely with the rites. When, quite by accident, God was quite near you – because he is omnipresent and his ways are inscrutable – you did not notice him, did not feel him. Once a high priest loses the spiritual intuition of the prophet he accepts nothing but what conforms to the ritual he established himself ...

From a letter to Stanislavsky
November 10, 1914

Since I wrote you that you were not simple enough as Vershinin in the last performance of *The Three Sisters,* it is now my duty and pleasure to state that your performance of yesterday scaled very great heights of genuine, artistic simplicity, sincerity, nobility and intelligence. It was magnificent!

A letter to Stanislavsky
December 12, 1914

...Now about Stockman.

Unquestionably, Konstantin Sergeyevich played him with utmost skill. It was the finest thing Konstantin Sergeyevich has done in the realm of theatrical art, the most consummate and incontestable...

From a letter to V. Kachalov
August 1923

Pity that the 500th performance of *The Blue Bird,* which I had kept for this season to make a triumph of it for you, though now over, was marred by your illness and, especially, by the lacklustre theatrical season – and, to be sure, by all current affairs.

The least I can do is send you this modest greeting in remembrance of that wonderful chapter in your theatrical career, which so vividly illustrates your wealth of imagination and dogged perseverance, your knowledge of the audience and your profound foresight.

Let me shake your hand most sincerely.

A letter to Stanislavsky
October 19, 1924

Jubilees call for a re-appraisal of one's relationships. Deep down in my heart, I am boundlessly grateful to you for everything I have received from you in my artistic development – the scintillating and joyful recollections about our joint work, and the sentiments of genuine friendship and fraternity. If I were ever to pray, I would beg Providence to keep you strong for many many years to come.

A telegram to Stanislavsky
January 17, 1933

K. S. Stanislavsky and V. I. Nemirovich-Danchenko, Varen, 1923

Stanislavsky dreamed of creating an art which would enable actors to perform so freely in a play as if they were doing it for the first time – free from all the hackneyed gestures and devices of the 40th, 50th or 200th performance. He dreamed, so to speak, that each performance would be fresh creation, creation not only free from the amassed *clichés,* but full of surprises for even the actor himself . . .

From an article,
"The Second Dimension"

. . . Why not call Stockman romantic?! One might even go farther: why not call Stanislavsky romantic – Stanislavsky, here, in his life? He is romantic through and through!

From an article,
"The Romantic
and Realistic Theatre"

On the Twentieth Anniversary
of the Stanislavsky Opera House

February 7, 1941

. . . In my enforced solitude I go over the chain of memories how 20 years ago this cause was conceived, so trifling in appearance, and so vast in content;

of your wonderful leader, who led you at once with vividly artistic daring and sagacious caution, of his fervid and passionate dreams to consolidate the opera on the strong pillars of genuine art, of the man through whom we are bound by an unbreakable spiritual kinship – of Konstantin Sergeyevich Stanislavsky . . .

From a letter to the company of the Stanislavsky
Opera House

Speech at Stanislavsky's Funeral

August 9, 1938

The comrades will forgive me if my speech is not smooth. I come directly from the railway station. I learned of Konstantin Sergeyevich's death at night, as I was entering the Soviet Union at Negoreloye Station. Furthermore, my memory is burdened by so many experiences over 41 years, so many experiences in the realm not only of art, but private experiences, too, that, overcome, it will not let me be eloquent.

In the 41 years of our association we did not simply deposit artistic ideas into the theatre, but, in the full sense of the word, all our lives.

Stanislavsky possessed a brilliant genius of leadership, which really induced people to dedicate themselves entirely to art. Creative work intertwined with life; all interests, all aspirations merged into something whole and harmonious, and it was impossible to see where private emotions ended and artistic emotions began.

All those people who launched the Art Theatre – Stanislavsky himself and those present here at this sad parting, his disconsolate widow, Maria Petrovna, his brother Vladimir Sergeyevich and his sisters Zinaida Sergeyevna and Maria Sergeyevna, or the illustrious Moskvin, Knipper, Vishnevsky and such of his comrades as Grigoryeva, Titov and the Gremislavskys – may the others forgive me for not mentioning them now – all of them put everything into their life's work, just as Stanislavsky did. Later, Kachalov, Leonidov and others dedicated their lives to this theatre. This was only the first stratum, galvanised by Stanislavsky's unbending determination to create an art of noble beauty, a realistic and honest art, profoundly truthful, taking hold of the very existence of all the people involved.

So many unrepeatable things have happened! No matter how much I thought lately of reviving the emotions that gripped us when the Art Theatre was being founded, I arrived at the conclusion every time that it was all unrepeatable. And not only because of the charm of the gifted men and women who created the theatre, but, which is much more important, if one might put it thus, because of the sacrificial devotion that imbued Stanislavsky. Yes, yes, sacrificial devotion and not mere veneration and appreciation of beauty.

This spontaneous longing to devote all of his being to the profound ideas that moved him, this sacrificial devotion that gripped all the others, was the earnest, the truest earnest of success for the Art Theatre.

As I weighed my recollections in the few hours of my train ride here today, the echo of this enamoured devotion which had filled all our lives, resounded constantly in my mind. Let me say once more that all these things intertwined and that it was impossible to perceive the line dividing the sentiments of friendship from the sentiments of the artist. Mind you, in our private lives we still managed to abandon ourselves to other passions and to satisfy other desires. As for Stanislavsky, there was art and art alone, and to the final minute of his labours and his life he belonged, and gave of himself solely to his labour of love.

I do not know the deep-going workings of Stanislavsky's mind. A realist to the marrow of his bones, he may have inclined towards idealism in the deep and secret recesses of his soul. I do not know what he thought of immortality. But for us that is just where immortality begins.

So long as my thoughts move within the walls of the Art Theatre, beside the things the Art Theatre has created, I shall always see the gaps between Stanislavsky's art and the other artistic trends of the theatre. Stanislavsky used to say that art is richer if there are different trends. It is important that the ultimate goal should be a true triumph for the truth. But where his rock-bottom ideas inclined outside the theatre and art, I do not know. Yet we are witness to the inception of real immortality.

How art overflows the bounds of the theatre, far and wide, how it penetrates the soul of the whole people, in what way, and what in particular reaches and fills the hearts – history will look into that. Immortality begins here. Enamoured and sacrificial devotion was the pivot in the creative life of the deceased.

And when I wondered what we should adopt in art, I decided it was most of all his attitude to art. We may argue over the artistic issues that we argued over when Konstantin Sergeyevich was alive. But this, his stupendous sacrificial attitude to art is something incontestable.

And what I would like is for all my comrades of the Art Theatre present here to make one vow beside the coffin: Let us vow that we shall treat the theatre with the same profound and sacred devotion as Stanislavsky did. Let us adopt that as the great motto left us by him. Let us vow to behave as he behaved.

K. S. Stanislavsky and Y. B. Vakhtangov. 1920-22

YEVGENY VAKHTANGOV

Dear Konstantin Sergeyevich,

I beg you to forgive me for troubling you with my letters, but it is so very hard for me now, I am so pained that I cannot help turning to you. I shall write to you what I never said to you aloud. I know that my time on earth is running out. I know that I shall not live long, and I needs must tell you, at last, what I think of you, of theatrical art, and of myself.

Ever since I learned to know you, I grew fond of you to the end; I believed you to the end, and you became what I lived by and what I gauged life by. Consciously and unconsciously, my affection and veneration infected everybody who did not have the privilege of knowing you personally. I am deeply grateful that I saw you in true life and that, albeit rarely, I had a chance to associate with an artist of world stature. It is with this affection of you that I shall die, even if you were to turn your back to me. I know of nothing and nobody higher than you.

In art I loved nothing but the truth you speak of, the truth you teach. It penetrated not only into that part of me, that modest part which serves the Theatre, but that part of me, too, which we call "man". It keeps at me day after day, and if I do not grow better, the sole reason is that there is so much I have to conquer within myself. Day after day, it tempers my treatment of people, the demands I make upon myself, my path in life and my views on art. I believe thanks to this truth which I have received from you, that Art is a service to the Supreme in everything. Art cannot and must not be the possession of a group, the possession of isolated individuals. It is the possession of the people. To serve art is to serve the people. An artist is not the valuable possession of a group. He is a valuable possession of the people. "The Art Theatre," you said once, "is my civic service to Russia." That is what enthralls me, a small man. It enthralls me, even though I may not be destined to achieve anything, even though I may not achieve anything. In this phrase of yours lies the symbol of faith for every artist.

As far as I am concerned, I have no faith in myself, I like nothing about myself; I never dare think anything audacious, and consider myself the least of your pupils. I am ashamed of every step I have made, and I always feel unworthy of showing my work to you, the Only and the Peerless.

This, briefly, is what lies in me.

Young people have come to you now from the group I worked with, whom I taught to love what I learned from you and Leopold Antonovich.* These young people have stopped believing me. I do not know what they say to you, and how they say it. I do not know what they say about me and my feelings for you.

I am writing you, because I want you to know the truth, because I want you to know that I "don't give myself airs", because I want you to get a first-hand impression of me. If you believe me, if you believe that a man has no cause to dissemble when his days are running out, if you believe that I have no ulterior motives in addressing you, please also believe that wherever you are concerned every step I make and every act I perform are

* The reference is to Leopold Sulerzhitsky (1872-1916) – Stanislavsky's closest helper at the Art Theatre and head of the Art Theatre's First Studio from 1912 to 1916.

Yevgeny Vakhtangov

marked by the compelling and unaltering demand upon myself and others to be decent, modest and reverent. I did not want to show you fragments, and now do not want to show you other works, because they are not worthy of your attention. I beg you to allow me two years to give personality to my group. Let me bring you not fragments, not a diary, but a production, a production that will show the spiritual and artistic make-up of the group. I ask for these two years, provided I shall be able to work, to prove my true affection for you, my true reverence, my boundless loyalty to you. Please believe me that my thoughts are far from making a career, from the wish to play some big important role, from any bold actions whatsoever.

I cannot go on without just a little of your confidence, not in my capabilities but in the purity of my intentions.

Affectionately yours,

Y. Vakhtangov

A letter to Stanislavsky
March 29, 1919

Vsevolod Meyerhold

VSEVOLOD MEYERHOLD

Dear Konstantin Sergeyevich,

As he was describing an episode in one of his novels, Nikolai Gogol had difficulty in putting down on paper what had just occurred in his tale. He stopped suddenly and exclaimed:

"No! I can't! Give me another pen! My pen is drab and dull, much too thin for this picture!"

As I begin this letter to you on your birthday, I am in Nikolai Vasilyevich's position.

My feelings for you, my dear teacher, are such that every pen I take is too drab and dull to put them to paper.

How to tell you how much I admire you?!

How to tell you of the immense gratitude I feel I owe you for what you have taught me in so little explored a field as the art of stage directing!

If I shall be strong enough to survive all the difficulties made for me by the developments of the last two months, I shall come to you and you will read in my eyes the joy I feel that you have conquered your illness, and that you are cheerful and strong again, and that you have again begun to work for the good of our great homeland.

I shake your hand. I kiss you.

My love to your household. My special love to Maria Petrovna. Tender greetings to your granddaughter, who moved me to tears by her tact when I asked about you.

Affectionately yours,

V. Meyerhold

January 18, 1938

Sergei Eisenstein

SERGEI EISENSTEIN

An Extract from "Autobiographical Notes"

Meyerhold!

. . . His affection and respect for Konstantin Sergeyevich was amazing, even in the fiercest years of struggle against the Art Theatre.

How often he spoke fondly of Konstantin Sergeyevich, how highly he prized his gift and skill!

Where, in what poem, in what legend did I read how Lucifer, the first of the angels to rebel against Jehovah, for which he "was cast down", continued to love him and "shed tears" not over his own debasement, but over not being allowed to see him! Or would that be from the legend about Ahasuerus?

There is something of the Lucifer and Ahasuerus in the mercurial figure of my teacher... absolutely lacking the patriarchal balance people take for harmony but bordering rather on philistinism, which Goethe believed essential in a measured dose in every creative personality.

Who has ever proved more conclusively than the dignitary of the Weimar court by his own biography that this measured dose of philistinism assured tranquility, stability, deep-rootedness and the honey of fame where a lack of it would doom an excessively romantic character to perpetual ebullience, perpetual quest, to ups and downs, to the tribulations of fate and, all too often, to the lot of Icarus, which culminated the life of the Flying Dutchman...

This longing for Konstantin Sergeyevich, that patriarch warmed by the sunny rays of endlessly burgeoning second and third generations of admirers and enthusiasts, contained something of Lucifer's tears and the unspoken anguish of Vrubel's Demon.

I remember him, too, in his autumn, the time of his impending rapprochement with Konstantin Sergeyevich. This coming rapprochement of two old men was very pathetic to observe.

I do not know the feelings of Konstantin Sergeyevich... who had turned in the last years of his life to the eternal source of creation, the rising generation, to which he dedicated the new ideas of his everlastingly young talent.

But I remember the glitter in the eyes of the "prodigal son" when he spoke about the new reunion of the two men "circumventing" all the paths foreign to the true theatres, from the anticipation of which one fled on the threshold of our century and of his own creative career, and which the other disowned dozens of years later...

Their association did not last long...

But in those long years when, having overcome my own hurt,* I made peace with him and we were friends again, it always seemed to me that in his treatment of his pupils and followers he kept reliving his own pain of parting with his own first teacher. Reliving his own harrowing

* The reference is to Eisenstein's own embroilment and departure from Meyerhold's theatre.

disappointment in the ones he cast down, and, as he cast them down, acting as the tragic Father Rustim who struck Zorab, seeking vindication and embellishment, as it were, to what in his own youth was performed without evil intent by the "father" and belonged solely to the creative "independence of spirit of the overproud son".

That is how I saw this tragedy.

Perhaps I was not objective enough. Perhaps not "historical" enough.

But to me it was too intimate, too dear, too much of a "family chronicle".

After all, in the context of "descending benefice", due to the benediction of the elder I am in a way the son and grandson of these past generations of the theatre.

Alexander Tairov

ALEXANDER TAIROV

Wherein His Genius?

What is genius?

I do not know if there is any clear-cut *theoretical* reply to that, but there certainly is a *practical* one.

It is Stanislavsky.

Stanislavsky's genius did not lie in his being a magnificent actor.

And not just in his being a magnificent stage director and craftsman.

And not even in his having had outstanding victories and devastating defeats as the big artist that he was, and not even in that many of his errors were more significant and fruitful than some of his victories, and those of others.

Stanislavsky's genius derived from the fact that at the turn of the century he imparted *a new life, a new rhythm, a new quality* to the theatre with *amazing creative foresight.*

Stanislavsky's genius derived from the fact that no craftsman of the theatre can any longer *ignore* this new quality, and from the fact that one can and must argue with Stanislavsky, one can and must surmount him, *but one can never escape him.*

This new quality imparted by Stanislavsky to the theatre may, roughly and schematically, be defined with the one word – *truth.* I know that many centuries before Stanislavsky some big artists spoke about truth and upheld it in their art.

I also know that individual actors, both in the West and in our own country, both in the remote and the recent past, made truth the cornerstone of all their endeavours. However, none but Stanislavsky made truth the fundamental essence and quality not of an individual artist or actor, but of *the theatre as a whole* in all the profuse variety and unity of its socio-creative substance.

Truth is a word that sounds unconvincing and indeterminate.

Indeed, *what* truth?

The truth of life or the truth of the theatre?

The truth of reality or the truth of performance?

The truth of emotion or the truth of fancy?

Abstract truth or concrete truth?

Idealistic truth or materialistic truth?

Yes, it is an indeterminate conception. Quite true. It is indeterminate. *But determinative.*

After Stanislavsky different artists, different generations, different epochs will with conviction and convincingly, doggedly and rightly search and assert this truth, each in their own way.

Everyone of us must and can partially or entirely accept or deny Stanislavsky's truth.

That is *life,* that is *progress,* that is *socially inevitable.* But none will ever be able to say, after Stanislavsky, that the theatre needs no truth, that it is conceivable without truth.

That would not sound as an aphorism even, but rather as a hopeless anachronism.

One more thing.

Stanislavsky's genius did not derive simply from the fact that he made truth part of the very concept of the theatre as a kind of *absolute.* It also derived from the fact that he himself, as an artist, was always and absolutely truthful.

This is why we hail in Stanislavsky not only his amazing talent and skill, not only his love of art, theatre and actor, but also *his severity, his intolerance, his fanaticism.*

This is why today, on his seventieth birthday and the fiftieth anniversary of his stage career, we are fond of him *as much for his errors as for his foresight.*

This is why we love him more, perhaps, not when we applaud him, but when we oppose him fervidly, unbendingly, deeply convinced, with a different truth, *our own truth.*

Olga Knipper-Chekhova

OLGA KNIPPER-CHEKHOVA

It is a hard and a responsible job to write about Konstantin Stanislavsky. We have lived a long time, our main creative years, in association with him.

What to write about? What instants to snatch out of the long succession of years to illustrate the many facets of Stanislavsky's personality? How to find the words that would tell what we feel for him?

My memory flies back to the remote time when I first saw him. It was the winter of 1897-98. I was in my last year at the dramatic school of the former Philharmonic Society. During an ordinary school performance of *Innkeeper* by Goldoni word spread of Stanislavsky's being in the audience... There were rumours in Moscow then that a new theatre would soon open, and our professor, Vladimir Ivanovich Nemirovich-Danchenko, had told a few of my school-mates and myself that it would engage us. You can imagine how excited we were, how furiously our hearts beat, as we peeped through the eye-hole in the curtain. That was when I gathered my first impression and was at once captivated by the imposing stature of this magnificent and in every sense beautiful man – captivated, and yet somewhat awed...

For the rest of my life I was captivated by him, feared him, revered him and at times "hated" him. To be sure, my "hate" referred to minutes of weakness, of a loss of faith, minutes when I thought he was inaccessible, when I simply could not understand him. He was a very strict man, and very exacting. It was at once a torture and a joy to work with him, but torture more often than joy, until one grasped what he was after, and what he wanted one to do to achieve the cherished goal. He was always immersed in big and pure art. He rose above the drabness of daily life, and the interests of narrowly theatrical life too. He required that the actor purge himself completely of all extraneous and petty sentiments, of vainglory. He was a fanatic in art. He told us, who were then still young aspirants, what thoughts and feelings we should take with us to the stage, so that all the humdrum, all the petty interests, be left outside the theatre, so that the actor, as though purged of everything that everyday life instils in him, should tackle his creative work and bring only the "worthwhile" that nature endowed him with to the stage. It is for all this that I still feel deeply and endlessly fond of Konstantin Sergeyevich, that I am immensely grateful to him for making me believe in all the beauty, the "realness", that nature endowed the actor with.

For all his usual kindness to me, he was extremely exacting and always rebuked me for my lack of will-power and self-control. I was, indeed, unbearable. I grew dumb, and instead of listening to what he said I gaped at him, at his unusual zeal, which repressed me. I felt I was quite unable to do at once what he wanted me to do, and hated myself for causing him so much annoyance. I was tormented by the thought that he had to expend so much of his vast store of energy upon me. He, for his part, brimmed with fervour, wishful and "infecting", and it never occurred to him that an actor could be unable at any given minute to perform what he so wanted him to perform, what he thought had to be performed.

Let me illustrate this with an episode from our work on Turgenev's *A Month in the Country*. The role of Natalia Petrovna caused me immense suffering. I was mastering it with untold difficulty. To be sure, I probably never mastered it at all. Oh, if it were now – but, alas, it is too late... So it was that when my suffering and the terror, my fears that I would never grasp the emotional subtleties of Turgenev's characters, gripped me, obscuring the charm and fragrance of the image, I broke into tears at one of the rehearsals and declared that I could not play. I went home. That was when Stanislavsky showed his extraordinary tact in his treatment of a confused and tormented actor. The following day I received a letter from him. It amazed and excited me, and caused still greater suffering – not for myself any more, but for him. Let me quote a few passages from the letter:

"I did not come to you myself because I do not want to annoy you. You have grown so tired of me that I must hide out for a while. Instead, I am sending you flowers. Let them tell you of my tender affection for your talent. This fondness makes me brutal to all that pollutes the beauty nature has conferred upon you.

"You are in the throes of artistic doubt. On the stage, deep suffering is born by such torture. Do not think I am indifferent to your ordeal. I am constantly troubled from afar, and yet I know that your torment will bear magnificent fruit.

"Let someone else, instead of me, tell you what nature has given you. I am willing to admire from afar how your talent will sweep away the redundant, how it will acquire freedom and assert itself with the force which the actor's craftsmanship is retarding for a while. Believe me, the things that seem so difficult to you are really trifles. Have the patience to understand, to think, to grasp these trifles, and you will experience the finest joys of living given to man in this world.

Konstantin Stanislavsky and Olga Knipper-Chekhova in I. Turgenev's *A Month in the Country*, 1909

"I promise that I will not frighten you with scientific words. That has probably been my error. I beg you to be firm and brave in the artistic struggle that you have to win, not only for the sake of your own talent, which I love with all my heart, but also for the sake of our theatre, which is the purpose of all my life...

"Look at your part again and establish clearly the elements of which it consists.

"Forgive me for causing you to suffer, but believe me that suffering is inescapable. Soon you will attain the true joys of art."

As I read this letter again, I experience the excitement I felt on that remote day when it gave me much pain and at once much consolation, because I realised that I was not alone, that Konstantin Sergeyevich had not abandoned me, that he was by my side and that I had to be brave and conquer myself for the sake of the play, and to live up to the standards of the theatre which was Stanislavsky's "purpose in life".

For all his exacting cruelty at work, Konstantin Sergeyevich was very kind to the actors. He helped them with advice whenever he could, and wanted to know how they lived. He often assisted them financially, and all in a kind of covert way. If an actor fell ill during the season, Stanislavsky saw to it that he was shipped at once to a health resort, if necessary, and if the theatre did not have the cash for it, he gave of his own.

Much has been written and still will be written about Konstantin Sergeyevich, the stage director, actor and teacher. As for me, I simply want to restore in my memory the production of Chekhov's plays, in which we were so closely associated with him, and which were especially dear to me. Konstantin Sergeyevich was tenderly fond of Anton Chekhov. It was very hard to produce Chekhov's plays. The company was still young, but inspired by a great love for Chekhov and the theatre, and our wonderful directors – Konstantin Sergeyevich and Vladimir Nemirovich-Danchenko, who had prevailed upon Stanislavsky to produce Chekhov.

It was a joy, a veritable holiday for me, the actress, to play and associate with Konstantin Sergeyevich in the Chekhov plays. What helped me was that I – the Yelena of *Uncle Vanya* and the Masha of *The Three Sisters* – was genuinely in love with both Astrov and Vershinin, that I loved brother Gayev fondly in *The Cherry Orchard* and can never think of Count Shabelsky, in *Ivanov,* without tears welling up in my eyes.

I see Stanislavsky clearly as Astrov in his grey jacket in the first act. I see him and hear him say with deep feeling:

"When I hear the rustling of my young forest, the forest I planted with my own hands, I realise that the climate is a little within my power too,

Konstantin Stanislavsky and Olga Knipper-Chekhova in Anton Chekhov's *The Sea-Cull*. 1898

and that if man will be happy in a thousand years, it will be a little due to me too."

And as I looked at the hands of Astrov-Stanislavsky, it seemed true to me that they really planted forests, and his eyes seemed to say that he did not live an ordinary life, that his gaze was fixed far ahead into the future. "Generally, I love life, but I can't bear and I hate our provincial, drab Russian life with all my heart,"* he says to Sonya. The words are Astrov's, but the voice is Stanislavsky's. It is his yearning one hears to hand down to the younger generation all that he had thought about, and realised, all his immense experience, all his gigantic effort in art, to which he had dedicated all his life – and all this to the future.

Konstantin Sergeyevich often said he was surprised at his success as Astrov. "I don't do anything, yet the public praises me." It was hard to believe, somehow, that he did not realise what a magnificent, poetic and manly character he had created as Astrov, and how light it was. I see him clearly in my mind's eye, coming on the stage a bit under the weather, with Wafer, dancing on the balls of his feet. Then, in the last act he comes up to the map of Africa, and says looking at it: "It must be boiling hot in Africa!" There was so much bitterness in that one phrase. He spoke it with bravado, or perhaps with defiance. When we heard the bells jingling as the carriage drove Astrov away, the heart contracted painfully at the thought of the drab life and hard work in store for this gifted and brave man in the provincial backwoods. One did not want to part with this unforgettable image that Stanislavsky had created.

I looked forward to the scene in Act III, in which I played with him, as to a holiday. When I felt his enamoured eyes on me, filled with roguish delight, and heard his loving, sarcastic, "You're cunning", I was always annoyed at Yelena, the "educated" girl who refused to go with him to the forester's home.

There was so much nobility, restraint and purity in the image of Vershinin, that lonely dreamer of *The Three Sisters*. His dreams of a life that could have been and a life that was sure to be, helped him live and suffer

* Anton Chekhov, *Uncle Vanya,* Act II.

the unprepossessing drabness of a joyless epoch and all the trials and tribulations of his personal life.

It is as if I hear him now, saying:

"In two hundred, three hundred or, perhaps, a thousand years – it doesn't matter when exactly – a new and happy life will arise. We are not going to be part of that life, it is true, but we are living for it now, working for it, suffering for it, and creating it – and in that lies the purpose of our being, or, if you like, in that lies our happiness."*

I, Masha, enjoyed hearing his voice, which I had learned to love, and looking in his eyes, fixed on something far away, and I chuckled quietly from some inner emotion when he spoke.

Vershinin-Stanislavsky spoke these tirades about a happy life, these dreams of how to start life anew, quite consciously, not with the inflections of a man who loved to philosophise. One felt that what he said came from inside him, giving purpose to his life, giving him a chance to rise above the drab environment and all the trials that he so patiently suffered. There was so much purity in Vershinin's love for Masha. "I am in a special kind of mood today. I want so much to live!" says Vershinin-Stanislavsky in the fire scene in Act III. He chuckled and sang. "All ages obey the calls of love, love's inspiration is beneficial." Then the faint "trum-tum-tum", with the glory of love beaming in Vershinin's and Masha's faces. Naturally, they both understood this "trum-tum-tum", and when, soon after, Vershinin's voice backstage sang "trum-tum-tum", Masha knew exactly what to do. She sang "tra-ta-ta" in reply and went to him with a heart overflowing with love. It was easy for me, Masha, to confess to my sisters my love for that kind of Vershinin:

"He seemed strange to me at first, then I pitied him . . . And then I fell in love. I loved his voice, his words, his troubles, and the two girls . . ."

I can't think without inner convulsions of the scene in which I part with Vershinin. I did not feel the ground under me. I did not feel my body as I went from my dressing-room to this parting on the stage, as

* Anton Chekhov, *The Three Sisters,* Act II.

Act I of Chekhov's *Uncle Vanya.* 1899

though some strange force was bearing me there. How good that Chekhov let Masha say just one word, "Farewell". I treasure this image of Vershinin in my heart, and am eternally grateful to Konstantin Sergeyevich for having helped me to live through the love which Masha had for Vershinin on the stage.

I remember Gayev of *The Cherry Orchard* and Shabelsky of *Ivanov,* as clearly as though they were standing before me. I cannot help smiling to myself when I think of Konstantin Sergeyevich in these parts, which he created with such consummate skill and grace, such a variety of colour and such ease. I close my eyes and hear the rise and fall of his voice, his words and expressions. I loved him dearly, as my brother, in *The Cherry Orchard.* The play sounded more important, more weighty, whenever he played in it.

I tried to grasp the ease with which he passed from one mood to another, and that helped me play Ranevskaya.

Take his famous speech before the cupboard. "As soon as I had done it, I knew it was stupid," he said soon after to Anya. Quite true, as he concluded that speech with his favourite billiard-room words, he looked somewhat embarrassed, conscious that it was silly. Or take his famous "What's that?" His big, somewhat awkward and at once elegant figure, his kind face, now turned to Anya with a tender smile and now listening with a kind of fastidious anger to Lopakhin's tirade about saving the cherry orchard, and his aversion to Yashka, the lackey: "Step back, you smell of chicken." I will never forget his appearance on the stage at the end of Act III, after the cherry orchard had been sold, when he handed the anchovies and Kerch herrings to Firs, and said, brushing away a tear: "I've had nothing all day. Lord, what I've been through."

Take his confused figure in the last act – the parting with the house where he had lived all his life, and his words: "I'm a bank clerk now, a financier . . . cannon off the red", which he spoke with a smile, trying to cheer himself up, and then his final lament: "My sister! My sister . . ." and then the exit . . .

When we played *The Cherry Orchard* the first time after Konstantin Sergeyevich's death, I heard his intonations with something akin to physical pain and it seemed to me through the tears that I saw his figure, his face, his smile, the motion of his arms – he stood in my eyes as a spectre throughout the performance. It was a torture and a joy at once, and his image is firmly imbedded for ever in my memory.

Take Shabelsky in *Ivanov,* that shabby and wretched count who had frittered his life away and was fully conscious of his shabbiness, a count turned parasite – how well Konstantin Sergeyevich showed in this depraved character a kind of private human dignity, a human emotion that still smouldered somewhere deep down in the man's heart.

I remember his big frame, ill-clad, ridiculous and wretched, in the last act . . .

. . . You should have seen Konstantin Sergeyevich sitting backstage with the 'cello, and then the two of us playing a duet as the curtain rose for

Act I. It was Konstantin Sergeyevich no longer, but Count Shabelsky in his short and shabby jacket, with Shabelsky's face and Shabelsky's gestures... Konstantin Sergeyevich Stanislavsky – it is a name that should sound like a bell, and not to us alone who knew and loved him, and worked with him, but also to the young men and women and the far-removed generations, calling upon all of us to treat art, to understand it, as a thing pure and exact. It is a name that should be our conscience.

Vasily Kachalov

VASILY KACHALOV

Not a Single Grey Hair

Stanislavsky is seventy. This big and luminous man has travelled a big and luminous road.

That is good. It is good, too, and joyful, to go in one's mind over this big and luminous road of a man. It is a road full of all "human" elements, a road full of everything that a man's life could yield – both good and bad. To be sure, the bad, I feel, becomes good in Stanislavsky.

The heart fills with radiant joy, understandable pride, admiration and warmth when you think about the life lived by 70-year-old Stanislavsky. But here is something I cannot think about without deep-felt emotion, without a catch in my throat, the kind one feels from height, depth, or a bottomless pit – I feel it whenever I think of Stanislavsky the artist, of his creative personality, for this personality is fifty years old today.

No matter how much, and how harmoniously, "man" and "artist" blend in him, it is true, after all is said and done, that his gift and his creative genius tower above his human side.

Stanislavsky's gift and his artistic genius is 50 years old today. That, too, is a lot. It is real fame. But whenever I think of Stanislavsky's talent I always remember Mayakovsky, who said of himself when young:

I haven't a single grey hair in my heart,
Nor tenderness of the ageing!
I've assaulted the world
With the might of my voice,
And go, handsome,
*Twenty-two years old.**

These lines of Mayakovsky are to me a subtle and most accurate portrait of Stanislavsky's talent. It is a fact, after all, that silver-haired Stanislavsky's talent truly has not "a single grey hair".

Neither is there any "tenderness of the ageing" in his talent. That, too, is quite beyond question: a young man's vim, irreconcilability, irrepressibility, tirelessness, boundlessness and severity, not softness and tenderness, those are the elements of his gift. No, there is no "tenderness of the ageing!"

"I've assaulted the world with the might of my voice" – quite true again. It is just that the might of his "voice", of his talent, is not some divine trumpet of Jericho, but a living and earthly voice, a voice appealing for its truthfulness, its loyalty to this earthly truth of ours, enamoured of this "truth" – and hence his talent is convincing and understandable to all the world. The whole world hears the echo of his footsteps.

* Vladimir Mayakovsky, *Cloud in Trousers.*

"And go, handsome, twenty-two years old" – that, too, is true. He "goes", really and truly. He walks, rather than marches over the boards. He does not drag his feet as time-honoured men of fame do, and he does not mince fussily in the pursuit of success. He "goes", he goes with powerful, impressive strides, he goes vigorously, filling his lungs as he breathes, squinting at the sun with joy-filled youthful eyes from under his heavy dark eyebrows, laughing hilariously, reprimanding the lazy, the weak, the dull, and the conceited in a voice of steel, a sharp, intolerant voice, and trampling pitilessly all sham and routine, looking at them guardedly and keenly as at his bitterest enemies.

Yes, handsome! Yes, twenty-two years old! With not a grey hair in his heart! That is Stanislavsky.

Vsevolod Verbitsky

VSEVOLOD VERBITSKY

Separately, the features of his face could not be described as classical, or even proportionate. Yet I never met a man more beautiful. There was something lionesque, something of the eagle, something regal about his imposing figure, his proudly-set silver-haired head with the black eyebrows, under which you saw the sparkle of his inspired eyes.

That is how I remember him in a crowd, where all the others seemed small and insignificant beside him.

But there were times when he was different – kind and simple. He approached people about to hold their entrance examinations to the Art

Theatre, faint with fear at the prospect of the impending ordeal. He shook their hand one by one, with a welcoming and kind smile, and spoke a few reassuring and encouraging words to them. People felt cheered, and there was never a person who did not fall deeply in love with him from that first minute – deeply and for ever.

Such was his charm! Such was his beauty!

* * *

Whenever he spoke about the immense significance of the theatre, about the high honour of being an actor and about the great responsibilities implicit in this honourable calling – about the endless difficulties of the path to genuine stagecraft, about the ceaseless everyday work one had to perform to become master of oneself, to master one's voice, one's body and one's elocution – one felt shamed for being a dilettante in one's attitude to art, for being no more than a craftsman, for one's clowning and affectation. After a talk with him it was inexorably clear that there were just two solutions – either to serve the theatre to the full extent of one's capacities, as he did, or to give it up.

Such was the impact of his high-minded influence, such his dedication to art.

When Vladimir Ivanovich Nemirovich-Danchenko relieved him of the part of Colonel Rostanev after the dress rehearsal of *Stepanchikovo Village** and gave it to Massalitinov,** the company gasped and held its breath in horror, wondering what would happen next. But nothing happened. He submitted without a word to the authority of the stage director, although he considered the part of Rostanev, like that of Dr. Stockman, the best he had ever played. We did not hear any intimation of protest, no word of discontent from him on this score. If Vladimir Ivanovich thought he was not good enough, then he wasn't.

* A stage adaptation of Fyodor Dostoyevsky's novel, *Stepanchikovo Village and Its Inhabitants*, first performed by the Art Theatre on September 26, 1917.
** *Nikolai Massalitinov* – Art Theatre actor from 1907 to 1919.

When Vladimir Ivanovich made critical remarks to members of the company after seeing *The Wise Man** Stanislavsky took down what he said neatly into his notebook like a diligent pupil, listening to the director with the look of a respectful and timid newcomer.

Such was his discipline, such his modesty.

It was evening. Two hours before the curtain. I walked into the empty, dark auditorium. The little lamp on the stage cast a dim light over the setting for Act I of *Ivanov.* A lonely figure was wandering about Ivanov's garden, now sitting down on the bench, now climbing on to the balcony, gesturing and murmuring something. I was stupefied. He was looking for something, rectifying, perfecting something in his matchless Shabelsky, a role he had played many times with unsurpassed brilliance, in his masterpiece of masterpieces.

Such was his thoroughness, such his ceaseless yearning for perfection.

A few of us green ones assembled in the men's dressing room backstage and fervidly rehearsed some passage or other. Then we heard rapid footsteps along the corridor. Stanislavsky appeared on the threshold. His visage was clouded, he was obviously in haste. But he noticed that we were rehearsing and that his coming had interfered. Instantly, his expression changed. Embarrassment appeared in his face for the inconvenience he had caused us. He rose on his toes, put a finger to his mouth, gesturing with his other arm that we should continue, and slowly crossed the dressing room. Noiselessly, he went away, leaving us thoroughly troubled, something he had not wanted at all.

Such was his tact, such his veneration of work.

* * *

It was night. The rehearsal had lasted for many hours. Various scenes and passages had been rehearsed an endless number of times. We got stuck on sentences, words even, for an endless number of half-hours. Some scenes were improved on. We were at the end of our tether. He alone, he who had worked more and harder than any of us, was still lively, fresh, brim-

* A. Ostrovsky's play, *Enough Stupidity in Every Wise Man.*

ming creative energy. At last, it seemed we were through. He summoned us from the stage to the desk and issued his final remarks. Surely, we would be free now to creep home to bed.

"Well, let's go over it once more now, from the beginning," he said suddenly.

Outside, dawn was breaking.

Such was his capacity for work.

* * *

He could be severe, rude almost, and kind, almost tender. It all depended on how you appeared before him.

His censure was scathing. His praise gave wings. False notes caused him what looked like physical pain. Sincere notes brought a happy smile to his lips. Watching his face at a rehearsal was far more interesting and instructive than watching the stage. All the developments on the stage were reflected upon his visage as in an invariably faithful mirror. His visage changed every second, and his expression magically presented thousands of different emotions. You saw his frame straining forward, his eyes sparkling gaily. He laughed loudly and contagiously. That meant the actors lived and performed true to life, that there was a holiday on the stage. Then you saw him leaning back, his eyebrows contracted. Boredom and indifference replaced annoyance on his face. That meant the actors had begun to play-act, that they had strayed from true-to-lifeness and there was drabness on the boards. It was impossible to deceive him on the stage.

Such was his unerring sense of true-to-lifeness.

* * *

We are a lucky lot. Succeeding generations of actors will envy us. Indeed, great luck has fallen our way. It was a privilege to have been his contemporary, to have seen and admired him for many years, to have learned from him, to have delighted in his acting, to have been his partners on the stage, to have revered him as artist and man to whom the lofty word Genius fitted so well.

Vasily Toporkov

VASILY TOPORKOV

When I was beginning to learn the art of acting (over 50 years ago), dramatic schools were already quite widespread. They were sponsored by the imperial theatres. There were also many private schools. But the theatrical world, especially the veteran actors, were prejudiced against schools. They said the art of dramatic acting could not be learned in a school – that one learned through practice only, on the stage.

In those days most actors had no schooling at all, and acted, so to speak "by the dictates of their heart". The sceptics, the opponents of learning, held this up as an argument.

But the schools gradually came into their own, and the opponents of dramatic schooling grew fewer. It was recognised that schools had a right to exist, that they had to exist.

By the time I met Konstantin Sergeyevich Stanislavsky the new school had developed to maturity and a new method, Stanislavsky's method, of training actors was universally accepted. Yet Konstantin Sergeyevich used to say that our art was not art, not professional art, that it was amateurish and lacked the firm and definitive theory possessed by music and the other arts. The actor had no idea yet of the rudimentary elements that comprised his art, and had no chance to practise them. He did not have sketches, gammas and exercises to train on.

"It would be absolutely incongruous," he used to say, "if an orchestra musician would play only in symphony orchestras and if this were all he did to perfect his technique. That is absolutely out of the question.

"It is just as incongruous for a ballet dancer to dance at performances only, and not exercise daily.

"Yet the dramatic actor is deprived of exercises, because he does not know what he should exercise, because he does not know the elements of which his art consists, because he does not have a theory. But for some reason this is considered tolerable in dramatic art. For some reason, the actor who plays in performances only thinks that this is quite sufficient for his artistic development."

Konstantin Sergeyevich would not suffer it. He examined the creative process of the actor very closely and devoted his life to a search for the more lasting foundations of training. He strove to determine the theoretical aspect, if only in an elementary form, for that, he hoped, would lead him to his goal along shorter and more reliable paths. What he wanted was to develop scores for the various parts and productions, etc.

By artistic technique Konstantin Sergeyevich meant a technique that would safeguard the creative essence and guide the actor to the threshold of the subconscious, to intuition. What always surprised me most in his treatment of actors was the way he used to warn them against all the cunningly placed pitfalls of theatrical routine and show them the path to live, organic actions. I was stunned by the results he achieved. They seemed a near miracle. Yet Stanislavsky had a thousand devices to achieve them.

This was what made me so much a votary of Stanislavsky's system.

Whenever we complained that our productions were too few and that we worked on them for years, Konstantin Sergeyevich agreed that this was not right. "But," he said, "to produce a new play every month we would have to close the theatre for a few years and develop our techniques. After the actors will have mastered stage techniques, the director need not take so much time to produce a play. Suppose someone comes to me and tells me he wants to learn an aria. I start teaching him and discover that his voice has not been set, so that before teaching him his aria I have to give him vocal classes. The aria has to wait until after I train his voice. I suppose you realise how much time that takes. Yet it is with untrained voices that you come to me for rehearsals. I do not get the material to create the living body of a production. Before cutting the costume I have to weave the cloth for it myself. Learn the necessary techniques, and we'll produce a new play every month."

That is the simplest, the most intelligible, the clearest one can mention when recalling one's work with Konstantin Sergeyevich, when recalling his ambition to create organic life on the boards, to create a living actor-and-man who performs organically.

Now that I have come this far, I would like to relate a few episodes from the practical classes we had at the Leontyevsky Lane studio. What I remember best is my work on *Dead Souls*. All attempts to adapt Gogol's poem to the stage had never had any success. There had been more than a hundred adaptations, but none of them, essentially, had the finesse of the poem. The same was true of the latest adaptation by the Art Theatre. It was very hard to work with the material we had. We started on it without Konstantin Sergeyevich. The grotesque was very much in the fashion then, and we laid an accent on external exaggeration, reckoning that Gogol had had an extremely keen pen. But what moved us most was the current fashion.

So we brought the production to the dress rehearsal, and Konstantin Sergeyevich came to see what we had accomplished. He did not like it. He said he had not understood anything, that nothing of what he had seen had reached him, and decided to tackle the matter himself.

We removed our make-up, took off our costumes and started all over again. That is, we came to Konstantin Sergeyevich's, seated ourselves round a table, and began from scratch.

Stanislavsky said to me:

"You wanted a razor-sharp form of embodiment. You wanted to seize the result at once, though you did not know and did not try all the ways of achieving that form. The outcome is that you've dislocated all your joints. You have failed to produce a keen outline. What is more, you're not a living being at all, and you have no idea of how to walk on the stage. Grotesque is a very keen form and I will be the last to deny it. Furthermore, it is the highest of all forms in art. But not all of us are destined to master it easily.

"I know of only one actor who performed it unfailingly, Varlamov,* and of only one writer, Gogol. You made the attempt while lacking the means. To achieve an image of consummate sharpness, laconic to the supreme, and to embody it organically, you have to begin with cultivating the soil, and the roots from which this splendid and living plant is to grow. Yet you did not bother about the roots. What you wanted was to grasp the flower, and that is absolutely impossible."

"When I was in Paris," Stanislavsky continued, "I saw an excellent comedian playing in a sordid play. When enacting a quarrel with his mother-in-law he took his trousers off on the stage and beat her with them. That was magnificent, and I watched it with pleasure because the comedian convinced me with his supreme and organic logic that in the circumstances he had had no other choice. But to do so one must either possess immense talent, for which everything is at once simple and clear, or work very hard on cultivating the roots from which the plant is to grow."

So we began cultivating the soil. I recall clearly that we started with the text. Konstantin Sergeyevich was of the belief that one should not begin with the text, but often went back on his own rule when he thought it best. This time, too, he began with the text. My first rehearsal boiled down to speaking just one sentence: "Having come to this town I deem it my duty

* *Konstantin Varlamov* (1848-1915) – famous actor of the Alexandrinsky Theatre.

to pay my respects . . .", etc. Stanislavsky would not end the rehearsal until he made me speak the idea in that sentence clearly, musically, consummately. As far as I remember, the rehearsal lasted four hours. But we did not get farther than that one sentence.

We worked hard on the text and on the movements, and advanced slowly but surely towards "relocating the joints". Only then did we start to build up the inner life, the inner logic of Chichikov's behaviour. What Konstantin Sergeyevich did with me is a classical example of what he called "cultivation of the soil" and "strengthening of the roots" of the future plant – the stage image.

Take one of our many rehearsals.

We were rehearsing Nozdryov's scene (Nozdryov was played by Moskvin*). After a long to-and-fro Nozdryov and Chichikov decided to end the matter with a game of checkers. The checkers take up a certain space of time, during which the players speak just two sentences: "It's a long time since I played checkers", and, "catch me believing you play badly!" That is one of the most difficult passages in the scene. How could we make it dynamic? Whenever we came to this point, there was a blank – we felt something was missing, something to capture the audience.

So we applied to Konstantin Sergeyevich. We told him we did not know what to do with the scene, how to fill it, how to make it expressive. His reply was: "It will not be interesting to the onlooker until you yourselves will show an interest in the outcome of the game. Don't people follow a game of chess with bated breath? See that you are interested in the outcome of the game; it is sure to reach the audience through your physical actions. Find the right logic of behaviour for two excited checker players."

Konstantin Sergeyevich could have sat down and shown us how to play, and we could simply have imitated him. But this would never have produced what he wanted. What he wanted was for us to find the right way by intuitive creation, without forcing the creative essence. He wanted living people in this scene, who would abandon their eyes, ears and nerves to their

* *Ivan Moskvin* (1874-1946) – a distinguished Art Theatre player, People's Artiste of the U.S.S.R.

Scene 6 of *Dead Souls,* stage adaptation of Nikolai Gogol's poem of the same name. Vasily Toporkov as Chichikov (left) and Ivan Moskvin as Nozdryov

part, rather than the hackneyed devices of stagecraft. That is why he did not show us how checkers are played. Instead, he suggested that we try to take an interest in the game. But nothing came of it. Then he asked me this question:

"Please, tell me, Vasily Osipovich, how much money you stand to gain if you beat Nozdryov in this game of checkers?"

"I don't know."

Konstantin Sergeyevich grew pale with anger, and said: "Well, how do you expect to play checkers, how do you expect to play keenly and tensely if you don't even know what you are playing for? What is going to feed your temperament? That is something you should have thought about first. You ought to know what you are risking. You ought to know what you are going to do with the money you win. And so forth. To begin with, a thousand questions. Let's figure it out, let's do some counting. Well, what do you think?"

I did not even know where to begin.

"Well, let's put it this way," said Konstantin Sergeyevich. "You need dead souls. How many of them is Nozdryov likely to have? Well, how many?"

Stanislavsky delved into all the details of Nozdryov's farm and proved to me that Nozdryov was bound to have very many dead souls. Ultimately, we calculated that Chichikov, who had staked a hundred rubles, would gain something like 40,000 rubles if he won.

"Do you realise now how eager Chichikov was to win? Think about it, think of what 40,000 rubles meant at that time. Do you realise how excited Chichikov must have been? Chichikov is not the kind of man to disregard the odds."

"What have we?" he continued. "We have this: you have to play excitedly, with great abandon. But what does that mean? What actions would express it? What does 'excited playing' mean, what does excitement mean, what physical actions does it involve? Have you ever gambled?"

"Yes," I replied (that was quite true, I had gambled much).

"Well, try to remember how you behaved when you played for big stakes."

It was thus, inch by inch, that we established that the closest attention to the game and the partner was the chief element of a game for high stakes. This close attention was the main thing.

Konstantin Sergeyevich said:

"Now we know that attention is the main thing. Please try to train your attention. See how you would act if you really had to win 40,000. That is not something you can simply tell yourself on the stage. You will have to find something that will make you be attentive. Sit down and play checkers. Let's play a real game. Try to make five moves in sixty seconds. Make those moves, and tell me exactly what they were and how you think your opponent will respond to them."

This was how Konstantin Sergeyevich made me watch the game with utmost attention for this brief spell, and gradually, unnoticeably, he turned this scene in the play into a real game of checkers for us. We were excited by it, and played it with abandon, eager to beat the other fellow.

After having created this real, true-to-life excitement, Konstantin Sergeyevich asked me: "Is the essence of this contest clear to you?"

"Yes, it is."

"Try to play once more. When you rehearse this thing, don't just play it, but try to plan a few moves before you start the game."

That was how he wedded me, man and "Chichikov", with all of Nozdryov's affairs, with all the possibilities connected with this game of checkers. He calculated to a kopek how much I was likely to lose, and established the substance of a game for high stakes. He made me play with a lively interest, and had me try various devices.

"This trifle of a truth," he said, "will open the door for you to genuine intuition, and you may do something you would never do deliberately, something you will never be able to repeat again as perfectly."

When we rehearsed the same scene with Livanov, Konstantin Sergeyevich employed another shrewd and cunning device to rouse our intuition, and suddenly we began to behave very organically and vividly. He was thrilled by our performance, and said it was wonderful. "That was true to life! It was a masterpiece! That's the way to act!"

He added: "If you want to do it all over again to the minutest detail, you will never succeed. What one does by intuition is unrepeatable. When you play this scene again, don't think of the results, but of the roots."

When he released the production, Konstantin Sergeyevich said:

"The production is by no means ready, but I am releasing it, because I see that the soil and roots have been cultivated. I see small, but living sprouts, which will, if you tend them, grow and yield real blossoms."

To me Stanislavsky said:

"Now, Vasily Osipovich, you have learned to walk on the stage and to do things on it, but you do not behave quite like Chichikov yet. You are a living being, but still a baby. Please continue learning to follow this path. In about ten years you will behave like Chichikov, and in another ten years you will be Chichikov's living image, and in still another ten years you will be able to play Gogol."

Such was the scope of Stanislavsky's thinking.

When he insisted that we embark on the path of true-to-life, organic actions, abandoning the variegated assortment of theatrical stereotype, he used to say:

"You have at most a hundred ways of solving a scene with stereotyped theatrical devices, even though you may be a big actor, while true life has a countless number. Theatrical acting expressed through devices of even a very good but purely theatrical technique of 'performing', differs as much from true-to-life organic behaviour born of the actor's intuition as false teeth differ from real ones, living hair from a wig, and paper flowers from living plants."

My association with Konstantin Sergeyevich has convinced me of this, and I am doing my best to master his techniques and to use them in my acting and directing.

Nikolai Khmelyov

NIKOLAI KHMELYOV

My highly esteemed Konstantin Sergeyevich,

Allow me to congratulate you, and to express to you, a brilliant teacher, my delight, my veneration and my deep respect.

Your name will always live in art and will stand for the unattainable beauty to which every actor who wants to serve the theatre seriously and thoughtfully, must aspire.

Your loyal pupil,

N. Khmelyov

A letter to Stanislavsky,
Moscow, September 12, 1936

Vasily Sakhnovsky

VASILY SAKHNOVSKY

In the latter years of Stanislavsky's life, no matter what play we rehearsed at the Art Theatre, whenever he released it there was always a special period in it – the rehearsals in Leontyevsky Lane. The Leontyevsky Lane home was Konstantin Sergeyevich's last home (the lane has been renamed Stanislavsky Street).

Whoever came to see Konstantin Sergeyevich at the small, old-fashioned two-storey Moscow house with the round garden before it, always felt his heart thump as he climbed the wooden steps to the door (as in *Wit Works Woe*).

In the upper storey hall all of us took our places round the table with the immense ashtray, on the benches near the windows between the low, pot-bellied columns, and conversed in hushed voices, smoking and glancing at the closed door as we waited. When the lot of us had arrived, the director of the play pressed the button beside the locked door. A few minutes later, Natalya Gavrilovna, Konstantin Sergeyevich's *major-domo*, would poke her grey head out of the doorway, then vanish to get her orders behind the oak door to Konstantin Sergeyevich's study, and invite us to come in.

Strangely, nothing in the study was associated with art. There were two official-looking mirrors on the walls, a silly-looking wooden partition, a hanger with copper hooks behind the sofa, four American cupboards with books (their broken panes replaced with glass from show-windows that still had shops' names on it), and two incongruous desks which nobody ever occupied. On one of them was a mock-up covered with cloth and paper. It was never shown to anyone, but everyone inspected it when Konstantin Sergeyevich's back was turned. On the other desk was a pile of neatly dusted but never read theatrical books – English, French and Japanese, with their authors' respectful inscriptions, "To Stanislavsky". There was also a museum piece, a little table no one was allowed to touch, and a few soft chairs and armchairs with shabby dust covers, on which both the Art Theatre and the Stanislavsky Opera companies rehearsed their plays. Rugs and leather suitcases, the companions of a recent voyage abroad, were stacked under the desks and the mirrors. There were household things behind the bookshelves – a children's chair, a baby bed, and something else.

It was always very clean in the study, the floor was polished to a shine, the room well heated, the Dutch stove breathing warmth, and baskets of recently sent or faded flowers dispositioned indiscriminately around the room. Perhaps it was because Konstantin Sergeyevich's study and all its appointments did not fall in with the usual notions of art, or perhaps because it was so unusually quiet in that old house in Leontyevsky Lane and all of us were, so to speak, all ears – perhaps those were the reasons why he achieved his most brilliant results in that purely and typically Moscow environment.

Konstantin Sergeyevich usually sat on the vast sofa covered with a bed-sheet, beside a small portable table on which he spread the manuscript of his "system". Often he added something to it with a fountain pen. He was always neatly shaven, always smart, specially clothed for the rehearsal.

At first we would all push about awkwardly and say our hellos incoherently, all of which took up two or three minutes. Konstantin Sergeyevich peered at us. The director of the play would sit next to him on the sofa, the prompter beside the window and the assistant beside the door. The players sat in the armchairs and in the chairs, in a semi-circle round Konstantin Sergeyevich.

At first we talked in "generalities". If Konstantin Sergeyevich was well, if he was not pale, if his eyes were shining, he would fling his pince-nez over his right shoulder and joke, make trifling compliments and ask venomous questions about the latest theatrical news.

Then he would smile officiously, straighten his back, clap his hands, and say:

"Well, let's begin!"

His face took on an alert expression. His eyes squinted a bit, the pupils grew sharp, and his lips and face seemed to follow the movements of the lips and face of the player, until there would suddenly come a minute when Konstantin Sergeyevich stopped following. A kind of sour look would appear on his face. It grew severe and ponderous. He twitched his lips nervously, and soon we heard his strong and angered voice.

The rehearsal would stop. Konstantin Sergeyevich would begin analysing the passage. The actor had to tell him how and why he arrived in the state in which the passage began.

After the pattern of the preceding events had been analysed, we began working on the immediate task which, as Konstantin Sergeyevich remarked, the actor had failed to accomplish.

Very often, when trying to make the actor perform his bit properly (Konstantin Sergeyevich did not differentiate between any of the Art Theatre veterans and the newcomers), he devoted the bulk of the rehearsal, sometimes all of it, to a search for what he called the "little truth". We were all struck by the variety and wealth of examples which Konstantin Sergeyevich suggested, we were amazed at his instructions, his digressions, his stupendous stock of experience, and his startling discoveries.

At these rehearsals all of us experienced a sense of exhilaration and inspiration. To be sure, those were not even rehearsals, but wonderful lessons filled with a profound content. Konstantin Sergeyevich would digress, speak about art, and at once gave examples of what he wanted, setting new assignments all the time. The others would prompt him or argue with him. At his rehearsals a few of us would always be taking notes, writing down the examples he gave, the things he said, and noting the results.

But there were other times when, no sooner had we begun, Konstantin Sergeyevich would stop us, and exclaim:

"I don't believe you!"

Sometimes – and this was especially "dangerous" for the rehearsal – Konstantin Sergeyevich would lean forward, put his hand to his ear and say quite politely:

"What did you say? I didn't catch it."

The actor would repeat his lines.

"What's that?" Konstantin Sergeyevich would ask again. "I didn't understand a thing."

After that he usually anatomised the sentence, wanting it correctly stressed and the idea properly conveyed, or would start working on the actor's elocution.

Frequently, Konstantin Sergeyevich would declare that the actor did not convey the idea, that he did not see what he was talking about. Then he would work hard on finding the "magic if", that is, the actions that would have occurred if the person rehearsing would really land in the offered circumstances.

By making the actors find the "little truths", Stanislavsky strove to make them behave true to life. And whenever they succeeded, if truth and simplicity captured them, you would forget, sitting there beside Konstantin Sergeyevich, that they were actors, for as they spoke their lines they seemed to speak for themselves, the author's words became their own.

Sometimes – and this was the most interesting part of the rehearsals in Leontyevsky Lane – Konstantin Sergeyevich would suddenly sense the truest and keenest line for the scene or act, and would start revising all that had been done before, moulding an entirely new inner pattern.

This part of the rehearsal always revealed Stanislavsky's amazing talent. Mostly, he would begin with an absolutely indescribable lecture, explanation or demonstration – I don't know how to qualify it best. He would put the actors on to the *rhythm* of the scene as he had suddenly grasped it by telling them various episodes from life, by startling improvisations. Everything else seemed to fade beside the vivid images, in which his immense figure would appear now here, now there. A minimum of motion, a minimum of gesture, just a little mimicry and a scarcely noticeable change of stature – yet an amazing creative transformation!

Scenic images arose easily and quickly, and they were not just external, but filled with an inner meaning, growing naturally out of the main task, out of the "grain", out of the common action of the role. Every such image lived in its own, individual rhythm which, merging with the rhythm of the general movement, became a solid basis for the intrinsic pattern of the scene. As the play developed, this rhythm captured the actors more and more strongly, prompting new situations and unexpected *mises en scène.*

Once he had found and shown the rhythmic setting, Konstantin Sergeyevich wanted the actors to produce a definite pattern. He made every actor demonstrate his rhythm. He denuded the scheme and gradually introduced the individual lines of the movement into the whole of the scene. He created complex counterpoints of action and then, like a conductor, followed the inner rhythm of every player until he achieved the desired pattern and the intrinsic image of the scene came into full evidence.

As he went on, he asked the actors to perform various exercises likely to excite the desired emotion or unconsciously rouse their feelings. He explained how they should seize upon the desired state, and pointed out various methods to the directors that would help obtain results from the actors. As he did all this he never betrayed himself, never indicated what he was leading up to. All the time, he protected the creative intuition of the actor and watched the processes in which the desired state arose in the actor.

I know of no actor, no director, who failed to experience a physical sense of Stanislavsky's artistic charm when working with him. It is hard to tell how this volitional influence was transmitted to the actor. While binding

Stanislavsky in 1926

him in some things, it led him insistently to the goal Konstantin Sergeyevich had set.

The rehearsals in Leontyevsky Lane were in the fullest sense of the word an actors' laboratory. When Konstantin Sergeyevich came to the theatre and took his seat at the director's table and began to mould the production, a different kind of artist-director-producer appeared.

The lighting, the rhythm, his finds, and his prodigious inventiveness, his immense imagination, invaded the purely histrionic realm.

The director-producer who saw the play as a whole was preoccupied with its style, with the super-objective, the idea he had to convey to the audience through the formal aspects of the production – the scenes, the settings, sets, costumes, and sound and light effects. This interfered with his duties as the teacher, the actor's mentor.

In this work, which was full of temptations for his boundless imagination, Konstantin Sergeyevich created productions where the actor's effort was the basic and chief element.

Stanislavsky maintained that the actor was the carrier of all the author's ideas, obscuring by his performance all the sets and subtleties of the director – all of which could exist so long as they did not interfere with the acting.

That was what we usually talked about after rehearsals in Leontyevsky Lane: the scene painters, the style of a production, the skill of behaving on the boards, the skill of wearing costumes, and the continuous exercises of actors, the training.

Usually, there was a crowd of people in the rehearsal room, because it was not only a place for rehearsing but because people came there to see, to hear, to take notes. Konstantin Sergeyevich's medical nurse looked in every hour in her white gown and brought a medicine in a large glass bowl covered with a clean sheet of paper. He had to swallow it, while she invariably remarked that creative tension was bad for her patient. Natalya Gavrilovna, the *major-domo,* reminded him over and over again that it was time for dinner, that he had been rehearsing for four hours without a break, and that the doctors had told him not to. But nothing could stop him.

Then, at last, the rehearsal was over. Those of us who were not playing that night would stay in the study. We would sit round Konstantin Sergeyevich, question him and hear his answers. He would recall the actors he had seen, various practical experiments, and draw conclusions that he promptly put into his book.

Then it would all be over. Weary, Konstantin Sergeyevich would say goodbye to us and keep someone behind for an eye-to-eye talk of 10 or 15 minutes. The door to the hall would bang shut, and the light would be switched off.

All of us who ever attended the rehearsals in Leontyevsky Lane, glance up unconsciously as we pass the house, at the three oval windows of the study and the two square ones of the bedroom, where the thread of continuous artistic thought was spun for so long and the fount of creative theatrical art gushed so richly.

Mikhail Kedrov

MIKHAIL KEDROV

The Last Experiment

The production of *Tartuffe* at the Moscow Art Theatre has a history all its own. It was Stanislavsky's last production, and was tackled on his initiative. The original idea was not producing *Tartuffe* so much as accomplishing certain experimental assignments connected with new methods and stage techniques. The rehearsals, therefore, were very different from those we had for other productions.

Konstantin Stanislavsky was much more than a magnificent actor, much more than a great stage director who made a science of the art of directing. He was also a great innovator and reformer, a penetrating explorer of the essence of stagecraft, the founder of a school of acting, a school known as "Stanislavsky's system".

The most trenchant feature about Stanislavsky was that he aspired tirelessly towards perfecting theatrical art. He was never satisfied with the standards of contemporary stagecraft. He looked for new ways and means of revealing the subtlest organic processes of human life on the stage.

The purpose of realistic art is to show man as he lives and breathes. But how to make the actor who performs in an invented theatrical environment, among thought-up sets, in the emotional climate of a public performance, how to make him *remain alive*, to make him act true to life, to see, to hear and to speak on the stage as a living being does off the stage – how to make him do it rather than "play-act"? What are the ways of relieving the creative personality of an actor from the fetters of stage conventions, how to help him employ his organic character in his stagecraft?

In his search for a practical solution, Konstantin Sergeyevich discovered a new method for the actor to develop his part and the director to develop his production. The actor's work is made more concrete. Indivisible unity between the physical and the mental in a man's life is taken as the point of departure, and the physical line of an actor's life on the stage is properly organised. The idea is to penetrate into the most elaborate, the most profound emotions through a properly patterned performance of physical actions, through the logic of these actions. The actor is induced to rouse these emotions within himself to create the desired scenic image.

This was the method Stanislavsky employed in instructing young actors, but there was another question that preoccupied him: Is it possible to apply this new method to an actor with ten, twenty, even thirty years of acting?

That was how the idea arose to make an experimental production with a group of actors who would try to realise Stanislavsky's ideas. Molière's *Tartuffe* was to be the material for it. Stanislavsky picked a group of actors and invited me to be the stage director and to play the title role.

Once he had us together, Stanislavsky said:

"Forget your seniorities and titles – they are out of place now. All of you are pupils. Your purpose is to master a new technique. We are not going to perform the play for the public. We have come here to learn."

He said he had no intention of putting the play on in the theatre. "I am not running after glory, I've had enough of it. It would be silly to end up by producing yet another play, no matter how brilliantly directed. I don't have long to live, and the last thing I want to do is to transmit my living experience, my knowledge, to those who want it. I want people to know how to do what I have done, after I'm dead. What I want is to give you guidance, rather than bask in the glory of yet one more production. Take all of it – I am here to give you everything I know."

He said that his *Tartuffe* was a testament he wanted to leave behind.

"The keenest and most understandable in our art," said Stanislavsky, "is the real thing, the thing that is true to life. I don't want you to 'perform' emotions or to 'act' an image. That would be the artisan approach I want you to avoid. Learn to perform the simplest physical actions on the stage correctly and organically. The succession and logic of these actions will induce the desired complex of emotions. In effecting the logic of physical actions you will come to the logic of emotions – and that is the core of an actor's work."

All this posed new tasks at our rehearsals and imparted a very specific character to them. Konstantin Sergeyevich did not speak of any "plans" and told me that I was not to speak about them either. He believed that, at least in this experimental production, the director should learn as much as the actors did.

Whenever I reminded Konstantin Sergeyevich that the hour was sure to come sooner or later when we would have to think of the stage production as a whole, and then relayed some of my ideas, he replied:

"I realise all that. Splendid, you may create still more interesting and intricate compositions, but I want you to remember that your roles will be 'out of tune'. What I mean is, the actors performing them will not have mastered the new techniques to a sufficient degree."

It was to the business of "tuning pianos", i.e., the roles, that we devoted our sessions.

We worked very hard. What else could we do – Stanislavsky was inexorable. He would not tolerate the least trace of unrealness, and pounced

Rehearsal of *Tartuffe* at Stanislavsky's home in 1937

severely on the actors for trying to play their parts "off the bat". The play itself, its various passages, were for a long time just raw material for our training.

We performed numerous exercises set by Konstantin Sergeyevich. The actors, most of them with considerable stage experience, had to stifle their impatience to play. When Stanislavsky saw it, he simply forbade us to work on the play. We trained our concentration in exercises and sketches, and learned to perform our actions true to life, to see and hear our partners, to watch their actions, to perceive their inner wishes and intentions through their intonations, their behaviour, the expression of their eyes, etc.

What we were after was a true-to-life, unconscious concentration, rather than an actors' formal concentration. Strange as it may sound, it is always very difficult to concentrate one's attention, and to use it, on the stage. It is far easier to "play", to enact an actor's attention.

Konstantin Sergeyevich refused to set any dates. He feared that that would encourage us to employ our old techniques. In his opinion it was liable to speed nothing but the professional process in the development of the production. An actor who lacks perfect technique, draws involuntarily upon *clichés* in his creative efforts and produces a hackneyed pattern, much to the detriment of his creative imagination. It is unquestionably desirable to reduce the terms of rehearsing and preparing a play, but not before you have actors with developed stage techniques. This was one of the reasons why he intended to impart his new method to us, for that method was meant to lighten the work an actor does in developing his part.

Konstantin Stanislavsky was deeply engrossed in our creative experiment and cut short all attempts by us actors to launch out into the production before the time was ripe. Whenever he noticed an actor's impatience, he said bitterly:

"Be honest about it, tell me before we go on which of you want to tackle your role at once. I don't need them."

He was bent on focusing our attention entirely on his new method, and avoided speaking at the time about images for purely pedagogical reasons. Whenever an actor tried to hint at an image, at the specific features of an image, he would reply:

"*You are neither Orgon, nor Tartuffe, you are you, acting in the suggested environment of Orgon or Tartuffe. Be honest with yourself: what would you do if you happened to be in their shoes.* At the moment I don't want you to do anything special, anything you may think best suited for the image, the play and the time, etc. All I want you to do is spot the simplest true-to-life logic of behaviour based on human nature and equally applicable to people of any epoch. I will not rest until you learn to behave like that."

We got our assignments from Konstantin Sergeyevich and did them on our own. "Don't expect Konstantin Sergeyevich to come and show every one of you how to play your parts," we were told. "What you want is initiative and patience – the difficult will then become familiar, the familiar easy, and the easy beautiful."

Our *Tartuffe* experiment lasted until the spring of 1938. Our last meeting with Konstantin Sergeyevich was on April 27, 1938. We had had something like 20 classes with him, excluding the three meetings with the scene painter and myself, the director. The rest of the time we had been on our own.

Konstantin Sergeyevich died in the summer of 1938. That put me in a most difficult situation. I felt that the burden of responsibility fell on my own shoulders now. No longer was I responsible for just my own part, and for the general director's line. From now on I was also responsible for the way we applied the new method and for bringing the experiment that Stanislavsky had begun to its logical conclusion.

We could not give the whole thing up, for all of us were morally obliged to Stanislavsky to bring it to its consummation. To be sure, we were all quite earnestly enthused over his latest creative ideas.

So we decided to take the matter to its consummation, whatever the risks of defeat. In the circumstances, we felt we had to proceed from pure training to actual production. Our experiment entered a new stage, the stage of artistic production.

The job was completed. The play was shown to the public. It was up to the public now to say what was good about it, and what was bad.

The method I just spoke about so much is no more than a means of producing a play. No method is good if traces of it are visible in the performance. What the audience wants is the result, nothing else.

What were the ideas that gave us guidance?

Molière's *Tartuffe* was, for us, mostly a play about hypocrisy.

Among the large variety of hypocrites, Tartuffe's image seems to me the most repulsive and dangerous. No wonder the name has become a symbol. Tartuffe is a hypocrite with the basest of instincts, a parasite pursuing selfish goals, a man capable of the foulest of acts, a traitor and a cynic devoid of moral principles of any sort. But he concealed all this behind a veil of high-minded ideals. He employed his camouflage with great subtlety, and was very hard to expose, because he was an excellent psychologist, he knew human weaknesses and the ways of exploiting them.

Hypocrisy and deceit presuppose yet another line in the play – the line of gullibility. It is brought out by the image of Orgon. Credulity is one of the most vulnerable qualities of human nature. Whenever excessive, it may cause a person to lose his capacity for critical thinking. Such credulity is no less dangerous than Tartuffe's hypocrisy.

Making the most of this credulity, knowing all human weaknesses, Tartuffe, a master of unprincipled time-serving in any environment, wears a mask of sincerity to achieve his base goals.

Molière wrote *Tartuffe* at a time when religion pervaded all the facets of life. It was only natural, therefore, that the mask of a devoted servant of the church, his piety, was the most fitting vehicle for the title role. Progressive for his time, Molière aimed his satire above all against the hypocrites of the church, but if tartuffeism were restricted to the church alone, Molière's play would lose much of its impact. The image is all-embracing. It should not be limited to just one trait. Indeed, the greatness of the classics lies in their universality. The point of their ideas is not dulled by time.

I did not think it right to regard *Tartuffe* as a play aimed solely against religious hypocrisy, against the seventeenth-century church. To accentuate the anti-religious aspect of the play would mean to give precedence to pure tendency rather than to its essence and idea.

By giving the play a purely anti-religious interpretation we would have reduced the range of hypocrites against whom Molière's satire could be aimed.

It is a pity that Molière's plays were often burdened in their theatrical embodiment by a profusion of *clichés* and ready-for-use devices of stagecraft. Things had come to a point where a set of special "specific" methods of performing Molière were worked out. These included a cascade of bows and gestures, without which, ostensibly, Molière was not Molière. There was an assortment of pseudo-French movements and a torrent of temperamental speech that blotted out the subtleties of thought. There were also all the other stage attributes, which totally obscured the human images.

We renounced all of that at once. We believed that Molière had written about living people, not masks. We believed Molière's play dealt with human passions, rather than false pseudo-theatrical emotions. What we wanted was to produce a play of genuine human passions and complex human relationships.

Tartuffe is a satire, but satirical laughter is not induced by exaggerated masks devoid of human sentiments. Most of all, satire arises when true-to-life human passions, while retaining their realness, grow to hyperbolical dimensions and living people enmeshed in these passions, get involved in ridiculous and incongruous situations.

The more sincerely and devotedly Orgon worships Tartuffe, the more desperately he defends him from his family. The more sincerely Madame Pernelle pours out her anger upon the family and insists on Tartuffe's piety, the more vigorously the family opposes Orgon's obsession, and the deeper the profundities of the play, its message, will be relayed.

I attach immense importance to a correct alignment of the conflicting forces. Tartuffe won Orgon. The rest of the family fights tartuffeism tooth and nail. There are defeats and there are victories on either side. The stage director must take account of it all, because he must organise the struggle properly. If he fails, the play will be robbed of its intrinsic dynamics. Its passions will be groundless and Molière's images static. There is no genuine, emotion-packed *Tartuffe* unless there is savage struggle unto death between the characters.

We wanted to achieve this genuine and passionate abandon, which fills the living images of Molière's play, in the manner expounded by our teacher, Konstantin Sergeyevich Stanislavsky.

Yuri Olesha

YURI OLESHA

A Great Man of the Theatre

1

I do not remember when I first heard of Stanislavsky. My childhood and youth passed in Odessa. Did the Art Theatre ever come there? Very likely it did. In any case, I heard the word "artists" far back in my childhood, and definitely in relation to some wonderful theatre.

I saw *Blue Bird* in Odessa. It was performed on the stage of the local Opera House, and in my memory the outward scale of the spectacle was immense. The scene showing the realm of the future is impregnated in my memory in the shape of a Gothic edifice. Later I learned that the production had been a copy of the Moscow Art Theatre production.

Stanislavsky was very much in love with *Blue Bird.* In *My Life in Art* he gives us a delightful description of his trip to meet Maeterlinck, about their acquaintance, and about the man himself. There is a lot to be said for *Blue Bird* being one of Stanislavsky's favourites. Was it only the scope it offered for various theatrical effects that enraptured Stanislavsky? No, of course not. It was the poetry of the tale that captured his imagination. How wonderfully he conveyed this poetry on the stage! I wonder if there is anything more superb in the theatre than the scene in the Land of Recollections where little children in caps of different colours appear suddenly at the table, banging their spoons. Watching it one feels that this once a fairy-tale is quite at home amidst the ponderous and straightforward nature of the theatre. *Blue Bird* is one of those plays that runs on and on. Indeed, *Blue Bird* is still running. Thinking back to my childhood, I cannot help remembering two little figures – those of a boy and a girl – so well described in Maeterlinck's remarks. The remarks say the boy is dressed as little Tom Thumb and the girl as little Red Riding Hood. In my mind's eye I see these two little figures walking forward with a cage into the thick of a fog – the past.

I have no idea how our children, most of whom are budding physicists and mechanics, react to this production. There is not much chance of their believing in reincarnation, but the message of the fairy-tale is sure to reach their hearts. Happiness, they will realise, is attained in that kind and simple environment where you work among people you love.

2

The first time I came to Moscow was in 1922. The comrade who showed me round the city brought me to Kamergersky Lane, where I saw the building of the Art Theatre. Moscow is changing so quickly that the memory stretching back no more than a decade reacts to the changes with an old man's incantations. "There still was then", and "there wasn't yet". But it is a fact of life. Kamergersky Lane was still cobbled then, and one of the doors had a shrieking green signboard showing a fat man sailing in a giant rubber shoe. I don't remember now what the signboard stood for.

The Art Theatre building with its modernistic bas-reliefs did not look attractive to me. It may be recalled that it had not been specially designed for the Art Theatre. When you look at it, you realise clearly that the Art Theatre was founded in a capitalist society, and that it worked and developed in spite of it. It was a cause, performed in this building whose fronton is reminiscent of the cover of a decadent magazine, a cause comparable to the life's work of a powerful writer whose writings influenced his time. No wonder two great literary names, Chekhov's and Gorky's, are so closely associated with it. The theatre put on triumphant productions of *The Sea-Gull* and *The Lower Depths.* The head of that theatre, who undertook to produce a rejected play* because he was convinced it possessed beauty that people had failed to see, will always stand out in magnificent relief.

Stanislavsky's daring in doing so is perhaps one of the finest chapters in the history of the Russian theatre. Considering the hurt which *The Sea-Gull*'s failure in the Alexandrinsky Theatre inflicted on the ailing Chekhov, its triumph at the Art Theatre illumines the latter with a special luminous glory. It is a theatre that put on a play far removed from any existing products of world dramaturgy – the delightful and truly unrepeatable Chekhov drama. How absorbed Chekhov was by thoughts of the dramatic theatre! How his own efforts in this realm diverged from the demands he made upon drama.

How magnificent the results of this divergence! His famous demand that the gun seen in the first act must on all accounts go off in the last, has very little in common with the trail-blazing Chekhov dramas which deny the need of a climax. After Chekhov nobody has ever written dramas like Chekhov's. The theatrical embodiment of Chekhov's dramas by the Art Theatre is a truly unusual phenomenon in the history of the arts. The innermost trends nurtured by the author were guessed by the director and his company, and this short episode in the history of Russian art has none, or few, others to match it in brilliance.

* The reference is to the failure suffered by *The Sea-Gull* at the Alexandrinsky Theatre.

How impressive the figure of the theatre director who takes his company to the other end of the country just to show a sick writer what he had done with his play! *

There is this episode in Stanislavsky's biography. And that alone is enough to make it a wonderful biography.

3

Konstantin Sergeyevich – that was how everybody called him. He went to the boxes at the rehearsals, stooping to enter them because he was very tall, and picked a seat with the lightness of a butterfly, because he did not want to distract attention. His face was puckered. People pucker their faces that way when they are about to see a spectacle they have looked forward to seeing.

"Konstantin Sergeyevich is here!"

His every appearance in the theatre, be it only a casual business call, was a big event.

Although my play for children, *Three Fat Men*, was produced by the Art Theatre, I did not have any discussions about it with Stanislavsky. I was introduced to him, though. Soon after, he went abroad for medical treatment, and, if I recall rightly, was away for over a year. *Three Fat Men* was produced without him. I have no more than visual impressions of our acquaintanceship. I peered with consuming curiosity at the grey-haired man who stood before me in his black suit. His appearance created an eccentric impression. This was due, perhaps, to recollections of the portraits and cartoons – that vast gallery of diverse Stanislavsky images – gracing the journals of an era.

To me, apart from everything else, Stanislavsky was also a writer. His book, *My Life in Art*, is written in what I consider excellent prose. It is a fragrant work of art. It was not written by a professional writer, but its

* The reference is to the Art Theatre's tour in 1900, when it went to Yalta and Sevastopol with *The Sea-Gull* and *Uncle Vanya* to perform for the sick Chekhov, whom the doctors had ordered to stay in Yalta.

prose is expressive and pure, the titles of its parts and chapters have been selected so discerningly, there is so much humour in it, and so much of the simplicity that evidences a complete command of the subject.

That fairly heavy volume is a most valuable gift to everyone employed in the arts, and especially to a playwright.

It is a book about the torments of a man who creates images. Stanislavsky has made a number of discoveries in this difficult business. His search for the truth, his efforts to make the image convincing, his quest for methods to make the image true to life, those are all the works of a scientist. There have been great actors of whom legends were composed. But there probably was something in the actor's art of the past – theatrical conventions, routine, untruthfulness and stereotype – that repulsed the artist in Stanislavsky when he began his reform. It was to remedying this situation that Stanislavsky devoted all his thoughts. He spent the rest of his long life thinking about it, and at the end of it was still unable to declare that he had found the solution. Drama and theatre. Poet and actor. How to make these expressions of the spirit equivalent? The gulf between the wealth of drama and the poverty of the theatre depressed him. He devoted his life to elevating the actor's art to the level of the qualities that distinguished drama – good drama, of course. The story Stanislavsky tells of how he worked on the role of Salieri is amazing. It is a story of how difficult it is to be an actor. Stanislavsky's work is unusual, because he was a combination of actor and thinker. His book is full of ideas, definitions, hypotheses and guesses. It is a book of an extraordinary scientist, a book groping for the rules of good acting. This "good acting" is treated by Stanislavsky with fanatical severity. How often, working on a play, one suddenly experiences the distressing feeling of "untruth".

"No, this isn't right, this isn't true, the character would not speak that way."

Stanislavsky's favourite "I don't believe it" is a precise indication of a precision instrument.

"I don't believe it."

When he said that, no one ever thought of insisting on the contrary. If Stanislavsky did not believe it, it was obviously untrue.

Stanislavsky in 1935

Our contemporaries are never fully appreciated. Yet to assess Stanislavsky's greatness, one need only recall that for many years – a whole epoch – not a single action of the man was ever pronounced wrong, and that whatever he thought, all his assumptions and conclusions, all of them, were weighty and accepted by all, accepted as the laws of science. Stanislavsky created a "system", and no man working in any one of the various arts, failed to realise that the "system" had a message for him as well.

4

Our generation – I speak of people who embarked upon life at the time of the Great Socialist Revolution – does not remember the young Stanislavsky.

I have seen photographs in which he wears a moustache. He is grey-haired, but his moustache is black. There are portraits in which Stanislavsky wears a canotier. Old fashions are always funny. It is funny to see Stanislavsky in a canotier – the Stanislavsky whose visage is to us so brilliantly blinding, like the visage of a statue.

We know only the old Stanislavsky. The notions of power and fame grow grander still when associated with the image of an elderly man. The figure of Academician Pavlov was made grander by this association. The human consciousness reacts gladly to the power and fame of an old man. Take Suvorov. One is thrilled by the thought of him not only because Suvorov was a great general, but also because he was an old man. Grand old men are numerous in the history of culture. Grey-haired, like time, they rise above their epoch.

Stanislavsky's old age – he worked until his last day, he worked with young people, analysing the eternal *Hamlet*. The scientist was not yet sure, there were still laws he had to verify.

The man's life was long. He writes that his childhood went back to the era of duels. His life was translucent and pure. His admiration of art bordered on that of the Renaissance painters. There is still another feature that makes Stanislavsky akin to them – his inclination to admire talent and craftsmanship in other men.

There are many passages to that effect in his book. One gets a delightful portrait of Chekhov by Stanislavsky. He depicts people who seemed gifted to him with a delicate brush. And he speaks of his own failings and weaknesses with an unfeigned sincerity that stems from within him. These are traits of a real genius.

The theatre he founded has become the treasure trove of our new socialist culture. The Art Theatre has invaded the life, the thoughts, the dreams and ambitions of every Soviet man. A big space of time, a torrent of events, separates *Anna Karenina* from *Tsar Fyodor.** Moscow, Russia, the whole world have changed beyond recognition. But the rule that art must be truthful remains unchanged in Stanislavsky's theatre. Years have gone by, and a new generation of people flocks to the doors of the theatre, noisy, excited, eager to enter them and see the art discovered by that grand old man.

5

Stanislavsky the man is magnificent. I have not had the privilege of hearing him speak about art, about drama. I saw him amid the sparkle of a social gathering, amid young faces, with a glass of champagne in his hand. It was a jubilee celebrated by the theatre. He left the city a few days later, and I never saw him again. But I have often heard actors speak about him. They said the simplest of all things – they loved him. Simply, they loved their teacher, they loved the man of whom they were pleased to be proud. They were willing to tremble before him, and willing to tell a joke about him with fond affection.

A great life has ended. A model of pious service to one's calling is complete. This model will serve new generations of actors. Stanislavsky's importance was so great, the impact of his personality so immense, that his death does not at all evoke any notion of the end. He will live on, just as drama, the theatre, and art will live on. Life has written a magnificent play about the life's work of a great actor and artist, a chronicle culminating in a scene in which the great actor, prostrate on his death-bed, hears the whole country pronounce his name.

* Alexei Tolstoi's *Tsar Fyodor Ioannovich* was the opening play in the Art Theatre's opening season. The *première* of *Anna Karenina*, an adaptation of Lev Tolstoi's novel by B. Volkov, took place on April 21, 1937.

Alexei Popov

ALEXEI POPOV

Fragment from "Recollections and Ruminations"

Soon after I returned from the Far East, during our tour of the South, we, and all the theatrical world, were stunned by the death of Konstantin Stanislavsky.

We had long learned to live with the knowledge that he no longer played on the stage, but all of us knew that he was brimming with creative energy, working hard in his studio, and writing books. So long as he lived, the conscience of the theatre was alive, the creative thought of a genius was alive, developing and enriching our art.

I had had no personal contacts with him for many years, but I did not feel isolated from him. I always knew what he was doing, what he was working on. I felt his presence, just as one feels the presence of one's father and mother, from a distance. But now the teacher was gone.

I could not inure myself to the thought for a long time, and as always in cases like that, I grew conscious of how much I lost only after Konstantin Sergeyevich was dead.

It would be impossible to reproduce now the torrent of thoughts and emotions that inundated my mind and heart in the autumn of 1938. Today, whenever I remember my teacher, whenever I restore his image in my memory, it is an alloy of everything I have thought about him in my life.

I have never parted from Stanislavsky in my heart for even a day. And now, coming to the close of my ruminations, I feel I have not yet said what Stanislavsky has been to me. It is farthest from my mind to describe him now as an actor or stage director. A lot has been written about that already, and many books are yet to be written.

Everyone of Stanislavsky's pupils has experienced the immense influence of his rich personality and great talent, but, only naturally, there was some *one facet* of his creative personality that impressed each one of us *specifically*.

We all know him to have been a director with a tempestuous imagination, an actor of a delicate psychological mould, a thinker and theorist, one who laid the scientific foundation of an actor's craft. But at once Konstantin Sergeyevich was a fervent proponent of the ethical fundamentals in an artist's education, a proponent of the *organic connections between an actor's spiritual wealth and his technological resources.*

Each facet of Stanislavsky's multifarious personality acted differently on different people. But I am sure that he will influence the life of coming generations with the wholeness of his genius.

"It is the duty of our theatrical art," he used to say, "to reveal the life of the human spirit." There is no more lucid and at once more exhaustive definition of the super-objective Stanislavsky set himself as an artist.

If some people today say that the theatre has begun to lose its place of honour in the life of our society, the blame for it lies in our forgetting this supreme task.

Like every genius, Konstantin Sergeyevich anticipated the paths of the science of stagecraft. A materialist by intuition, he kept pace with Ivan Pavlov, the great physiologist.

L. Leonidov* said aptly about Stanislavsky:

"How lucky we actors are that it was not Salieri but Mozart who decided to verify harmony by algebra."

An artist with a sensitive intuition, inexhaustible imagination and immense inner temperament, Stanislavsky spent his life probing and learning the laws of creative art. Yet whenever this analyst, this thinker, stepped out on the stage, he dominated it like a charmer, a magician.

We could never decide accurately what X-rays he employed to perform his magic upon our hearts, making us suffer, rejoice, laugh, ponder on life, on the purposes a man should serve.

Chekhov and Gorky lived at one time. The first produced a magnificent description of intellectual Astrov, a country doctor. The other produced the portrait of Satin, a tramp and rogue. Astrov and Satin are both mutineers. Both of them protest against torpor in life and man. But how different and matchless Stanislavsky was in those two parts!

Yet we saw that the noble human essence of the artist sparkled through his prodigious art of transformation. There was always the feel of this beauty of a man in all his theatrical creations.

Paradoxical as this may sound, Stanislavsky never achieved anything easily in spite of his genius, never without harrowing torment. That is probably the source of Stanislavsky's consuming wish to teach the actor to surmount difficulties. He himself was an object lesson of how the difficult is made familiar, and the familiar is made easy.

Stanislavsky was not a man of letters. It was a torment for him to write an article, even an address. But towards the end of his life he wrote several books, one of which – *My Life in Art* – is a model of superb literature and comparable to such books as Herzen's *The Past and Thoughts.*

Stanislavsky's ethical standards were very high. Questions of morals, ethics and discipline were for him part and parcel of the elements of artistic creation. He used to say:

* See *Notes,* p. 293.

"The baser your thoughts and feelings, the more of the bad you see around you, because you still have to be elevated to the good, while you see the bad easily. So may you develop your good will, and don't let yourself follow the example of theatres where whole companies hate each other... Take a closer look at the great creators of our art. Their faces are always inspired, calm, and joyously vigorous."

Stanislavsky's favourite formula, "Love art, and not yourselves in art", contains a veritable programme of artistic education. How many gifted people we have lost who placed their ego above the purposes of art! How many theatres have gone to waste just because their people were fonder of themselves than they were of art and of their colleagues! And, what is most important, how many creatively underdeveloped actors we have even now, sometimes whole companies, who murmur instead of shout and work at half strength just because of that!

Stanislavsky was a model of profound loyalty to art, oblivious of his own ego and prestige. Let me relate the following example.

After a long interval we were resuming performances of A. Ostrovsky's *Enough Stupidity in Every Wise Man.* After the dress rehearsals Vladimir Nemirovich-Danchenko gathered the cast round him to make his remarks. There were Stanislavsky (Krutitsky), Kachalov (Glumov), Germanova (Mamayeva), Leonidov (Gorodulin), Moskvin (Golutvin), and the rest of the cast. There were also other Art Theatre actors not occupied in the play.

In this exciting and festive environment on the eve of the opening night, Nemirovich-Danchenko praised the cast and said the production had improved considerably. He lavished praise on Kachalov, Germanova, Leonidov and Moskvin. But to everybody's surprise, he pounced on Stanislavsky savagely. "The acting is stereotype. We only see the outlines of the image. Deplorably, Konstantin Sergeyevich has turned from the once strongest performer of the cast into the weakest. You are unrecognisable, Konstantin Sergeyevich."

A tense silence followed. It had not been easy for Nemirovich-Danchenko to make this brutal attack on Stanislavsky, and it is easily imagined how Stanislavsky must have felt.

He was pale, and his eyes were lowered.

The two leaders of the theatre were obviously upset.

After a harrowing pause, Konstantin Sergeyevich said the play should be postponed, that he would work hard, but did not know how much time he would need.

The play was postponed. A month or six weeks later we had another dress rehearsal, at which Nemirovich-Danchenko took back his words and declared that Stanislavsky had played Krutitsky as wonderfully as before.

The company gave full credit to the courage and artistic integrity of its two leaders.

In his earliest period, our teacher was extremely exacting in his demands upon the actors, and all too often his insistence verged on despotism.

After Konstantin Sergeyevich realised how damaging his method was, he changed his tactics at once. The new truths he had discovered in the realm of organic laws governing stagecraft ruled out coercion. But even the insistence of the early Stanislavsky was always whole, pure and trusting.

I recall the following episode.

At a rehearsal Stanislavsky tormented actor M. He kept interrupting him with his annihilating: "I don't believe you!" The actor tried a bozen times to speak his lines, and the murderous "I don't believe you!" resounded again and again from the hall.

All of us others present at the rehearsal were distressed. At last, actor M. could bear it no longer. He lost his temper, cursed under his breath, and said:

"I don't understand you, Konstantin Sergeyevich. Show me what you want."

He climbed down from the stage into the hall. Somewhat embarrassed by the actor's curt words, Konstantin Sergeyevich coughed lightly, and ascended the boards.

The stage was lit up, the hall was in darkness. Actor M. decided that he would prove to Stanislavsky that it was wrong to be so despotic and not let a man speak his part. He sat down deliberately with his back to the stage and waited.

Stanislavsky came out, and as soon as he opened his mouth to speak M. shouted: "I don't believe you, Konstantin Sergeyevich!"

Stanislavsky in 1933

Stanislavsky began again. Once more the exclamation resounded from the darkness of the hall.

Stanislavsky started a third time. "I don't believe you, Konstantin Sergeyevich!" M. shouted once more.

The people watching this duel held their breaths, dreading the moment when Stanislavsky would realise what was happening. But, alas, Konstantin Sergeyevich was accustomed to trust whatever came from the director's table: it never entered his head that he was being ridiculed, although actor M. did not mean to make fun of him. He merely wanted to show him that this was no way to behave. After the sixth or maybe the eighth attempt, Stanislavsky said in confusion: "Hm, well, all right, I'll work on the passage at home and show it to you tomorrow."

All of us were embarrassed. The confiding trust of the great artist disarmed and shamed us.

But even in the years of his "despotic" rule, when he made so many actors shed tears, those tears were never in vain. In deep torment and suffering, the actors instructed by Stanislavsky mastered the most secret facets of their art. They were eager to work with him. They looked up to him. They adored him.

His unceasing creative search was Stanislavsky's most striking feature. From the first days of the Art Theatre and until his dying hour Stanislavsky worked untiringly with deep inspiration. At 60, at 70 even, he managed to "drive" the young people so hard that, as the saying goes, they rushed around with their tongues hanging out. He never knew the meaning of complacency in art. And that largely explains why he gravitated so much towards the youth. Owing to their young age and their reserves of strength, the young people were more congenial to him because of their enthusiasm and rhythm. But, unfortunately, the young people never lasted more than 5-8 years, then grew complacent and self-satisfied. As for Stanislavsky, eternally young, always seeking perfection, forever looking for the great truth in art, he found new youngsters to work with, established new studios, new schools. And so on, to the end of his days.

He was so enthusiastic about his creative ideas, so thirsting for a response to his new creative discoveries, that he was often blind and overtrusting, associating at times with actors and actresses who were quite incapable of absorbing the true substance of the truths that excited him, Stanislavsky. And quite often he had to pay dearly for his trust with the pain of disappointment. But his pain was always short-lived. He ended his attachments with determination and brutality, and marched on. That, too, was a special feature of his character.

His gravitation towards the youth, I must say, was at once beneficial and a source of pain. He used to say sadly:

"Oh, if the young knew how, and the old could."

The young gave him amply of their temperament and enthusiasm, but they had to be taught from scratch. While those who were *trained*, were all too often *unable* or unwilling to sacrifice themselves to art, as Stanislavsky was able and willing to do. Konstantin Sergeyevich was the one to suffer most from his perfectionism. He "piled" into the actors, but that was not all – he also "piled" into the play and the directors, although, in all fairness, he had a knack of watching rehearsals and performances with good will. Before a review he always managed to create an atmosphere of good will between the excited actors and himself, Stanislavsky, who had come "to see them act". He grinned broadly, or laughed contagiously, suppressing the exacting critic in himself, yet making mental notes of all the actors' and directors' errors.

After seeing a rehearsal with benign cheer, Stanislavsky would suddenly grow serious at the end of it.

"Well, now we can look into it," he would say. "The play is titled *The Truth Is Good, but Happiness Is Better*. Is there any 'truth' in what you just told me? Yes, a little. But have you managed to convey that the truth is 'good'? I didn't catch it. There is a counterposition in the title – the truth is good, but happiness is better. Have you managed to convey this 'but'? I don't seem to have noticed it.

"Let's go on. Was there any 'happiness'? Yes, but too little of it. And I did not happen to see that it was 'better'."

I must admit that his criticism was not as laconic as I retell it. It was far more exhaustive, and furnished with many examples. It impressed the actors and directors that they were still far removed from their final goal.

At times we thought that Konstantin Sergeyevich attached too much importance to certain trifling facts, that he was, as the Russian saying goes, "shooting at sparrows with a cannon". But the fact was that the lofty principles of an actor's training were, to him, an artist of genius, inherent in all things, and a seeming trifle assumed the proportions of an act of fundamental significance.

There was a young actress, Sophia Golidei, in the Art Theatre's Second Studio. She did extremely well in one of the performances with the monologue from Dostoyevsky's *White Nights*. At the Art Theatre, Golidei was considered a newcomer. The episode I want to relate now was told to me by her:

"Once, when I came to the theatre I was met with panic-stricken exclamations – 'What have you done? Stanislavsky is looking for you everywhere. Go and see him at once!'

"This was enough to strike terror into me. I found Konstantin Sergeyevich on the stage. He was obviously restless.

" 'Aha,' he said to me, 'so you've come! I have a two-hour rehearsal. Don't go away – wait for me.'

"I spent those two hours in deep alarm.

"When the rehearsal was over Stanislavsky called me to his dressing-room and put this confounding question:

" 'Who are you?'

" 'I don't seem to understand what you ask of me, Konstantin Sergeyevich,' I murmured.

" 'No, I ask you – who are you? Are you Knipper'?

" 'No – I am Golidei.'

" 'You – you are a swelled-headed brat. Nemirovich-Danchenko and I spent all our lives creating the Art Theatre. Then comes Golidei and scuttles the cause of our lives!'

"I had begun sobbing by then from fear and the total ignorance of my fault.

" 'Stop slobbering! Were you photographed at the Sretenka Studio?' Konstantin Sergeyevich asked me.

" 'Yes, Mother wanted a picture of me, so I had a photograph taken at a cheap photographer's.'

" 'So that's it. Well, follow me!'

"Tears rolled down my cheeks. We came out of the theatre. Konstantin Sergeyevich hailed a cab and said: 'Sretenka!' The cabby named the price – 20 kopeks. Konstantin Sergeyevich replied, 'Fifteen!'

" 'Get in,' said the cabby.

"I pressed myself into the corner of the cab. Stanislavsky got in beside me and off we went to Sretenka, to the photographer's.

"When we arrived, I saw to my horror that an enlarged photograph of myself was displayed in the show-case, inscribed, 'Art Theatre Actress Golidei'.

"Stanislavsky led me up to the show-case, and said:

" 'See how you have disgraced the Art Theatre?'

"We entered and Stanislavsky, after bargaining with the photographer, bought my portrait.

"All my attempts to vindicate myself, to tell him that I had never authorised the man to enlarge my photograph, let alone title it, were ignored by Stanislavsky.

"He climbed into the cab and put my portrait in the frame at his feet. I sat beside him, weeping unhappily. Stanislavsky was silent all the way. Just once he exclaimed: 'Damn it! A brat of a girl makes me ride all over Moscow buying up her portraits! What am I going to do with it? I suppose I'll let Maria Petrovna have it.' "

There was much merriment at the theatre over this episode, but Stanislavsky was true to himself. On account of a trifling fact in which he espied an actor's egoistic itch for glory, he did not spare his nerves, nor an hour of his time, to go and remove the portrait of an Art Theatre actress from a photographer's show-case.

This anecdotical episode reveals Stanislavsky as a man who refused to ignore trifles, who entered the lists in behalf of the high-minded principles of an actor's ethical development proclaimed by the Art Theatre.

He maintained the self-limitation of actor and artist as the rockbottom basis of art. "In art," he used to say, "the simplest things are the hardest;

the simple must be meaningful; without substance it is senseless. To be important and to stand out in relief, the simple must enclose the whole range of complex life phenomena, and that calls for genuine talent, consummate skill and rich imagination, since there is nothing more boring than the simplicity of a poor imagination."

This artistic wisdom supplies an answer to what Stanislavsky considered innovation, what he considered richness and what he considered poverty of artistic imagination.

Stanislavsky will always excite the theatrical world. He will always prompt it to make new discoveries, to study life continuously, to study human nature, to advance all the time.

Sergei Obraztsov

SERGEI OBRAZTSOV

A Fragment from "My Profession"

That was as long ago as 1927. I was asked to take part in a concert arranged by the Association of Friends of the Stanislavsky Studio.

I knew that there was a possibility of Stanislavsky turning up at this concert and for that reason did not accept the invitation at once. In those days I respected Stanislavsky's pre-eminence in the theatre world no less than I do now. If his verdict on my puppets were to be unfavourable, I would take it as a severe blow. On the other hand, if he liked my performance, his approval would make me feel enormously happy. In the end my wish to show Stanislavsky my puppets overcame my fear and I accepted.

I showed *Just a Minute, The Titular Counsellor* and *The Deacon,* in short, practically all my repertoire at that time.

After the concert Stanislavsky came up to me and congratulated me on my work. I was happy.

However, when eight years later, in 1935, I had to perform once more before Stanislavsky I was, if anything, even more alarmed at the prospect. That was understandable. In 1927, after all, I was only twenty-six, an age at which one takes risks lightly. Besides, at that time I did not feel that puppeteering was the one and only thing in my life. It was a side-line, an interesting one, of course, but definitely a side-line; whereas now in 1935 it was my work in the legitimate theatre that I considered a side-line and the puppets the main thing. So I was risking very much in submitting my puppets to Stanislavsky's judgement once more.

I had the more reason to feel alarmed because my second appearance before Stanislavsky was not a regular concert one. It took place in Stanislavsky's house in Leontyevsky Lane. A group of actors, members of the Theatre Club, were going to see Stanislavsky in order to have a talk with him about the theatre and to tell him what we were doing; afterwards, as a mark of gratitude, we were going to put on a short concert.

That is what made me feel more anxious than anything else. We knew each other's repertoires by heart. I was afraid that my comrades would not react to my puppets, that they would watch them without a single laugh. In the absence of a reaction from the audience I might act badly, and then Stanislavsky would think I was never any good.

And that is what would have happened if Stanislavsky had not possessed that quality – rare among producers – of being absolutely direct in his reactions as a spectator.

He laughed as sincerely, as loudly and merrily as I could have hoped for from the best audience, though, really, my audience on this occasion consisted of Stanislavsky alone.

It was a wonderful day from beginning to end.

All of us entered the house in a mood of solemn exaltation.

We gathered in the big room which was fitted up for rehearsals, as Stanislavsky's state of health confined him to his house, where he used to hold his classes.

At Stanislavsky's

We took our seats quietly and spoke in whispers: we felt moved at the thought that we were going to see Stanislavsky in the flesh.

Stanislavsky came into the room. We rose to our feet to greet him, feeling even more excited. And, indeed, he did look extraordinary. His frame was enormous, very gaunt but well-proportioned, and somehow he seemed to glitter. His white hair glittered, the skin of his face glittered, his eyes glittered under the white brows.

We greeted him and sat round a big table. The conversation started. The oldest of us was young enough to have been Stanislavsky's son, yet Stanislavsky was the youngest of us all.

Every phrase, every thought was young. Though he had dozens of years of professional work behind him, Stanislavsky spoke about the theatre as if he had only just started working in it and the most important and significant work lay ahead, with all that he had done being mere preparation for it.

One cannot learn to be a genius. One cannot learn to be a Stanislavsky. All the same one must learn from him. But not only how to "work with actors". Of that nothing will come though you master all the rules of the "grain", and the "subtext". Nothing will come of it unless the student possesses the main thing that Stanislavsky possessed: youthfulness in the perception of life, a keen sense of the truth, the will to struggle uncompromisingly for it, and an absolute faith in one's cause. Those things, of course, are not easily learned, but on coming back from Stanislavsky's house that day I could think of nothing else. I thought how necessary it was for every artist to see the world with open eyes, without fear or prejudice, and to believe in his cause, in the path he has chosen, not because it is his but because it is the only right one for him.

Nikolai Okhlopkov

NIKOLAI OKHLOPKOV

Fragments from "To All the Young"

Stanislavsky and Nemirovich-Danchenko created a new school for an actor's training, with new principles of directing and instructing, on the finest traditions of the past and, above all, the firm, dependable Shchepkin foundation.

That was how a theatre of deep-going creative collaboration between actor and director developed, campaigning all the time for artistic purity, in contrast to the "director's theatre" where the director had dictatorial powers and the "actors' theatre" which denied the immense culture of directing accumulated over the decades.

It is to the actor that the director should devote his imagination, his creative experience and knowledge, and his inspiration. It is a truly artistic pleasure to appreciate the actor, to grasp the width and breadth of his creative personality, to convey to him the ideas of the author, and your own, to help him grasp the content of his part, to rouse his creative imagination and initiative, and to guide them in the desired direction, and at once absorb all that emanates from the actor, his thoughts and emotions and his own particular appreciation of the author, and of his part. This pleasure is probably best known to treasure seekers, to prospectors, inventors, and to pathfinders and seafarers, to the discoverers of new stars and, in a nutshell, to all true artists and poets, no matter what their occupation.

You, the director, are not alone when you work.

No matter where your thoughts and feelings take you, no matter what you do in working with the actor and playwright, you are always in the fine company of those great teachers, Stanislavsky and Nemirovich-Danchenko, those wonderful reformers of theatrical art, the renowned directors and connoisseurs of human nature, subtle analysts and psychologists, those true innovators in the training of actors.

It is inconceivable that in our day any serious-minded man of art could ignore Stanislavsky's system in his theatrical work. One need not be a member of the Art Theatre company or a pupil of the great director and teacher, but it is absolutely inconceivable to get along without a profound study and knowledge of the basic principles of Stanislavsky's system, no matter what theatre one belongs to and no matter what theatrical beliefs one holds.

Stanislavsky's system is really a collection of different inner and outer techniques. They help to improve the art of the actor and stage director. But they are not hard and fast prescriptions. They are not dogma. Many of them need to be critically tested, amended, or developed. Stanislavsky's system is a decisive turning point in the exploration of an actor's art, for it sums up the best and the most progressive elements in the wealthy creative experience of the great masters of the Russian stage and reveals far-reaching prospects for new growth and new development in the psychology of artistic creation as a science based on the materialistic world outlook.

The conclusions drawn by Stanislavsky from his theoretical and practical investigation of the processes and the rules governing the art of acting, are not final at all. On the contrary, they cry out for the most vigorous and audacious continuation and development of all the truly positive experiments made by Stanislavsky.

Stanislavsky is great because he was the *first* in our own theatrical world, and in the world theatre, to chart a vast programme of scientific theatrical exploration, the first to outline a new, most important trend for the science and art of acting with an amazing amount of knowledge and with brilliant insight into the nature of acting.

Just think, we speak today of a *science*, of which the most complex processes of an actor's art in their various stages are the subject.

Only recently this had appeared to be beyond the reach of science, something that did not yield to scientific reasoning.

Quite beyond question, Stanislavsky based his creative investigations of the art of acting on the all-important achievements of psychology and physiology that marked the victory of the materialistic standpoint in science over the idealistic.

Stanislavsky's thinking as a stage director doubtlessly followed the path illumined by the genius of Ivan Pavlov.

"The human being," Pavlov wrote, "is a system (more crudely, a machine), which, like any other in nature, is governed by laws inevitable and single for nature as a whole."

While combating all the elements that confused the creative processes of acting, Stanislavsky sought to impel our nature to act, for, he thought, nature was the "finest of the arts". He taught the directors what they had to suggest to the actor in order to create in him a correct inner emotion. He sought to develop a science about the creative processes, and to define the rules governing them. He urged an appreciation of the secrets of theatrical transformation and the creative "living the life" of the image. He found, tested, and elaborated numerous means and devices of the actor's inner and outer techniques, and their purpose was just one – to help the actor live on the stage and embody an image correctly, profoundly, truthfully and naturally, to help him probe the deepest feelings and emotions, to help develop the actor's inner rhythms, and to provide an outlet for the actor's temperament, etc., etc.

Stanislavsky was the first to dissect and examine the existing trends in the art of acting, making use above all of the experience of the finest actors of the Russian stage, from Shchepkin on. Shchepkin's name was constantly on his lips, which was also true of Nemirovich-Danchenko and Meyerhold.

While following the development of such theatrical giants as Yermolova, Fedotova, Sadovsky, Yuzhin, Lensky and many others, and treating them with due affection and respect, though without blind worship, Stanislavsky looked at the same time for ways of combating all the ossified elements that repeated themselves and clung tenaciously to the stage of all theatres. Stanislavsky crusaded against conformism and drabness with Shchepkin's name on his lips, with the slogan that could best be worded as: "Learn from Shchepkin." What he meant by that was: "Away with *clichés* and stereotypes, with grandstanding, with play-acting, with playing 'at images', with innuendoes and gestures."

Stanislavsky maintained that there were three aspects to theatrical art – the art of artisanship, the art of performing, and the art of feeling.

Artisanship is called artisanship rather than art because it lacks human emotion. Artisanship emphatically denies the truth of emotion, genuine sincerity, and depth of feeling. That is its chief and basic error. The artisans do not believe in showing their inner feeling to the crowd, since they doubt that it would ever reach the crowd. Therefore, they think, it will not look convincing. They believe the actor should "play", rather than "live" on the stage. That is why they perform purely external actions. In performing their role they employ existing stereotypes, imitate the greater actors blindly, speak bombastically, and make many false, psychologically unjustified gestures.

"The artisan actors," Stanislavsky said, "deal in motions, not in true-to-life human motions, but in purely professional, theatrical motions, more simply, in play-acting.

"They like to speak bombastically about their non-existent emotions, that is, they want to fill the inner, spiritual vacuum of their acting with external theatrical effects. It is always more profitable to perform a role one does not intrinsically feel with a lot of outer trimmings to a round of applause. But no serious actor is likely to want theatrical acclaim in scenes conveying his most cherished thoughts and emotions, his intrinsic spiritual essence.

"If an actor sacrifices this and stoops to debasing a festive minute, this only goes to prove that the words he speaks are devoid of meaning for him, that he has failed to fill them with anything dear and cherished. As for the thought and the feeling itself, for the sake of which the play was written, such kind of acting will convey them only 'generally' sadly, 'generally' gaily, 'generally' tragically, etc. Such interpretation is dead, formal and artisan."

The art of performing assumes that the emotional process is only one of the stages in the quest for the forms of a role. The exponents of this art believe that one should emotionalise just once (in the early stage of rehearsing), to register the external form of this, and to present it (the form) on the stage.

They do not believe in emotionalising on the stage itself. What is more, they believe it to be dangerous. They say that emotions on the stage interfere with their acting, that they deprive them of the essential self-control. The need to record the external form of an emotion spurs them to hard work on developing their technique, which, though highly developed, assumes the shape of a *cliché* as time goes by, and becomes unconvincing. Clearly, no fake, no matter how technically perfect, can equal a genuine creative emotion through which the actor seeks to grasp the texture of his role every time and in every kind of work.

Stanislavsky was always a most consistent and vigorous opponent of artisanship and of the art of performing, no matter how well an actor's formal skill succeeded in concealing the inner frigidity of this art.

The art of emotion presumes the actor to be a genuine creator, a true artist, an heir to the gigantic creative wealth left us by famous actors of the past, a continuer of the great behests of Shchepkin and Fedotova and, above all, a follower of Stanislavsky's genius.

There is no real art without emotion. This art strives to reveal the inner world of man in truly artistic theatrical forms.

The art of emotion is concerned mostly with depth, with creating the actor's inner life, whereby the actor must live, feel and perform consciously on the stage in presenting his theatrical image.

Actions are employed for "being", rather than "seeming to be" a character on the stage, to act not purposelessly, but for the sake of something quite definitely determined.

This principle in art lives up to Pushkin's formula about the "trueness of passions and truthfulness of emotions in offered circumstances".

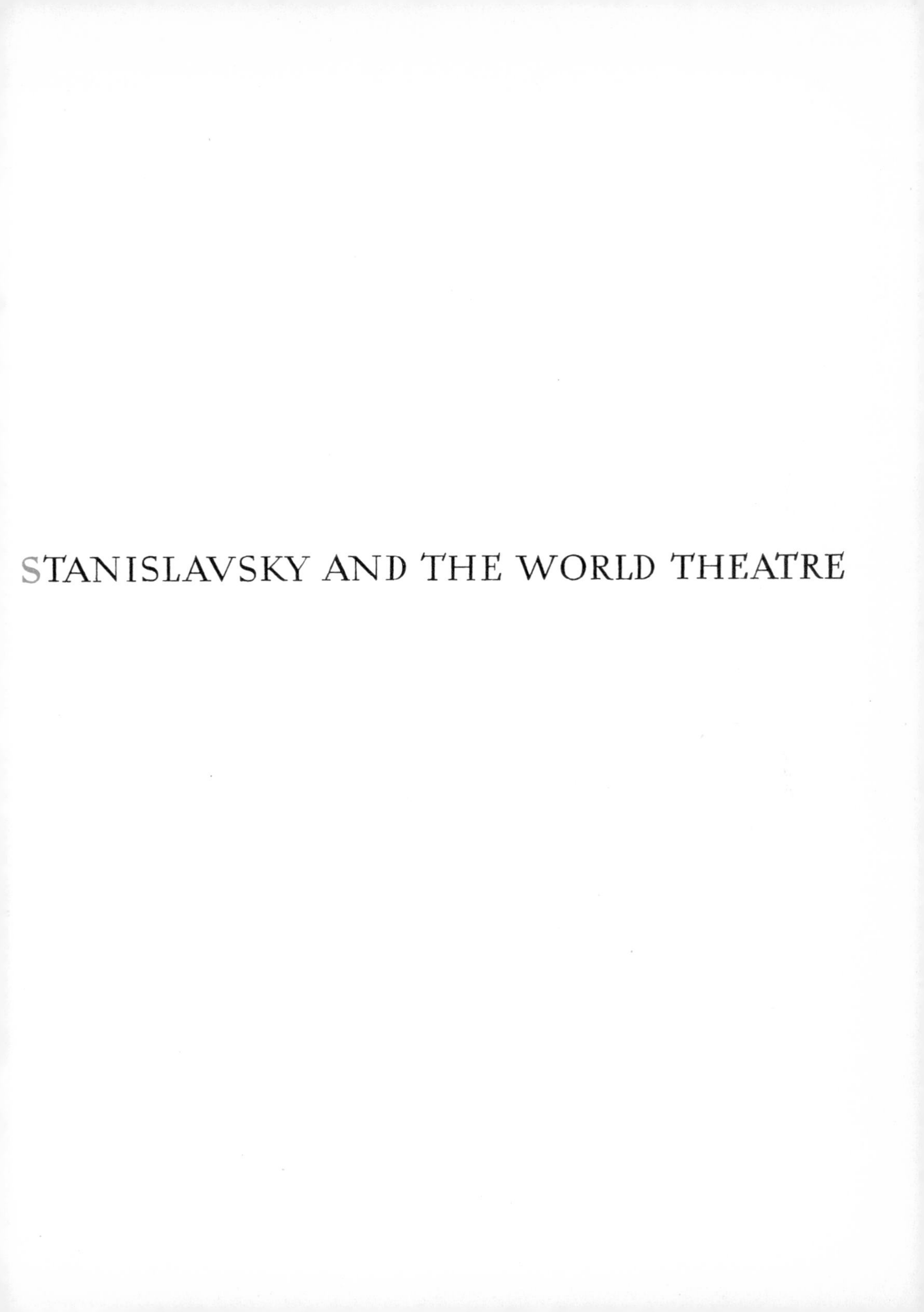

STANISLAVSKY AND THE WORLD THEATRE

ERNESTO ROSSI

Dear Mr. Alexeyev,

In thanking you for your kind invitation to the Hunters' Club to see the production of *Othello*, I want to ask you to convey the great pleasure it afforded me to all the amateurs who played their parts with the intelligence and devotion of true artists.

Be good, dear sir, to accept the expressions of my high esteem and respect.

Devotedly yours,

Ernesto Rossi

Hotel Metropole, Moscow,
January 23, 1896

LUDWIG BARNAY*

Moscow, December 4, 1896

My dear and kind Mr. Alexeyev,

It appears that you are a man of pleasant surprises. At first, you afforded me pleasure by your courteous visit, taking the lead in the matter and affording me the joy of meeting a most attractive and kind man. Then you surprised me with your truly excellent and creditable accomplishments as a dramatic performer and a first-class stage director. I may tell you frankly that the performance of *The Polish Jew,* which I saw in your theatre, delighted me. This applies both to the performances by yourself and other actors, and to the magnificent production of the play, especially the picturesque scenes in the second act. Finally, your third surprise: the magnificent wreath, whereby you marked my first performance yesterday.

* The inscription on the photograph says: "To my revered friend, distinguished actor and director, Mr. Alexeyev-Stanislavsky. Ludwig Barnay. Moscow, November-December 1896."

Allow me to express my most cordial and sincere gratitude for all this and to beg you to be just as kind to me in the future, as I shall for ever remain your true and loyal friend,

Ludwig Barnay

Berlin, December 23, 1906

My dear Colleague,

I recall your excellent production and performance of *Uriel Acosta.* Please send me portraits of the performers and pictures of groups as quickly as you can.

Thanking you in advance,

Your old and loyal admirer,

Ludwig Barnay

IDA EMILIE AALBERG

April 22, 1905, Petersburg

I have just returned to the hotel and am absolutely stunned by the impression I got from *The Three Sisters.* How much beauty there is in that admirable play!

And how much irony there is in that poem, how much pitiless and depressing, and yet endlessly beautiful irony, beautiful to the point of tears. It is a tragedy of our spirit, so intimate and delicate in its sweet pain, and there is so much faith, warmth and immensely vibrant idealism in it!

I beg you to relay all my admiration to Mme Knipper. I wept today together with her.

And you, what exquisite finesse, what depth, what genius you displayed as you re-lived the whole of the play. Thank you heartily for these unforgettable minutes.

I have just returned to Petersburg and was very happy to learn that you are here.

Ida Emilie Aalberg

ELEONORA DUSE

Moscow, Hotel Metropole, February 16, 1908

Mr. Stanislavsky,

Work –

Work, nothing but the responsibilities I bear prevented me from being at *your theatre* today.

I regret it very much,
very much,
very much.

Yesterday, I again found *Truth* and *Poetry*,

Poetry and *Truth*, those two *profound sources* for your soul of art and artist.

Believe me, believe me that *I have understood,* that I am *worthy* of understanding your effort. All the *perfection* which your effort exhales. Here is all *my joy* of having understood – and my confidence of coming again and being with you to admire and enjoy once more the same joys, pure and profound.

Eleonora Duse

JAROSLAV KVAPIL *

Fragments from "Of What I Know"

Early in 1906 we learned that the Moscow Art Theatre company was coming to Berlin. Berlin was to be its first stop-over, and it then planned to visit other West-European cities. I did not want them to miss Prague on their tour and went to Berlin posthaste before Stanislavsky's company got there...

We saw four Russian plays performed as we never dreamed of seeing them performed. It was a revelation for the Western theatre. It was not simply a theatrical performance. Rather, it was a divine service. It was not simply brilliant playing, but enlightened and high-minded proof, without the least admixture of stereotype. Everything in it was imbued with excellent national traditions...

In Berlin... the Art Theatre company scored a brilliant success, the like of which has not been seen there since the early performances of the Mei-

* The inscription on the photograph says: "To the great and brilliant Stanislavsky, with heartfelt gratitude. Jaroslav Kvapil, Prague, April 10, 1906."

ningen Theatre in the 1870s. The Art Theatre actors came as ambassadors of their people, to disperse the ill-fame which spread in the West about Russia after its military defeat and the suppression of the revolution. Stanislavsky told us then: "The war was lost, the revolution failed, and if we were to fail too, I would never go home as Kuropatkin did!"*

The inimitable Konstantin Sergeyevich! He was 43 then, but all his hair was grey. He did not look like an actor at all. His bushy moustache made him look like one of those noble and handsome men we see in the audience, not in the theatrical dressing rooms. There was nothing theatrical about this great stage artist, director and actor, not only on the stage but in life as well. An aristocrat in body and soul, he was aristocratically simple... He spoke piously of his artistic mission, as a priest does about religion. His thinking is a creative process. His life is genuine self-sacrifice. That was what he was like when I saw him backstage in Berlin, and when I met him in Berlin and Prague. That was the Stanislavsky I yearned to see for years, and that was the kind of man I saw in the long and heartfelt letters he wrote to me before the war...

...The wonderful spring days of the Prague guest performances are a glorious, truly revolutionary chapter in the history of our theatre. Since the spring of 1906 we can divide the major developments in our theatrical world into those that occurred before and those that occurred after the first guest performances of the Moscow Art Theatre.

* * *

... They came, we saw them, they conquered! It was in early April 1906... We saw the gate to Russian life open before us. We saw not only Russian plays and Russian actors, but all of Russia. It was a theatre in which tradition and innovation merged in sublime harmony. There was not a grain of stereotype in this new art of directing, acting and producing. All these elements were deeply rooted in their national soil, based on wonderful theatrical traditions and rising high from the earth...

* *Alexei Kuropatkin* (1848-1925) – commander-in-chief of Russia's land forces in the Russo-Japanese War of 1904-05, who lost the Mukden battle disgracefully.

... Of the five plays, the small repertoire which the Art Theatre took with it on its Western tour, neither Chekhov's *Three Sisters* nor Ibsen's *Enemy of the People* were shown in Prague.

... I saw the Art Theatre perform *The Three Sisters* in Berlin and was bold enough to produce the play nine months later in a Czech translation at the National Theatre. I was naturally very strongly influenced by the Art Theatre from beginning to end, and my heartiest thanks are due to the great Russian teachers for their lessons, for what I picked up from them in Berlin if this first Czech performance of *The Three Sisters* is still recalled with praise many years later. We learn from each other, one generation from another, and must not conceal where we learned and from whom we learned. One should not pretend to have made a discovery when one says: Thrice five is fifteen. The example of the Muscovites reveals that foreign soil, too, may be made fertile, and that even the fleeting art of an actor may be immortal ...

Stanislavsky as Doctor Astrov in *Uncle Vanya* and as the imposing Satin in Gorky's play, ruled supreme on the stage. In a play by A. Tolstoi, *Tsar Fyodor Ioannovich*, playing the small part of the patriarch not even listed in the cast, he stayed modestly in the shade of the other big actors, showing a model of submission to the collective discipline totally lacking in our theatres. He, the performer of leading parts, the director of boundless power, pottered about backstage with the trifling details which are entrusted in other theatres to the stagehands, helping to move stage property and produce various sound effects. Once, during the performance in which he delighted us as Doctor Astrov, I stumbled upon him at a moment when, huddled in a corner, he imitated the barks of a dog which the sorrowing Uncle Vanya heard in the middle of the night ...

Although Stanislavsky had invited me to come to Moscow the following year, and to practise a bit more, I parted from him with such great sorrow as though we were never to meet again.

ISADORA DUNCAN*

Petersburg, February 4, 1908

Dear Friend,

I have just come back from Mme Duse's. She is so pretty. We spoke about you. She said she would be delighted to see you in Moscow, and that you did not need any letter of introduction. She is very fond of you.

I danced last night. I thought of you and danced well.

I have received your cards, and today I received your telegram. Thank you. How good and great you are! And how I love you!

I feel a surge of new, extraordinary energy. Today, I worked all morning and put many new ideas into my work. Rhythms again.

It is you who gave these ideas to me. I am so glad I feel like flying to the stars and dancing round the moon. This will be a new dance which I will dedicate to you.

I have written to Gordon Craig. I told him about your theatre and about your own great art. But couldn't you write to him yourself? If he could work with you, it would be *ideal* for him. I hope with all my heart that this can be arranged. I will soon write to you again. Thank you once more. I love you. I still work with joy.

Isadora

P. S. My tender love to your dear wife and children.

* The inscription on the portrait: "With love, Isadora."

EDWARD GORDON CRAIG

Florence, Italy, September 5, 1909

. . . The more I read *Hamlet* over the more I see your figure. *I cannot believe for one moment that anything more than the simplest rendering of this character can ever reach those heights which Shakespeare seems to touch* and the nearest to those heights that I have seen in the acting in your theatre is your performance in *Onkel Wanja* . . .

How can there be anything higher and grander than the simplicity with which you treat your roles in the modern plays? I mean your personal acting.

Does not the thought in *Hamlet* develop itself and find its words through precisely the same process as the thought in Chekhov's plays. If there are passages in *Hamlet* in which the words are less simple than in Chekhov surely there are other passages which are the very essence of simplicity . . .

How much I would like to see you as Hamlet I cannot possibly tell you. I can conceive no more ideal thing on the stage and each time that I think of the play being performed in Moscow I am grieved to think of what the stage will lose without your presence. I am sure Kachalov will be very good indeed and that everyone in Moscow will think so. But I have a deep-down conviction that I cannot change that the whole of Europe would be moved and set thinking if they could witness your performance of this part . . .

MAURICE MAETERLINCK

Paris, November 25, 1910

Dear Mr. Stanislavsky,

My wife has come back from Moscow absolutely staggered by what she saw there. She told me with tears of admiration about the incomparable and brilliant miracle that you have managed to make from my humble poem.

I knew that I owed you a lot, but I did not know that I owed you everything. I can do nothing but bow low before one of the purest and greatest artists of the theatre of our time, thanking him from the very depth of all that is best in my heart.

Maeterlinck

P. S. And what to say to you for so noble and so generous a permission as you were kind enough to give to copy the sets for *The Blue Bird*. It is one of those acts for which one cannot find words of gratitude. But at least we will try to prove our gratitude by our deeds, showing religious respect for the creation of your genius.

M.

EMILE VERHAERN

Moscow, December 24, 1913

Dear Sir,

When I was brought your visiting card, I came down at once hoping to detain you and to chat with you for a few minutes. Unfortunately, you had just left the hotel.

I would have confessed to you that I had never loved the theatre as much as I did in Moscow, that you, especially you, have performed a kind of new magic and that I thank you for all the joy which I experienced here thanks to you and those of whom you are the teacher.

Please ask your kind secretary to remember about me, and accept all my affection, gratitude and friendship.

One of your admirers,

Emile Verhaern

Memories of Moscow

(Excerpts)

... When I saw *It Tears Where It's Thinnest* at the Art Theatre, I could hardly believe my eyes: the lucid warmth of the summer day that bathed the curtains and the furniture of a country parlour was so true to life and animate. It bordered on magic, it created an illusion, it really seemed an amazing accomplishment effected by some unknown means . . . Yes, Moscow is the seat of supreme theatrical art. Neither Paris, nor London, nor yet Berlin hold such festivities, and produce such beautiful, vivid and lofty artistic impressions. Max Reinhardt is unquestionably a producer of genius, but Alexeyev-Stanislavsky has climbed a higher rung, and, what is more, he did it earlier. Stanislavsky is indeed the most prodigious of magicians. He was the first to do the impossible. He was the teacher of those who in turn became teachers and now transmit his lessons to all the theatres of Europe.

JAQUES COPEAU

Foreword to the French edition of Stanislavsky's "My Life in Art"

The legend of Konstantin Stanislavsky has lit the way for me for many years from a distance that seemed out of reach. It is from Gordon Craig's book and from the stories of travellers from Moscow that I knew a man of genius was realising art to perfection, and that he was surrounded by a group of grand actors religiously devoted to his cause, that his theatre could, thanks to immense material support, indulge securely in research, that this theatre was a source of culture and of enthusiasm for crowds of people who streamed to it from all points of Russia.

That was how the glory of the Moscow Art Theatre reached us too. Without having ever seen it, we derived encouragement from its example. It was one of our ambitions to be worthy of it . . .

* * *

I met Konstantin Stanislavsky in Paris in December 1922.

During the fortnight that he stayed among us I saw him as often as his work and mine permitted me. Whether at the Gare du Nord, the evening he alighted like a patriarch among his people; whether on the stage at the Champs Elysées, where we bid him welcome, Antoine, Jacques Hérbertot, André Levinson and myself; whether on the stage of the Vieux-Colombier, surrounded by my comedians, who wished to fête him; or when he played his role, when he reposed backstage and when we chatted intimately, what struck me most in him was his nobility, his mighty frame, the way he carried his head, the inspired expression of his face, which all gave him an air of dominance tempered by the kindness of his smile and the exquisite manners of an aristocrat. There was something of the sovereign in him, in this simple man. I also found a bit of aloofness in him, of detachment, perhaps of lassitude, and, even in his courtesy, a sadness that did not surprise one in a grand artist who had just witnessed the birth of a new world.

I recall from my conversations with him three things that seemed to absorb him. He said: "Our theatrical art is extraordinarily behind all the other arts of the epoch. But it would be an error to apply the methods of the other arts to it artificially. We should not pretend to be able to express what is essentially out of our reach." At other times this man, so reserved and even a bit mysterious in his ways, put his hand on my shoulder and said profoundly, looking me squarely in the face: "Believe me, we, the artists of the theatre, we who believe in our art and who live for it, we of all countries of the world should unite and work together instead of wasting ourselves needlessly on people who want no part of us . . ."

I have heard this said in almost the same words by Gordon Craig. It did not astonish me, coming from him. But I was astonished to hear it from Stanislavsky, from this lucky man who, alone among us, seemed to have the means to attain, who seemed to have attained the summits of theatrical art. What was that? Was it possible that this acclaimed master was still looking for his place in the sun and for his destination in our art?

Finally, on the day we parted, when saying adieu to me, Stanislavsky repeated several times, almost in a whisper but with special emphasis: "Now I know; yes, it is true, I think I know what an actor should be taught . . ."

The emotions of the actor and the whole problem of interpretation, his methods and means, his possibilities and his limitations, the need to find a solid basis for his research, his need for collaborators, for worthy companions, the torments of dramatic art, with the very profound but very vague sense of the fact that the theatre of our time has not yet found its form and does not know where to turn nor where to begin – that is the tragic element in this noble Stanislavsky, that is what I grasped in a few intimate conversations with him in 1922 and what he revealed in his book two years later.

* * *

It was in New York, in 1927, that I made my first acquaintance with this book, with its American version. But I read it much later, because, having opened it on the ship, on my way home, I shut it again at once, startled by a few phrases in it.

I quit the stage three years before, and I could not endure hearing a voice, so true, reciting an experience so very much like my own, which had led me into a blind alley. It reminded me that my own resources were perhaps no longer employable . . .

What Stanislavsky presents in his memoirs is not a compilation of dogmatic affirmations and prophecies, but the confession of a consummate artist, a realist. It is an inventory of experiences which the human spirit elevated to the summit where they suddenly appeared worthless to him after he had always believed them to be infallible.

The visions of theory, innumerable trifling facts accumulated in practice, intimate notions suggested to the actor by the exercise of his profession, rules tested in practice, methodical exercises, lucky chances, errors, abuses and weaknesses – in this book he has covered them all. He identified and described them, a man of whom one might well say that he suffered in the purely Russian manner from an excess of devotion to art, but a man who is honest, sincere, modest and conscientious, who knows what he is talking about because he has done it all, and because he is a living master of his art, a man who creates and judges what he creates "from the standpoint of what is eternal in art".

Stanislavsky's theatrical experience extends over nearly seventy years of his life. He has seen the stalls in his theatre occupied by the privileged classes of the old tsarist regime. He has seen them invaded by the peasants, the workers and the soldiers of the Russian revolution. Not only has he himself lived a life in art, but he has witnessed, and still witnesses, the careers of his disciples and imitators.

He is the father of the modern Russian theatre.

* * *

If the narration, *My Life in Art*, had appeared a few years earlier, and if I had been lucky enough to have read the book before meeting the founder of the Moscow Art Theatre, it would have helped me immensely to come closer to him. Yes, and if he himself had during those few talks in Paris wished to take me into his confidence as regards his experience, I would have been better prepared, with the help of his clearer and more enlightened spirit, to settle the problems which alienated me from my companions. The tour he then made of America and, later, his grave malady, from which he recuperated so slowly, divided us completely. But I knew he would return to his work, and the news we got from the Soviet Union gave us reason to believe that he resumed his place of preponderance to which he has a legitimate right, in the theatrical life of his country.

Dear Konstantin Stanislavsky, I have never had a guide in my art. I have never known that living, familiar and redoubtable presence, rude and tender, which every day, giving of itself to us, has won the right to demand of our best. The thought that could have come to me, as it has to many others, to question this privilege, to be irritated by its constraints, to misunderstand it, is the only thing that attenuates my regret of never having served under some elder. But among the people whose words instructed me, whose example sustained me, it is you, dear Konstantin Stanislavsky, whom I should like to name as my dear teacher. Perhaps you will reject this title, you, who wrote at the end of your book:

"I know that I know nothing . . ."

Then I will say to you that I love you for your modesty, for your grandeur, for your fearlessness.

ANDRÉ ANTOINE

The memory of the all too brief sojourn among us of the Moscow Art Theatre group will never fade in those who are animated by a passion for dramatic art, and people like that are far more numerous than one would suppose, as one could see at its magnificent performances to unfailingly full houses.

The French, actors and theatre-goers, showed themselves more assiduous and attentive than one could have hoped, considering the barrier of a language unfamiliar in the Occident. As Jacques Copeau and myself had the honour of saying that evening, when we greeted our celebrated colleagues in a crowded hall at the fine Champs Elysées theatre, we had expected a lot from them, but they gave us much more than we had expected.

The magnificent legend about the Moscow Art Theatre reached us a long time ago. Those who had been to Russia relayed to us their admiration of the exceptional quality of its dramatic productions, which, even next to those of the celebrated Max Reinhardt, appeared unique in the whole world.

In 1915, having been engaged to play at the Mikhailovsky Theatre in Petrograd, then still St. Petersburg, the last performances in my acting career, Stanislavsky, who learned of my presence, did me the honour of inviting me to Moscow to speak at a conference. The war, alas, undid his plan. We were all filled with anguish, and my concern for my two sons took me post-haste to Paris. It was thus that I lost the precious opportunity of making a pilgrimage to the home of the art, which other people, more fortunate than I, have made. I will never forgive myself for it.

With what great attention we followed the development in Russia of an art so close to our own, and what great interest we showed in that small Moscow theatre, of whose establishment we learned almost at once and which we applauded with unfeigned enthusiasm. It seemed that the future, the true progress, had made it their home from now on, and the enthusiasm that we had felt for the German effort headed by Gerhart Hauptmann and Sudermann shifted to the new playwrights and the productions of the Moscow Art Theatre.

Quite understandably, I speak of that home of art with a certain concern and timidity because I have never seen it. I have piously amassed documents and my library is long enriched by albums and publications about it. But it is familiar to me solely from my reading, and nothing can supplant the unmediated impressions of seeing and hearing. All the same, the scenic accomplishments of the Art Theatre, so curious, so novel and so original, hold no secret for me. Through attentive study of documents, and from what I have been told by eye-witnesses, and, last but not least, from what we recently saw in Paris, I have perceived and remain proud of the fact that we have followed the same path towards the truth and that we saw the same goal on the horizon, that is, the goal of elevating art, which had in the final years of the past century bogged down definitely in the routine of outworn tradition.

Sometime in 1888 or 1889 I published a propaganda brochure, in which I attempted to define what we were beginning to see. It was a plan, a somewhat summary plan but sufficient, of a model stage that would embody all the new ideas floating around us. Stanislavsky remarked kindly to me later that this document – it reached him, because the indefatigable seeker never stopped learning – had in part confirmed his own conception.

It is an amazing coincidence that the company of the Moscow Art Theatre and that of the Théâtre Libre were both at first recruited from among amateurs. Eternally, in a period of decadence, at the very hour when sordid and shabby forms breathe their last after having lived too long, when prolonged prosperity engenders *insouciance* and laziness, troubling the pure waters of the living source – always, in all countries, and this recurred in Moscow, it is the amateurs who save the theatre by returning to its origins.

It was the same in Russia as in France. Our own Henri Becque who, towards 1887, was still misunderstood and barred from working on the bigger stages, became the guide and the model for our generation when in Russia Chekhov and his *Sea-Gull,* repulsed by the official theatres, made the fortune of the Art Theatre.

We saw the same objectives as ours, etc., consistent with the brilliant formula of Stanislavsky, the same ambitions of "chasing the theatre out of the theatre", of beginning from the beginning, of forgetting the outworn habits and professional artifices, and the same longing to pay homage to the author and his work which the actor, excessively honoured and excessively adulated, had stolen from them. Last but not least, there was the same longing to reconstitute life, truth and the proper milieu round the dramatic personages on the boards . . .

But when in the two countries contemporary authors elevated the drama to true splendour, and when in our country Becque, Porto-Riche and François Curel, to mention just the most illustrious of them, had triumphantly consummated the long-awaited renovation just as Chekhov, Gorky, Andreyev and many others did in Russia, the two countries confronted the problem of staging theatrical productions of a novel, true-to-life and sincere kind, capable of faithfully interpreting the new plays. The greatness of Stanislavsky and his company lies in their having completely realised the necessary revolution in the art of producing and the art of acting, indispensable for consolidating the conquests.

Certainly, we others, too, at the Théâtre Libre, searched half by instinct and half by deduction for new formulas that would bring back the natural, the simple and sincere to our performances. To some degree, our good intentions, which made only a breach at first, were crowned by victory. But the epoch, the circumstances, the obstacles, prevented us from realising them completely, and in France we are only half-way to our goal after a few years of triumph, with the result that the men who devoted themselves to this great task succumbed to the circumstances, discouraged and dispersed, so that at present, the Théâtre Libre being dead and its successor, the Théâtre Antoine, having disappeared, all our past work seems to have been defeated and we have returned to our old routine.

It is essential that a whole generation of actors and directors get back to work as in 1887. At this hour, Jacques Copeau and his Vieux-Colombier, and Charles Dullin and his L'Atelier, both newcomers already appreciated, have applied themselves to the goal, and the prosperity of the leading theatres gives us some hope for the future.

But I repeat once more, it is Stanislavsky, prompted by his firmness, his lucidity and faith to carry the task to its end, who remains our teacher and model. Our admiration for this grand man of the theatre is doubled by our knowledge that he, too, had to combat financial obstacles, submit to the tyranny of the moneybags and fight the selfish official art, and that in spite of it all he managed to triumph completely in a milieu which was still harder to conquer than our so brilliant Paris.

Thus, everything we dreamed of and vaguely foresaw, this revival of the theatre, this re-creation of the decorative art of costumes, this devotion to the play and to the author, all this research, this exultation over nature and the truth, this humility of author vis-à-vis his personages, and, lastly, all these elements which constitute superior art, pure beauty – Stanislavsky has achieved them all without any show of weakness.

We felt it very well recently in Paris and witnessed absolute perfection during the marvellous performance of *The Lower Depths*, although the work, put into too big a frame that violated the proportions, was a revelation to us with its prodigiously described milieu, and during the performance of *The Cherry Orchard,* although the hastily organised tour inevitably caused all sorts of complications. To be sure, we admired a perfect company during the Meiningen tour . . . But in applying the great principles of equality, submission of the actor to the play achieved a complete abnegation. Thereby Stanislavsky attained perfection in *Tsar Fyodor*, the sparkling production of which he showed in Paris, and has gone much farther, I think, than the famous German theatre. He did not limit himself solely to the historical theatre and to stylised plays. After having proved that he was no worse than his predecessors, he triumphed on ground which they had not walked, to wit, with a modern repertoire and realistic plays.

All this goes to show that the director of the Moscow troupe is the most integral man of the contemporary theatre, and that after having traversed the different cycles of style, of realism, he had also triumphed in the new conceptions of lyricism and pure beauty, producing scenes without precedent, like those in *Blue Bird* and those in *Hamlet*, which we would have liked to see in Paris if material circumstances had permitted. It is by this, by the variety of his art, which represents all the shades of the aesthetical, that Stanislavsky's true genius rules supreme.

DAVID BELASCO

New York, December 29, 1924

My dear Mr. Stanislavsky:

My deepest appreciation and thanks for your letter from far-off Moscow.

I wish you and the Company of the Moscow Art Theatre a happy, prosperous New Year – with every blessing.

We miss you and hope to see you and your band of great artists again.

With warmest admiration and happy memories of you, which I shall always cherish

Faithfully,

David Belasco

New York, July 23, 1927

Dear Mr. Stanislavsky:

Morris Gest* has given to me the precious medal and papers telling of the honour the Moscow Art Theatre has done me. Nothing could give me

* *Morris Gest* – organiser and manager of the Moscow Art Theatre tour in Europe and the United States in 1922-24. Gest and Belasco were made honorary members of the Art Theatre company and conferred the *Sea-Gull* badges worn by members of the Art Theatre.

quite as much pleasure and pride as being a member of that organization of great artists whose fame is world wide and who brought to my country a knowledge of the superb art of yours.

I know that your personal efforts did much towards procuring this honor for me and I thank you with all my heart. A letter of acknowledgement to the organization accompanies this.

I look forward to the time when we may have the joy of greeting you and your associates again.

Cordially and with deep and sincere regards and admiration, I am dear M. Stanislavsky

Faithfully,

David Belasco

MAX REINHARDT

Berlin, October 1928

Dear Konstantin Sergeyevich,

On behalf of the actors and on my own behalf I ask you to accept the attached address as an expression of our affection and deep respect. The title of Honorary Member of the Deutsches Theater was conferred only once since its establishment, and we have no higher token to express our admiration of you and your work.

For me personally it is a special joy to confer this honour upon you. Our encounters and my experience with you, the actor, the director and the man, briefly, all that the name Stanislavsky stands for, will always be among the memories that have made my life richer, more beautiful and purposeful.

Heartily faithful, your friend

Max Reinhardt

Berlin, 1933

My supreme veneration of the artist and my love of the man in you prompt me today, more than ever before, to associate myself with your art. I wish

I could warm you with my good wishes just as I am always warmed by the magic of the unforgettable hours I have had the good fortune to experience thanks to you.

Yours,

Max Reinhardt

A telegram to Stanislavsky

FIRMIN GÉMIER*

Paris, May 11, 1928

My great Teacher and Friend,

I could never tell you how happy I was to see you, to speak to you a little, too little I thought, and how touched I was by your marks of affection during my stay in Moscow. I have had to rest up after my return and to treat my rheumatism. I have just come back from the country and am once more here in Paris.

I would like now to maintain contact with you. You should write your thoughts about your art, your opinions about the theatre of your epoch. You must do it. I would like to find a way of obliging you to do it, for it would be so precious for us all.

I did not ask Max Reinhardt, but he himself suggested writing his ideas about the theatre, so that his report could be read out at the next international theatrical congress, which we plan to hold in Paris in the latter half of June.

* The inscription on the photograph says: "To Stanislavsky, the greatest man in the Russian and world theatre. His admirer and friend, Firmin Gémier. Paris, May 15, 1928."

Why don't you write, you too, your opinion either about the world theatre or the Russian theatre, or about producing, or yet about any of the questions of particular interest to you. We would read your paper to the congress, and we could even discuss it if you authorised us to do so. Your lofty personality, so admired by all, would be present among all the representatives of the theatre of all countries.

One of these days I am going to see Gaston Gallimard, to find out how far he has come with the translation and publication of your book. I am also sending you the photograph you have asked me for.

I beg you, my dear and great teacher, and my very dear friend, to accept my fond admiration of you.

HAROLD CLURMAN

From "The Fervent Years"

* * *

. . . My passage through Paris was made memorable by my meeting with Stanislavsky . . . When I visited Copeau . . . he told me that Stanislavsky was in town and that I ought to meet him.

Stella Adler and I called on him. He spoke at once of what was uppermost in his thoughts: the theatre. Every afternoon he went out for a few hours to get the sun in the Bois de Boulogne. He had been suffering from a heart ailment and had been spending the past year in Italy under the care of a physician supplied him by the Soviet Government. Stanislavsky asked us to accompany him to the Bois. Stella and I asked many questions. Stanislavsky answered all of them cordially and carefully. He asked us to come again. We went to the Bois again the next afternoon to take up where we had left off the previous day.

Stella Adler had been worried for three years over certain aspects of the Stanislavsky system or method. She no longer found any joy in acting, she avowed; perhaps this was due to that cursed method. Stanislavsky said immediately: "If the system does not help you, forget it. But perhaps you do not use it properly." He offered to work with her on some scene that she had found difficult.

Day after day we returned . . . Stanislavsky was not only a great man of the theatre but a fine human being, strong and simple, urbane and warm, thoughtful and relaxed. *Yet I felt I had to get back to New York and the Group. Stella urged me to stay on. I left.* She continued seeing Stanislavsky daily for five weeks, during which time she worked with him on a scene from *Gentlewoman . . .*

From "Lies Like Truth"

. . . The Method, I have said, is the grammar of acting. There have been great writers who never studied grammar – though they usually possess it – but no one on that account proclaims grammar a fake and instruction in the subject futile. A mastery of grammar does not guarantee either a fine style or valuable literary content. Once in command of it, the writer is unconscious of method. It is never an end in itself. The same is true of the Stanislavsky Method.

There was grammar before there were grammarians. Great acting existed before the Method and great acting still exists unaware of it. A theatre-goer who pays to see Michael Redgrave or Laurence Olivier cannot tell by watching them in performance which of the two was influenced by the Method.

The purpose of the Stanislavsky Method is to teach the actor to put the whole gamut of his physical and emotional being into the service of the dramatist's meaning. What Stanislavsky did was to observe great actors and study his own problems as an actor. In the process he began to isolate the various factors that composed fine acting. He systematised the way actors could prepare themselves for their task – the interpretation of plays. He detailed the means whereby actors might give shape and substance to the roles they were assigned . . .

The Method has influenced no theatre as much as the American. I have suggested one reason for this. Another has to do with one particular element of the Method – "affective memory" or the memory of emotions. I need not dwell here on the artistic validity, the use and abuse of this device. Suffice it to say that in the exercise of affective memory the actor is required to recall some personal event of his past in order to generate real feeling in relation to a scene in his part in the play.

This introspective action which – to an unusual degree – rivets the actor's attention on his inner life frequently strikes the novice as a revolutionary discovery . . .

Most young actors who come upon it eat it up. Some it tends to make a little self-conscious, melancholy, "nervous", tense, producing a kind of constipation of the soul! Those with whom it agrees not only use it but often become consumed by it . . . The actor being the ordinary neurotic man suffering all sorts of repressions and anxieties seizes upon the revelation of himself – supplied by the recollection of his past – as a purifying agent. Through it, he often imagines he will not only become a better actor, but a better person. It makes him feel that because of it he is no longer a mere performer but something like a redeemed human being and an Artist. In this manner, the Method is converted into something akin not only to psychoanalysis but to "religion".

This was not Stanislavsky's aim nor does it represent the purpose of the Method teachers in America. It is, I repeat, an accident of our local scene to be explained by the psychological pressures and hunger of our youth. Where cultural activities are a normal part of daily life – as in most European countries – where self-expression is natural and habitual, the Method is taken as any other form of technical training – something to be learned and then "forgotten" – as grammar is forgotten when we have learned to use language properly.

Culture with us is still considered something apart from the main current of our lives. This is especially true of the stage. Since we have no national theatre, no repertory companies, no widespread stock companies, no consistent employment for the actor and since, too, channels for serious discussion, examination and practice of acting as an art are rare, the American actor clings to the Method and its ever-expanding centres of instruction as to a spiritual as well as a professional boon. It becomes manna from heaven.

I am glad the Method has "caught on". It has been of enormous benefit to our theatre and acting profession. Now that it has been established I hope to see it more or less taken as a matter of course. There is very little that is intrinsically controversial about it.

What the American actor really needs is more plays and productions in which to practise what has been preached. What actors of every kind need is a broader understanding of the Theatre as a whole; a general education in its relation to the world and to art in general. Young actors imbued with the Method have become so engrossed by what the Method can do for them that they forget that the Method exists for the Theatre and not the Theatre for the Method. What they must finally understand is that the Theatre is here for the pleasure, enlightenment and health of the Audience – that is to say for all of us.

MEI LAN-FANG

To the Memory of Stanislavsky

I saw Stanislavsky in 1935 when I first came on my guest tour to the Soviet Union. He was over seventy. His honesty and inner purity attracted me from the first. We met a few times and spoke at length about our joys and griefs, our successes and failures in art.

When I performed in Moscow, Stanislavsky came often to my performances and I, too, went to the Art Theatre to see the plays he produced. He asked me politely for my opinion.

Stanislavsky fought consistently for realistic art and opposed formalism, which leads you away from life. He took the fine national legacy close to heart and selected the best from the art of other peoples very skilfully. He believed that education of the younger generation was an all-important task and his work reflects deep concern for the youth.

When I came to the Soviet Union the second time, Stanislavsky's pupils told me that fifteen minutes before his death he spoke to them about art. Such devoted service to art, such penetration, is a model we should follow.

Stanislavsky used to say that to be a good actor or director it is necessary to work hard and master the theory and technique of theatrical art, with equal emphasis upon both. At the same time the actor must imperatively appear on the stage all the time to test his skill, lest he be like a tree without roots.

Stanislavsky's kindness to me inspired me and is deeply imbedded in my heart. When I returned home I kept remembering the great artist, his perseverance and determination.

Seventeen years have passed. Late in 1952 I attended the Vienna Peace Congress. On its way home, the Chinese delegation stopped over in Moscow as guests of the All-Union Friendship Society. I visited the Stanislavsky Museum on January 7 and the image of the great actor was still more deeply imbedded in my soul.

On the first day of my arrival in Moscow I was told by Komissarzhevsky, the prominent stage director, that Stanislavsky used to mention me to his actors and pupils when working on his last production. I was embarrassed by what he said, and at once deeply thrilled. Last autumn I reread Stanislavsky's famous books, *My Life in Art* and *An Actor Prepares*, which gave me a still deeper insight into Stanislavsky's system. I shall learn still more perseveringly from this great artist in future.

ROMAIN ROLLAND

Villeneuve, Villa Olga, May 28, 1936

Dear Comrades Nemirovich-Danchenko and Stanislavsky,

It is four months that I am tormented by remorse for not having thanked you yet for your cordial salute of January 29. Please pardon me, because I was prevented from doing so by my work and ill health.

Your warm words and appreciation of my work are very precious to me and do me honour. I am very grateful to you.

Dear Nemirovich-Danchenko, I treasure the memory of our friendly meeting last June at the Bolshoi Theatre. And you, dear Stanislavsky, whose glorious name is for me that of a teacher of psychological truth on the stage, how I would like one day to see one of your true-to-life and profound theatrical creations!

I shake your hand cordially,

Romain Rolland

INTERNATIONAL PEACE CAMPAIGN

Paris, July 12, 1937

My dear master,

The International Peace Campaign, headed by Robert Cecil and Mr. Pierre Cot, has hundreds of millions of adherents in all countries.

Its annual congress, organised by the French Committee, is to take place on August 6 in Paris at the Palais de la Mutualité.

At the opening session we want to read out declarations by outstanding personalities in support of the Crusade of Reason Against War. We have specially asked Romain Rolland, one of the promoters of our immense movement, to send us a letter about the duty of every person in face of the current developments imperilling peace, and we have also asked other intellectuals of world fame.

We know the magnificent generosity of your sentiments. Could you send us your declaration on this score at your earliest convenience? It would be read out not only at the congress, but also at the open-air Peace Festival on August 1, which is expected to attract more than 300,000 people.

Be so good, dear master, to accept our homage and respects.

Paul Gsell
President of the Arts Committee

Louis Dolivet
Secretary of the International Peace Campaign

Guy Menant
Secretary of the French Committee, International Peace Campaign

BERTOLT BRECHT

What, Among Other Things, One Can Learn from Stanislavsky's Theatre

1. Appreciation of the poetic essence of the play.

Even the naturalistic plays which Stanislavsky had to produce to keep pace with the tastes of the time, acquired a poetical touch in his interpretation. He never stooped to wingless reportage. Yet in Germany even the classical plays often lose all brilliance!

2. A sense of responsibility to society.

Stanislavsky taught his actors to understand the social mission of the theatre. Art was not a goal in itself for him, but he knew that no goal could ever be achieved in the theatre without art.

3. Casting of "stars".

Stanislavsky's theatre had nothing but "stars" – big and small. He showed that the acting of every individual actor achieves the greatest effect in an ensemble.

4. The importance of the main line and the details.

The Moscow Art Theatre approached every play with a thoroughly considered conception and contributed numerous subtly fashioned details. The one is nothing without the other.

5. The obligation to be truthful.

Stanislavsky taught that the actor should know himself and the people he is to play to the most trifling detail, and that the one follows from the other. What the actor has not gathered from observation and cannot confirm by observation is not worth the public's attention.

6. Harmony of true acting and style.

Magnificent truthfulness combines with deep content in Stanislavsky's theatre. A realist, he has never been afraid of showing the ugly side of things, but he always showed it attractively.

7. Depicting reality as being full of contradictions.

Stanislavsky was aware of the complexity and diversity of social life and knew how to show it without being sucked in by it. All his productions were saturated with ideas.

8. Man is the most important thing.

Stanislavsky was a convinced humanist, and as such he led his theatre along the road to socialism.

9. The meaning of the further development of art.

The Moscow Art Theatre has never rested on its laurels. Stanislavsky worked out new theatrical means for each production. The theatre trained such artists as Vakhtangov, who developed their teacher's art quite independently.

STANISLAWA WYSOCKA*

My Recollections

A man has departed from us of whom it was always good to know that he existed somewhere in the world. A void has appeared, which no one and nothing can fill – the wise man of the theatre is gone, a chapter of theatrical history has closed. As usual, people who had the privilege of meeting a great man, think after his death that the minutes they associated with him were the most important. The rest is history. But to make these memories more intelligible one must stir the healed wounds of one's own life over and over again.

Much time has passed since I first met Stanislavsky. It was in autumn 1906, the time of my fruitful, enthusiastic work at the Krakow theatre. I could have made every sacrifice for that work. I would not shrink from any difficulties at all. Yet the voyage from Krakow to Moscow was not an easy one at the time, and doubly so for me, a Russian subject, who had lived for years without a passport and had to cross the border under an assumed name with someone else's Austrian passport. But the wish to see the Art Theatre, of whose successes I had read so much during its Berlin tour early

* Stanislawa Wysocka as Hamlet.

in 1906, the wish to see it in its own home, was a big enough stimulus. Perhaps I was prompted most to make the trip by Ibsen's *Brand*, which had just been produced by the Art Theatre. In any case, in autumn 1906 I came to Moscow.

The theatre building was not at all like any other theatre of the time. Its plainness, and the harmonious combination of grey and brown, looked severe and cold at first to the eye accustomed to red plush and diverse embellishments. Tickets were sold out months in advance. People from all over Russia came to see them play, but when I came asking for a ticket I was very courteously supplied seats for two plays; I was also promised that Stanislavsky would receive me.

Due to the endless stream of out-of-town visitors the Art Theatre had a big repertoire, and showed all its plays in rotation. It so happened that they were showing *Brand* the first night of my stay. Stanislavsky had nothing to do with it. It was directed by Nemirovich-Danchenko.

I was disappointed. The production was reminiscent of an opera spectacle. Knut Hamsun's *The Drama of Life* was shown the following night. It was produced by Stanislavsky, and he also played in it. It was a revelation to me. A fresh wind wafted from the stage. All things looked non-material, unreal, elevated to a plane where men's souls associated among themselves. I was delighted.

That night, during the interval, I was to meet Stanislavsky. At last came the moment when I entered his study. A tall man with a charming smile rose from behind the writing-desk and walked across the room to meet me, a visitor from afar, with an outstretched hand. The supreme simplicity, the kindness and cordiality of him, gave me courage. I felt as though I had known him a long time, as though he was a close and dear friend. We talked right through the interval, and I begged for permission to return after the next act to continue our conversation about my impressions. I learned at this point that Stanislavsky was deeply grieved. He had come back from the foreign tour with the intention of stamping out the influence of naturalism on his theatre. *The Drama of Life* was the first such experiment, and had run into very severe and hostile criticism by most of the press. In response to my sincere and deep-felt delight, Stanislavsky showed me a newspaper, and said: "Here, read what they write about me. Why should I break my back for nothing? Better stick to the old." The offence did untold harm, it roused doubt and vacillation in this eternal searcher for new values, because the old could no longer satisfy him...

On that visit to Moscow I also saw *Tsar Fyodor* and *Uncle Vanya.* I realised why the Art Theatre was called "Chekhov's Home". The acting in Chekhov's plays was marked by inner concentration, by an intrinsic rhythm and poesy, something the other plays lacked, and but for the excessive accent on purely external effects, such as the crowing of cocks and barking of dogs, and similar sounds of everyday life, which in my opinion intruded upon the general mood, these performances would have been the summit of inner truth. This is why I was very surprised when Stanislavsky said to me between acts, when introducing me to the cast of *The Cherry Orchard*: "Here you see the interior of our house." He put his arm on the bookshelf on the right side of the stage, and added: "If this shelf were moved to some other place I would not feel I was Gayev any more." It struck me that the outer arrangement meant a lot to these masters of naturalism.

I left Moscow very much enriched. New horizons opened to me. Not only what I had seen, but also what I had heard from Stanislavsky, gave me guidance in my further work. How wonderfully Stanislavsky changed when he spoke about the actor's role, when he explained what the actor should do to achieve inner truth. What he told me had nothing in common with naturalism. On the contrary, it was a negation of all external spectacular effects.

A few years passed. I got married and took up residence in Kiev with my husband, Dr. Gzegosz Stanisławski. I did not leave Kiev, except for tours. All this time I wrote often to Stanislavsky about my doubts and disappointments, and about my modest achievements. Out of the kindness of his heart, he always replied to me and gave me useful advice...

I met Stanislavsky when the Art Theatre came to Kiev on tour and was happy to receive him in my home. He spoke at length about his work of the past few years, but without enthusiasm, as though making a report. When I remarked that the acting in the Chekhov plays seemed to have lost some of its magic, he replied:

"We've come to a dead end and don't know where to go."

"We are conscious that what we play has ossified and become a *cliché*. But what is the way out of this dead end? I am a naturalist, and unable to change, though today naturalistic form is hateful to me."

It was the ebbing of the joyous creative uplift, which began in 1906, and the disavowal of the achievements of that time that caused the present state, thought I. The theatre had great success. All seats were sold out days in advance. Yet Stanislavsky grieved over the future, because he did not see the road that lay ahead. That would have been inconceivable in our own theatre, where good proceeds were a vindication of all ills. Kiev gave Stanislavsky and his theatre an enthusiastic reception. Festivities were held in their honour. At these socials in Kupechesky Garden, actors from among the public performed scenes from different plays. The impression was breathtaking. It was something one would never forget.

On my next visit to Moscow . . . I met Stanislavsky again . . . He told me that he had begun training young actors to reinforce and rejuvenate the Art Theatre company. The matter was being handled by Sulerzhitsky, Stanislavsky's constant associate, who was enthralled by his ideas and his "system". The training by that "system" yielded excellent results, as I could see on my subsequent visit to Moscow.

The historic upheaval of war found me in Kiev, soon after my return from a tour. It was a risk to go to Warsaw, which was soon likely to be occupied by the Germans, and I went to Moscow to seek advice from Stanislavsky.

"I'll show you something tonight," he said, "and then we'll talk."

In the evening, he brought me to a crowded and noisy place, a small hall with an amphitheatre reaching almost to the ceiling. The stage was no higher than the first row. All seats were occupied. Stanislavsky seated me in his own, vacant chair, and found a place for himself somewhere in the corner, beside a curtain. He did so often, I was later told, when he came unexpectedly to the "studio". This, I learned, was the Art Theatre's First Studio – a magnificent and thrilling summing-up of the work done with young actors by Stanislavsky's "system". I was present at their first public showing, for which they had selected Dickens's *Cricket on the Hearth*. Their previous work, Herman Heijermans's *The Good Hope*, was as yet thought incomplete.

The curtain rose on the indescribable delight of carter John's home and Baby puttering about in it. The sight captivated the audience and held it in its power until the curtain dropped on the final act. I can safely say that this was the strongest theatrical thrill I ever experienced, second only to Duse's acting. Tear-stained and excited, I did not leave my seat until I regained my composure. Smiling and pleased, Stanislavsky came up to me, and said: "Let's go to the dressing-rooms. Your tears will be their reward."

The auditorium was empty by then. Stanislavsky spread the curtains apart and we ascended the stage where, as usual after a performance, the actors assembled in expectation of his appearance. He introduced me to them. One of them was Vakhtangov (Tackleton), who was destined to play so big a role in the history of the theatre. Stanislavsky showed me the arrangement of the stage, and I could see how happy he was and how he loved his brain-child. The stage facilities were simple and expressive. The ceiling was covered with a wire net, from which the sets were suspended. In the *Cricket,* in which the sets were made of rough canvas, different shapes could be given to the stage. Simplicity was the hallmark of the *Cricket* in general. There were no external effects, just the subtle movements of the soul, and an inward concentration, which drew the audience into the orbit of Dickensian life.

That night I was provided the answer to my question:

"Establish a studio like that for the future renovated Poland."

Stanislavsky spoke these words at the end of 1914. Only a great free-thinker like Stanislavsky, an enemy of tsarism and of all oppression and slavery, would dare speak them in the Russia of that day. I acted on his advice readily, and since that time Stanislavsky was doubly dear to me. On coming back to Kiev, I gathered some young people round me and began working with them on the same play, *The Cricket on the Hearth.* After almost a year's work I gave a public performance, which was a big success . . .

The founder and the soul of the Moscow Art Theatre, Stanislavsky composed veritable poems on the subject of art, and one could listen to him for hours, enthralled by the charm of what he said, the charm of his personality, illumined, as it were, by an inner light. I remember our conversation in connection with a Pushkin social. Stanislavsky was to play Salieri in Pushkin's one-act drama, *Mozart and Salieri.* What depth of thought and feeling there was in what he said! He composed a veritable treatise on Salieri's attitude to Mozart. He spoke about form vividly, in a new way. I was deeply interested in everything he said. But some time later, I read very critical comments about that social as a whole, and especially about Stanislavsky. Confused, I decided to see for myself what could have happened and why the execution conflicted so with the idea.

So I went to Moscow and attended the performance, which consisted of three plays – *Mozart and Salieri, The Stone Guest* and *A Feast During the Plague.* The curtain rose on Stanislavsky-Salieri seated in a deep armchair. He spoke his long monologue. A few minutes later the auditorium began to cough and to fidget, something never witnessed before at the Art Theatre. I felt a chill running down my spine – it was not poetry but some unintelligible prose. When he put poison into Mozart's glass, doing it covertly under the table as though he were some thief in an inn, my indignation was so great that at the end of the play I rushed into his dressing-room and exclaimed: "How could you do it, Konstantin Sergeyevich!" He responded with a disarming smile, and said quietly: "But mustn't I emotionalise, mustn't I pause between emotions?"

I could never bear naturalism before, and from then on I began to hate it deeply. What a terrible enemy it was of the art of acting if it could so monstrously pervert and destroy so wonderful an idea! But his failure made Stanislavsky look for some new truth, and he found it, of which the chapter "The Voice" in *My Life in Art* is a witness. Stanislavsky ends this chapter with the following passage:

"Isn't it strange that I had to live almost sixty years before I understood, i.e., before I felt with all my being, this simple and well-known truth – a truth that most actors do not know"...

It is highly instructive for our actors to learn how a man at so elevated a peak confessed his errors modestly and candidly, and how he searched tirelessly, dissatisfied with what he had achieved.

ALEKSANDER ZELWEROWICZ*

When I was in Russia I made the acquaintance of two great people – Maxim Gorky in Kiev and Konstantin Sergeyevich Stanislavsky in Moscow. My encounters with these amazing people, honest artists in the loftiest and noblest sense of that word, left an indelible impression on me, eternally fresh and alive, as though they had occurred only yesterday.

A young actor and a still younger stage director of the Lodz Theatre, I went to Moscow with an express purpose. I went there, to this Mecca, well prepared, having read studiously everything I could get about the work and character of the Moscow Art Theatre, and having studied the current repertoire (Andreyev's *Anathema*, Chekhov's *The Cherry Orchard* and *Uncle Vanya,* Shakespeare's *Hamlet* and Turgenev's *A Month in the Country*).

I arrived in Moscow with a thumping heart, deeply moved. The exotic appearance of this, I daresay, most typical Russian city, in which Byzantine austerity, the mysterious charm of the East and the bubbling vivacity of the Slavs create a bizarre and magic mosaic, like the ornaments and colours of the faery cupolas of St. Basil's Cathedral, added to the tension of my expectations, which staggered, blinded, captivated and conquered me completely and for ever.

* Aleksander Zelwerowicz as the Inspector in Priestley's *Inspector Calls.*

From the railway station, almost, I rushed directly to Kamergersky Lane, to the box office, for that night I was determined to see the much spoken of drama by Leonid Andreyev, *Anathema.* But there was a notice at the box office announcing that *Anathema* was struck out of the repertoire (after 38 performances) by order of the censors, and that instead there would be Chekhov's *Uncle Vanya,* and on the following day Turgenev's *A Month in the Country,* and that (to my consternation) all tickets were sold out (that is, all owners of tickets for *Anathema* would unquestionably agree to see *Uncle Vanya,* whose 143rd performance this would be in three years). A few ticket scalpers loitered near the box office, naming exorbitant prices for front-row seats. I could not stay longer than 5 days in Moscow, and the loss of an evening would have been a disaster. Yet the lowest price the scalpers named was 20 rubles (a seat in the 10th row, nominally priced at 7 rubles), a sum that equalled the cost of a two-day stay in Moscow in my budget. In face of this peril, I decided to fight like a lion: I pressed a scalper who seemed the most intelligent and pliable to me, against a window and explained to him as lyrically as I could that I was an actor, a foreigner, and that I had specially travelled 1,200 versts, etc. The gentleman was probably strongly moved, because he sold me a ticket in the 12th row for 12 rubles (the nominal price being 6 rubles). At once, I rushed to the administration with the object of securing admission to four evening performances and one matinée. I was told there with exquisite politeness that one could get admission to the special guest-box free of charge but that this required Stanislavsky's personal permission. I was also told that I could see him in his dressing-room backstage after the second act.

I don't quite know the main reason for the excitement I felt and the red spots on my jowls. It may have been the magic of the profound emotion that had gripped the audience and myself, and of which I was almost a co-creator on the stage. Or perhaps it was the joyous anticipation that in an hour, in half an hour, in five minutes, I was destined to see and shake the hand of the brilliant teacher, the director and actor who had founded the modern theatre.

At the fixed time I was approached by an attendant who told me that the director expected me to visit him after the performance, since he did not want to break into the wholeness of my impressions. I could barely wait until the play was over, although I never regretted so much to see the curtain drop in the *finale.*

I came to this great man with two roses in my hand. There was as much of charm in him as of spontaneity and of extraordinary simplicity, as much of delicacy as of strength. I saw a well-built man with a handsome and noble face, with soft and full-blown lips, wonderfully white teeth, with large blue eyes, dark, almost black eyebrows, a big forehead and brushed back silvery-white thick hair. He had the smile of a child and a deep throaty baritone. My shyness vanished as soon as Stanislavsky began to speak. He asked me to visit him at home the following day between five and six, and said I would have seats for all the performances, and that a junior associate of the theatre, a capable actor and a Polish colleague, Riczard Bolesławski (subsequently a prominent theatrical and cinema director) would be my guide.

On the following day at half past five sharp, after a bath and a shave, with a bouquet of beautiful roses, I rang the bell at the door of the old two-storey house, the family home of Konstantin Sergeyevich. I did not feel the excitement of the day before. Simply, I was happy that a minute later I would be speaking to the man whom I worshipped and who embodied my ideals. An old servant opened the door for me (much like Firs in *The Cherry Orchard*) and took me up to a spacious hall on the first floor with the condescending smile of a *major-domo* accustomed to this sort of pilgrimages. A few seconds later I was seated in a carved armchair, facing Stanislavsky. A soft light fell on his head. For all of twenty minutes, completely free from any official ceremony, we conducted a dialogue, simple and lively, about the Polish theatre and Polish playwriting, which Konstantin Sergeyevich knew quite thoroughly. His knowledge of the Polish romantic writers, I would say, was almost complete. I learned that the Art Theatre was planning to produce *Balladin,* but I don't remember whose translation was to be used, and that rehearsals were soon to begin.

At the end of our talk Stanislavsky asked with the cordiality of a hospitable man whether I would like to stay the rest of the season at the Art Theatre as an associate to supplement the group of about a dozen Russians, Swedes, Bulgarians, Serbs, Germans, Hungarians, and Englishmen, who were something like "assistants" at the Art Theatre at that time. Stanislavsky said he would gladly arrange it with the immediate head of the "assistants", Nemirovich-Danchenko, promising the warmest of support. I was breathless ... The prospect of taking part in the work of the Art Theatre, of being among its people, of attending its rehearsals, breathing its air and, most important, having personal contacts with Konstantin Sergeyevich, made my head reel! I was on the point of forgetting all my obligations to the Lodz Theatre, of tearing up my contracts and, putting it plainly, acting like a pig for the opportunity to be next to this man and to take part in his work ...

The host saw me to the door and shook my trembling hand cordially. Five days later, I left Moscow utterly stunned, brimming with the loftiest of impressions and the most daring and ambitious of plans.

Since then, I can at any moment rouse in my memory the image of this man. I can see, hear and feel him beside me almost as distinctly as then, twenty-six years ago, when he said to me in parting:

"Farewell, and come to us more often."

JEAN VILAR

Introduction to the French Edition of Stanislavsky's "An Actor Prepares"

This book, this great book, is a total reconsideration of the art of acting.

A restless practician and a severe moralist, Tortsov-Stanislavsky dispossesses the performer of his vanities step by step. He divests him of his embellishments. He analyses false authorities pitilessly. He destroys conceit, and its cousin, *cabotinage.* Having done that, he offers the actor an orderly method of work, certainly the only one and the always effective.

However, one cannot practise the art of acting unless one deepens the demands with some preponderance of feeling over the clarity of the intellect, without a confusion of our faculties. That is why Tortsov's dialogue with actors is sometimes obscured by clouds of thick fog. An uninitiated reader may here and there run into passages which are unclear. I foresee even that he will lose his way in the endless labyrinth of the "system". Furthermore, the actor's Odyssey is an incessant voyaging within himself, isolated, masked, obscured, full of follies and doubts, of mortally dangerous adventures, a voyaging which sometimes culminates in the actor's physical disappearance.

In any case, no real actor ever fails, sooner or later, to assume, consciously or not, some paths of analysis so thoroughly worked out by Konstantin

Stanislavsky in his book, whose title, I believe, means: "I am an actor, I am a clown, I am illusion, I prepare..."

* * *

It is essential, too, that the reader should know a little of the character, the unusual outer appearance of this scion of a rich Russian merchant family. Oh no, believe me, our author has nothing in common with the fools, the "theatrical monstrosities" racked by a thirst for fame. His glory is pure. It is the glory of a hard-working man.

Konstantin Stanislavsky, unbending and severe to himself, was courtesy itself in his treatment of colleagues. Throughout his long career at the head of his theatre he has not committed a single imbecile act, let alone a discourtesy with regard to a fellow-actor. No, Stanislavsky does not yell at people, he does not insult anyone, he does not roll on the floor and break porcelain vases. A handsome man, with an open intellect for everybody and everything, a man devoted entirely to the exigencies of his profession, he exercised an influence on all Europe when he died in 1938. He served as a model for Jacques Rouché, Jacques Copeau, Appia, André Antoine, and many others. Meyerhold and Vakhtangov came from his studios. It would be futile to try and list the names of all his followers in this Introduction. He has influenced the theatre for all of seventy years, and continues to do so. Thousands of theatre-goers attending performances in Moscow, New York, Rome, Paris, Berlin and London are ignorant of the fact that what they delight in on the stage, from the actor's playing to the details of the production, stem most often from Stanislavsky's lessons.

I confess that I have always had a very special devotion for this man. And each day, each new production, turns my thoughts with greater veneration to his lessons.

I do not think it is necessary to speak here about this book, about this summing-up. I repeat that the reader is likely to lose his way in it at once. And in a way this will do him good. None but the people who manage to come along to the final sentence of these dialogues, will appreciate what severe obligations our profession imposes upon us.

* * *

Yes, I see how patiently, meticulously, fighting exhaustion, he suppresses his inevitable anger, how he forces himself to smile. He is goodwill personified!

The man is tall, handsome and affable. He has an open face, a big forehead, and he is well built. He has all the physical gifts of an actor from birth. Yet how many actors no less generously endowed by nature, have foundered! Not he! He also possesses the major virtue of the actor: character; and his demon is restlessness. As a boy he was crazy about the theatre. He founded his first company. His aged relatives, ensconced in their armchairs, were his first audience. The others were on the stage with him. But a remark, no matter how amiable, made by a sceptical relative would suffice to plunge him into doubt, to torment him and to rob him of his sleep, a remark such as this: "Do you think this scene was well played, Konstantin Sergeyevich?"

He would at once return to work.

He did not cease to reconsider his roles to the end of his life, even if they were quite insignificant and wordless. There are many anecdotes on that score. Admirable Konstantin Sergeyevich!

* * *

Beauty, force of character and grace of heart, a devilish taste for work – what else? Ah, yes, he had extraordinary luck – in a world bogged down in naturalism, he met the only poet of the stage, a compatriot. Stanislavsky was the first interpreter of Anton Chekhov. Lucky man! Years will pass before so happy an alliance will occur again in our art.

To be sure, Chekhov believed that Stanislavsky betrayed the spirit of some of his plays. And a letter to that effect by Dr. Chekhov to his patient was a cruel one. The diagnosis is brief, the prescription concise. But the actor does not protest. Not a single word of annoyance about the poet passes his lips. Not one. He tackled his task again. Just as before, at the family theatre. Yet he had to reread the letter over and over again, and to repeat to himself some of Anton Chekhov's sarcastic sentences. I see him sad and alone in the evening after the performance. Because he was the first, much earlier than his actors, much earlier than all of us, to fall in love unquestioningly with Chekhov and his works.

* * *

The more one considers the life of this man, the more one is inclined to believe that, save for a few inevitable losses, he was pampered by good fortune.

Son of a wealthy merchant, he at once had the first necessary resources and his first public. He was then fifteen or sixteen. Later, he met Nemirovich-Danchenko, a reliable and faithful man, an ideal reader, a discoverer of talent, a writer. They founded the Art Theatre for everyman, the prototype of the modern theatre. Quite soon, he assembled in his company Russia's best actors, actors as scrupulous as he himself. Then he met Chekhov, as I have already said. Furthermore, the Russian theatre was still very young. It was not weighed down by old traditions. One could create anything. The socialist revolution, which forgot of Stanislavsky for all of the first five years, reinstated him in his proper place – the first. And since then his style, his example, his school, his method of formation, his moral, spread throughout Europe, throughout the world.

* * *

To be sure, it is up to us to criticise his "system" and, in our turn, to reconsider the precepts, the prescriptions, the arguments, the spirit even, which he inspired. However, I have regret for the actor who, reading this book, will see nothing in it but schoolboy exercises or useless discourses. If, here or there, one may reproach Konstantin Stanislavsky of the wish at all costs to put in order the inexplicable, let us actors render him once and for all due credit: when studying these pages the well-intentioned reader will realise that although the art of acting is by nature unclear and inconsistent, it will always be one of the most inconceivable in scope and the most necessary of arts for the pleasure of others.

CHARLES CHAPLIN

Stanislavsky's book, *An Actor Prepares*, helps all people to reach out for big dramatic art. It tells what an actor needs to rouse the inspiration he requires for expressing profound emotions.

Comment on Stanislavsky's book "An Actor Prepares"

VITTORIO DE SICA

I should like to consider myself the Italian pupil of Stanislavsky and Nemirovich-Danchenko, the founders of modern theatrical art. I feel that my art really developed under the influence of the Art Theatre school, a school that teaches one to penetrate deeply into the essence of the image, to reveal it, to carry it to the reader.

From an interview in 1956

EDUARDO DE FILIPPO

In this house I should like to recall the name of Konstantin Sergeyevich Stanislavsky, that artist of genius, whose name is dear to all of you and to us. Stanislavsky's doctrine of the theatre is a basis on which all the theatres of the world aspiring to real art, could unite.

From a speech at a meeting with Soviet theatre workers at Friendship House, Moscow, 1962

LEE STRASBERG

The Stanislavsky system is no continuation of the textbooks of the past or present. It represents a sharp break with traditional teaching and a return to actual theatre experience. It tries to analyse why an actor is good one night and bad another, and therefore to understand what actually happens when an actor acts. His actual methods have more than vindicated themselves wherever they have been used. Theatres and actors of great variety and diversified form have created outstanding works on the basis of the training acquired by use of Stanislavsky's principles. The works created are never copies or imitations of one another, but are original creative achievements. That is the purpose of the Stanislavsky idea. It teaches not how to play this or that part, but how to create organically . . .

. . . The work of Konstantin Stanislavsky is the single most important influence in the modern theatre.

... After his death in 1938 his ideas continued to spread and now serve as a guide and inspiration to theatre people all over the world.

... Stanislavsky's strength, by all accounts, lay in his practice, in his wonderful insight and ability to understand and excite the actor's imagination and experience.

... The method is a tool. But one must be able to use it, not just to understand or appreciate it.

MICHAEL REDGRAVE

Extracts from "The Stanislavsky Myth"

Whatever his qualities as an actor, he (Stanislavsky) is known chiefly, and did I am sure wish to be known, as a man of the theatre, a director and the creator of an acting method which has exerted incomputable influence throughout the Western Hemisphere. Of his production those of us who have not seen them must accept the judgement of those who did . . . Many of the actors who worked with him before the revolution are scattered, though one catches occasional glimpses of them (Akim Tamiroff and Michael Chekhov, for example) in certain Hollywood films, where one longs to put them back into the setting to which artistically they belong. But even had not Stanislavsky and Nemirovich-Danchenko's Moscow Art Theatre survived to this day as a living tradition and a contemporary force, we should still receive Stanislavsky's influence through the pages of his book *An Actor Prepares.*

Quite a few actors have, I know, read it and have found it immensely stimulating. Other actors have read it, or partly read it, and find it fairly frustrating. Some others again say they have read it when what they mean is that they have always meant to read it. Some have read some of it and will frankly have none of it. Some would sooner be seen dead than reading it. For all I know some may even have died reading it. Very few have read it again.

It is because I have read it again several times and because I find myself returning to it that I am writing this. But first let me continue in a personal vein for a little. I have written about it once before, and I find that to become identified with a subject about which there is misunderstanding and prejudice is to invite these things on oneself. I do not mind being greeted with "Hello, Stanislavsky", or "Hi-ya Konstantin", or receiving anxious enquiries as to the state of my "superobjective" or whether "my units" are in order. Only my friends dare do this and in any case it is not unflattering.

. . . But I have derived great stimulus from the book, and constant reference to the high standards it demands can help check, to some extent, the varying quality of one's work. When I have directed plays I have tried to apply its first principles; that is to say I have tried to dissuade actors from flying at their parts "like French falconers", hoping to give a performance at the first rehearsal, but instead to encourage them to find their way into a part by degrees, and to try to make sure that they supply themselves with a good imaginative foundation to the part.

For again and again we see actors who start off well but who can never give a full expression of the character because they have not imagined it fully and actively and laid its foundations well; or others who have given a good performance on the opening night, while their imaginative powers were still at work, but who gradually lose life and conviction as the run proceeds, repeating maybe each move and inflection with expert precision but finding that they need the stimulus of a "good house" or "someone in front", or a particular scene in which they know they are especially effective to help them give their best. They are aware that something has gone out of their performance, but they do not know what it is. They know that certain scenes become increasingly difficult to play and they do not know why. At worst, they begin to indulge in private jokes which even the audience can see are not part of the play. Even the actor will have recognised some if not all these symptoms in his own or other actors' work. Nor are these flaws primarily caused by long runs. They are caused, quite simply, by the actors losing sooner or later (some lose quite early) the "offered circumstances", on which their part, not to mention the plot, depend.

Every actor knows how the impact of a first night audience adjusts his sense of the play as a whole. Some less thorough actors are never so good as on opening nights. The audience reactions supply such actors with the impulses which should have come earlier. But although audiences vary they do not vary to the extent of supplying a fresh stimulus every night, and then such actors become morbidly dependent on their audiences and cannot give their best except on rare, and unpredictable occasions. Such actors need to go back to the beginning and start again, trying to revive that imaginative faculty of believing in what they are doing. For that is part of what Stanislavsky taught: belief. Not half-belief. Not make-believe. Belief that does not begin and end by an intellectual process, but which is so deep-rooted that it fires each movement, echoes in each silence, and penetrates beyond "the threshold of the subconscious", where it becomes creative...

The best short summary of the Stanislavsky method is to be found in Norris Houghton's admirable *Moscow Rehearsals* which prospective and past students of the method would do well to get from the library. As Houghton says: "The Stanislavsky system is really only a conscious codification of ideas about acting which have always been the property of most good actors of all countries whether they knew it or not. Its basis is the work of the actor *with himself* in order to master 'technical means for the creation of the creative mood, so that inspiration may appear oftener than is its wont'."...

It is not my purpose here to re-examine or condense the system. But I would like to sweep away one or two of the prejudices which ignorance and fear have created round that thunderclap of a name: Stanislavsky.

Fear? Yes, where some actors are concerned. For there are those who feel that the very existence of this book implies some criticism of their own achievements and acting experience. Well, it does and it doesn't. It doesn't, for the reasons Houghton gives above. It does, I think, because there is no actor or actress living or dead who could sincerely read this book and not find some chink for doubt if not despair...

...If an actor can master the self-criticism which reading *An Actor Prepares* will bring, he has gone some way towards the reconciliation of such doubt. He may go further, he may effect a reconciliation with his own exhibitionism, that quality in every actor which none can lose without losing the desire to act, but with which somehow or other he must come to terms, to the point at least of knowing when he controls it or when it is controlling him.

I have said it is likely he will receive some shocks to his self-esteem but for these he is more than recompensed by the startling corroboration and, be it stressed, simplification of many of his own vague and fluctuating ideas and feelings about his craft. It is a truism to say that acting cannot be taught. Certainly no book can teach anyone to act. But no one would deny for a moment that to come in close contact with a great actor working at his craft must be illuminating, and to read *An Actor Prepares* is to be privileged to be in close contact with a great actor-director not in "a fiction and a dream of passion" but in the great evening of his life, still in active contact with what is probably the greatest of living theatres, telling us again and again, with all the clarity of a great intellect, the simple truths of our art.

Foremost among these is the dictum that our three masters are "feeling, mind and will", that feeling comes first but can never effectively operate without the other two. Many great actors have arrived at much the same verdict; notably Talma, who insisted that "sensibility and intelligence" are the two indispensable qualifications for acting: sensibility, the power to apprehend emotionally the entire content of character and action; and intelligence, the power to reduce that emotional experience to a technical formula which can be repeated at will. Sensibility cannot be consciously acquired, which is why acting cannot be taught. Intelligence, one might say, is the power to see the relationship of things, the power to keep these relationships in perspective. Stanislavsky's book is like some great mirror, wherein a man can see, standing close to the glass, the first mirrors of his soul, his own eyes, and in them, the tiny shape of the surrounding countryside; standing further back, he sees his setting reduced into a frame, and somewhere in that frame, looking curiously impermanent, the figure of himself. But, of course, the mirror can only reflect what the man can see for himself. All it constitutes is a sense of nearness, a sense of distance, a relationship, some proportions. For to read *An Actor Prepares* is like going on a trip abroad: a man can receive from either experience only in proportion to what qualities he brings with him. But to read it at all implies some degree of serious respect for his craft and for whatever else he finds in it, the actor-reader will receive the most sustaining reassurance that has yet been put on record that his work can at its best be creative and achieve not merely *réclame*, but dignity. It will probably make him profoundly dissatisfied with the conditions of work prevailing in Britain. All the better.

And for audiences? I find it hard to imagine that any but the most ardent amateurs of acting will find the patience to read the book. It would be worth their pains. It will perhaps induce them to try to distinguish between the actor and his part, a distinction seldom made by audiences, rarely by critics even. It may help them to realise that the abiding necessity for every actor, as for every artist, is the avoidance of *cliché*, the easy, effective, conventional mode or trick of self-expression. *Cliché* is like a weed: no garden is free from it all the time. The greatest performances are those which are most free from it, those in which every detail has been freshly conceived and which retain at each performance enough of that freshness. It is this freshness which contributes whatever is most exciting and at the same time satisfying in the theatre.

To take an extreme example: "He dies," says the stage direction. If we did not know Olivier to be a great actor by other tests we should know it from the manner of his deaths. Each one is in character. His Macbeth died violently, convulsively, as he had lived, but in spite of his defiant last words we knew that he had lost heart. His Richard III had no heart to lose and fought on and on, his muscles still twitching when all sense had left them . . .

As with death, so with a thousand other commonplaces of life . . . and of the theatre: an embrace; a hasty entrance; the light shock to which we react quickly; the deep shock which our feelings, in order to protect us, at first reject; the manner of starting a quarrel; the manner of saying a long farewell. When these things are well and truly acted they seem simplicity itself. "But," says the reader, like the student in Stanislavsky's book, "all this is obvious!" To which his master retorts: "Did I ever say it was anything else?" Yet how often do we see these simple truths really convincingly performed? Do not a great many audiences prefer, or at least feel more comfortable when witnessing, the artifices and the *clichés* to which they are accustomed. ... They would often rather see an actor "acting" acting, which I suppose makes them feel they know where they are, than acting the part without concession to convention... But just as for an actor to give himself up to conventional acting will in time dry up whatever imaginative powers he may possess, so it is with audiences; they become lazy, bored and only the most violent stimuli will satisfy them. Hence, amongst other things, the appetite for "pace" for its own sake, to which must be sacrificed one of the essentials of any artistic performance, rhythm.

There are in England today, roughly speaking, two styles of acting: the acting in which the effect springs from the cause, and that which begins with effect and which rarely, and only in part, seeks the cause. The latter style is still very much the preponderant. It is very seldom we see a production in which more than a few actors are faithful to the author, the director and their artistic conscience.

... By loving themselves in art and not the art in themselves they have, paradoxically enough, left much of their art unused. It is one of the virtues of Stanislavsky's method that it encourages actors not to let this happen.

JOHN GIELGUD

From the Introduction to the U.S. Edition of Stanislavsky's "An Actor Prepares"

Stanislavsky's now famous book is a contribution to the theatre and its students all over the world. The barrier of language is always a handicap in our ability to share and appreciate the fine work of the foreign theatre. Music, ballet, films even (with the help of translated titles) – these we can more easily enjoy. But one is apt to distrust one's judgement when one sees a play in a language one does not understand. It is easy to be too greatly impressed by the unfamiliar. After all, one says to oneself, the French, the Italians, the Russians are volatile expressive people – they convey so much with their eyes and hands and shoulders – their languages are more musical, more rhythmic than our own – they are trained in the grand style. Training – Ah, there it is – the eternal argument for and against dramatic schools and the necessary apprenticeship for our profession which can never, unfortunately, be sealed by a diploma. The skill of a player – in his early years at least – is so hard to assess in concrete terms.

But here, in this book, a fine actor and consummate director has found time to explain a thousand things that have always troubled actors and fascinated students, things that all of us players have discussed in our clumsy egotistical way at rehearsals and between performances all our lives, but that we have never been able to express in a simple, practical way in general constructive terms.

Stanislavsky, an elderly man when he wrote this book, can look back on his life as an artist with a wise and tranquil vision. He is an authority. You know he has no axe to grind. He is not concerned with the commercial theatre as we know it in Western Europe – not for him the smash hit or sensational failure, the unions, the gossip, the publicity, the star system, the three-year run. He is an Olympian, a specialist in every department of the theatre, who cares so passionately for his art that he wishes to bequeath something from his great store of experience and knowledge to anyone who cares to read what he has set down. And, because he is an expert, writing of what he knows and loves, he is also a fascinating and lucid writer. The book is absorbing. One is enthralled by it – one cannot put it down.

In it there is much wonderful understanding and advice – both for those who practise acting and direction, and those who only study it. How to relax, to control the body. How to study a part, to work with imagination, to build a performance from within. How to work with other actors, the give and take, how to regard the audience so that one may control their reactions at certain times and allow them to take control at others. The style of playing in classical and realistic work, the art of concentration. All these matters are discussed and examined with masterly clearness and simplicity.

Stanislavsky's theatre is a legend. Few are old enough to have seen it, and some of us may think, perhaps, that in perspective it has acquired too great a posthumous reputation. We are sometimes inclined to smile when our elders hold forth on the famous days that are no more – expatiating on the great Shakespearean productions of their youth, the theatre of Booth and Ada Rehan and Irving, of Ellen Terry, Sarah Bernhardt and Eleonora Duse – and the revolutionary struggles of the stage designer and director in the early nineteen-hundreds – Craig and Appia, Serge Diaghilev, Jacques Copeau, Max Reinhardt, Granville-Barker and Stanislavsky.

But in this book, and in the author's earlier biography *My Life in Art*, we cannot help feeling how universal are the problems, the anxieties and difficulties of the theatre all over the world, in whatever language, for every succeeding generation. The theatre needs leaders, and in our own day, when leading figures, in the theatre as elsewhere, are no longer able, owing to world conditions, to dominate as autocrats, where syndicates govern and unions dictate, the counsel of a great artist who is also a great authority is doubly precious.

They say that Karsavina and Nijinski, at the height of their talents and success, went daily to their classes, under the great maestro Enrico Cecchetti, and were dressed down and disciplined with the same severity that was meted out to the youngest students of the Imperial Ballet School. Similarly, the great musical virtuosi of earlier generations would return each year to Paris or Vienna to study with their teachers. Only in the theatre does the successful star, whether young or middle-aged, work without steady disciplined supervision. A fine director may influence him, especially during rehearsals. An occasional criticism from a casual friend or a discerning critic may strike him as helpfully constructive. If he is an artist of integrity he may improve through his own watchfulness and concentration. Actors are, on the whole, conscientious creatures, but the strain of long runs without expert supervision is a danger to their emotional natures. Players trust their instinct, both in creating and sustaining a performance – but instinct can lead them astray when repetition has dulled the first creative invention. It is even easy to lose all spontaneity through an excess of conscientiousness. To whom shall the successful actor turn for true criticism and constructive advice as he encounters the perils and continual problems of his career? To whom can the student go when he embarks on the first perilous seas of stage experience?

In spite of their self-centredness, actors are uncertain in their hearts, though they may appear boundlessly confident before an audience. A tactless director whom they do not wholly admire, or whom they think prejudiced or personally hostile, can destroy their belief in themselves easily enough. Their knowledge is picked up haphazardly over many years, and they hardly dare to advise each other about acting because they feel that for every player the problem is a different one, a private secret to be jealously preserved. There are few set rules, except the most elementary – audibility, imagination, concentration. Actors fear lest they may become old fashioned and stilted, on the one hand, or slapdash and new-fangled on the other. The basic craftsmanship – the five-finger exercises, the physical dexterity, the quickness of eye and hand and lips, these things are not easy to achieve. They are not practised or perfected in a daily routine as they are by executants of the sister arts, whether they are successful virtuosi or struggling beginners. Often players do not realise their own limitations or possibilities until they find themselves rehearsing a part which makes big demands upon them. Then they are not prepared – they lose their voices, find their costumes too heavy, their tongues become twisted in trying to sustain long speeches, they clip their words or find themselves out of breath. They do not excel in costume and modern dress to equal advantage – they are juveniles or character actors, but seldom both. Rarely are they equally at home in several different types of play. Stanislavsky is aware of all these difficulties. He describes them vividly. He has tried to answer many questions. There are people who will say his method is not practical for the commercial theatre. But this book is not a set textbook. It merely discusses difficulties, presents problems and suggests solutions.

Of course there are no practical directions in the book for the staging of the average commercial modern play. But the theory is what is important.

One can apply the Moscow Art theory, the art of living every moment of the part, to Shakespeare and the classics. But, you may say, apply it to *Hay Fever* and it easily becomes ridiculous. I am not so sure. I am pretty certain that the actor trained in the Stanislavsky school would carry a tray in a farce comedy *better* than any actor trained in the normal Anglo-Saxon manner . . .

In Russia and on the Continent the theatre is taken seriously as an art. In Anglo-Saxon countries, it is, if you generalise, a business. The actor's looks, his sex appeal, his personality, count for far more in our theatre than in Stanislavsky's. People drift into the acting profession for a dozen reasons besides real ability. There is not, at present, the same opportunity to build up a serious repertory theatre. There is no theatre for the classics in America – and it is deeply needed for the good of the theatre itself, as well as for the actors and for audiences – and without it an actor has very little chance to play the great parts. The actor, in these days, has often to make up his mind whether to be popular or to be a good actor. And often it is hard to gauge the difference between popularity and real talent. Alas, the modern commercial theatre is bound to be a bitter disappointment to those trained in Stanislavsky's theories. But it is our theatre which is at fault and not the training.

Of course, a great personality, a really great "star" actor, would be liable to disrupt Stanislavsky's type of theatre. I should like to have asked Stanislavsky how he could reconcile the supreme art of many of the great players of the past with the bad companies and the bad plays they often appeared in. Actors' taste in plays is seldom discerning. They are too fond of personal success, the limelight, the round of applause as they go off the stage. When they are offered a part they count their "sides" instead of reading the play.

This book gives some of the reasons why such ambitions are unworthy, why a great artist should seek for truth and dignity and style in acting, why he must have a true appreciation of the quality of the play itself, and try to understand the intentions of his author and director, and help the efforts of his fellow players to work with him to interpret these intentions properly.

Many leading actors try to influence their companies by directing the plays in which they appear. Stanislavsky himself did so, but often he played a supporting role rather than the leading part. In our day Laurence Olivier, Noel Coward, Maurice Evans, and myself have followed his example. Irving and Bernhardt directed, but always played the star part themselves. To combine two such important functions is exhausting and hazardous – but if it succeeds, it does often produce unusually successful results, and the presence of the director at every performance improves discipline and an adherence to the original mood of the rehearsals, which may otherwise deteriorate in a long run.

Are the Russian and the Continental theatres the only ones that produce great actors with true genius for direction also? Though the great actors of the last generation were often good directors, their attention was usually concentrated around themselves. They could not, or would not, have directed or acted in great productions of *The Cherry Orchard* or *Love for Love*, plays which were not written to show off individual stars.

Stanislavsky's book is amazingly modern. We move very slowly in the theatre, almost imperceptibly changes come about. This book was published in New York in 1936. It must have been written over many years. How little the technique of production has changed in all that time! With the sole and honourable exception of Mr. Thornton Wilder's two plays, *Our Town* and *The Skin of Our Teeth*, we have seen little in England or America which creates any kind of revolution in the actor's craft or the director's problems. In other fields violent changes have set in – Technicolour, the talkies, television follow on one another's heels. But in the living theatre we lack writers, and above all, writers who can work with directors as Obey worked with St. Denis, as Heggen has worked with Logan, Williams with Kazan. If only there were companies of actors who would stay together under the same director, with authors working to provide them with plays and preparing them in a settled repertory theatre.

No, say the managers, the authors demand full royalties on a continuous run – No, say the actors and directors, the temptation is too great. Times are hard. We need money. We must make films, do radio, keep ourselves free to put up our price as soon as we become popular. This was not Stanislavsky's way – Popularity, success, those were not his slogans. He was a true artist in the deepest sense, and when you read his book, you feel how much more he had to give to the theatre than the mere trappings which so often delude its most ardent followers.

ROBERT LEWIS

From the Foreword to the U.S. Edition of Stanislavsky's "Creating a Role"

Here, almost a quarter of a century after his death, are some more nuggets dug up from the vast gold mine of Stanislavsky's continuous search for a truthful and artistic method of training actors and working on roles. So rich is the substance of *Creating a Role*, so provocative, that one feels it is possible to take many of the ideas presented and expand them into essays or books.

The first of the three parts of this book is a particularly brilliant breakdown of how to work on a part. This study of Stanislavsky's approach to his role of Chatsky in *Woe from Wit* will be a revelation.

. . . The most important, and least understood, aspect of the work, the search into one's own experience to arouse feelings analogous to those required in the part, gets a thorough airing.

Don't think that "feeling" is all that is stressed here. Unlike some modern self-styled practitioners of what they call "The Method" (no such arrogance will be found in Stanislavsky's own writings) there is more than lip-service paid to beauty of language, lightness of verse, rhythm, imagination, and all the theatrical and artistic means of expression.

. . . But he also knew the *importance* of voice, speech, movement, and so forth. If it ever was needed, here is proof that gives the lie to the argument that anything in Stanislavsky's method leads perforce to sloppy speech and slouching. "Every living organism," he says, "has an outer form as well, a physical body which uses make-up, has a typical voice as to manner of speech and intonation, typical way of walking, manners, gestures, and so forth." What a blow to self-indulgent actors busy squeezing out a bit of private feeling, who care not a jot how they look, whether they can be heard, and so forth.

. . . It cannot be said too often that Stanislavsky's method is not a style and not applicable to one particular style of theatre, but is an attempt to find a logical approach to the training of actors for any play, and an artistic way of preparing for any role.

But we do have a chance to see Stanislavsky trying his rehearsal procedure on two other roles: Othello, and Khlestakov in *The Inspector-General.* Again he approaches these parts from the "inside" and the "outside" simultaneously. He discovers, in fact, that finding the correct physical truth of the part feeds his inner truth better, as he says, than "forcing" feeling.

. . . All through the three sections of this book you get a picture of a real artist at work, sometimes failing, but without despair, and always seeking truthful answers.

. . . Here, then, is more word from the master, than from his disciples. It is a book for all theatre professionals as well as students. Whether you are in agreement or disagreement with all, or parts, of it, you cannot help being stimulated and enriched by it.

STANISLAVSKY'S LETTERS

TO LUCIEN BESNARD

Moscow, July 20, 1897

Dear Sir,

Allow me to address you in Russian. That will enable me to speak to you at greater length and more freely.

... I agree with you that I failed as Othello, but I disagree with one of your remarks, namely, that we played and produced the play at variance with Shakespearean tradition. I adore Shakespeare and therefore consider it my duty to stand up for him. My opinion is this: Shakespeare's traditions are expressed by him in Hamlet's monologue to the actors. These traditions should be sacred ground for every actor. I revere the French for their tradition which, by the way, has now become a simple uninteresting routine in light comedy and drama. But their tradition in tragedy – what can be more terrible, and what has it in common with Hamlet's words? The French call their way of acting a tradition, and it is thus that Mounet-Sully plays Hamlet.* Where does this tradition come from? People say that Talma played that way.** But does any one of us remember him? I do not doubt that, perhaps, he did shout, but his shouting was the effect of an immense artistic temperament. He shouted because his expressiveness was so great that his voice, too, so to speak, grew and expanded proportionately to his temperament. I did not hear Tommaso Salvini shout,*** because his voice is the truthful and natural effect of his temperament. But when the miniature Mounet-Sully blows himself up and shouts as loud as he can to affect his own nerves and the nerves of his audience, I cannot help remembering the fable about the frog and the bull, and I say: "What a pity

* *Jean-Sully Mounet* (1841-1916) – famous French tragedian.

** *François-Joseph Talma* (1763-1826) – French tragedian and stage reformer of the time of the French Revolution.

*** *Tommaso Salvini* (1829-1915) – famous Italian tragedian who frequently toured Russia.

that this great talent is perverted by false tradition created not by genius, but by giftless people." And this is really so: genius is inspired by truth, by beauty, by life itself, while giftless people need a screen to obscure the poverty of their talent and imagination, and for this reason invent tradition. By now they have invented so many traditions and different rules, that Shakespeare is not understood by the ordinary public, and Molière is no longer funny. Who does he owe that to? I say, to tradition.

Judge for yourself: could Shakespeare be satisfied with Mounet-Sully's performance of Hamlet if he made Hamlet say the following lines:

1. "But if you mouth it, as many of your players do, I had as lief the town-crier spoke my lines." (Act III, scene 2.)

2. "O, it offends me to the soul to hear a robustious periwig-pated fellow tear a passion to tatters, to very rags, to split the ears of the groundlings; who, for the most part, are capable of nothing but inexplicable dumbshows and noise." (Act III, scene 2.)

3. "With this special observance, that you o'erstep not the modesty of nature; for anything so overdone is from the purpose of playing, whose end, both at the first and now, was and is, to hold, as 'twere, the mirror up to nature; to show virtue her own feature, scorn her own image, and the very age and body of the time his form and pressure. Now this overdone, or come tardy off, though it make the unskilful laugh, cannot but make the judicious grieve; the censure of the which one must in your allowance o'erweigh a whole theatre of others. O, there be players that I have seen play, – and heard others praise, and that highly, – not to speak it profanely, that neither having the accent of Christians nor the gait of Christian, pagan, nor man, have so strutted and bellowed, that I have thought some of nature's journeymen had made them, and not made them well, they imitated humanity so abominably."

Compare the above with what Mounet-Sully does and you will admit that he errs in his false tradition, just as all contemporary interpreters of Shakespeare. A terrible mistake, an inexplicable misunderstanding, has arisen with respect to Shakespeare. You will recall that Shakespeare's contemporary, Ben Jonson, also a theatrical writer, preached word for word what is now imputed to Shakespeare. Yet the latter never agreed with him. It was Ben

Stanislavsky as Othello and Christophore Petrosyan as Iago. 1896

Jonson, not Shakespeare, who loved ostentation, play-acting, and false theatrical effects or, more precisely, heroics. He ridiculed Shakespeare for gravitating towards simple characters. Shakespeare, on the other hand, was carried away by the characteristics of the part, but thanks to his extraordinary talent he depicted his heroes so vividly that they acquired universal significance. If in our time Ostrovsky is described as the writer of ordinary life, Shakespeare was such too for his time. I am sure you will understand that I am not comparing these two talents, and that all I say is that they are somewhat alike in their attitude towards art. For does not Hamlet say in Act II, in the scene with the actors: "They are the abstracts, and brief chronicles of the time"?

Last but not least, the revision of *Hamlet* as it is played by Mounet-Sully, is it not conclusive proof that Shakespeare's spirit has been misunderstood? Those Gervinuses* and other learned critics are Shakespeare's greatest foes. They approach the living, artistic and inspired work from the dry, scientific standpoint and take the life out of it. If there had not been this vast scientific library about Shakespeare's heroes and plays, everybody would regard them more simply and would understand them perfectly, because Shakespeare is life itself, he is simple and hence understandable to everybody. However, if one took exception to his every word and looked for different wise underlying meanings, Shakespeare would lose his brilliance, passion and beauty . . . and would become a boring philosopher and talker, of interest only to scholars.

Briefly, the more simply we treat genius, the more understandable and intelligible he will be. Genius must be simple. That is one of his main virtues. So, on the one hand, we have traditions that someone has invented, and, on the other, we have the brilliant lines by Shakespeare himself about dramatic art. Who to believe: the learned Gervinuses or William himself? Believe who you like, but I believe Shakespeare and say with conviction that all tradition which departs from the lines of the genius is trash and should be quickly forgotten.

So may you abandon tradition and routine more quickly, and we shall follow your example. This will be a help to me, because I am waging a fierce

* *Georg Gottfried Gervinus* (1805-1871) – German historian and literary critic.

struggle against routine in our theatre, in our modest Moscow. Believe me, it is the task of our generation to banish from art outmoded tradition and routine, and to give more scope to fantasy and creation. That is the only way to save art. This is why it pained me to hear you advocate what I believe damaging to living art, and why I have now written so much.

Wishing you success,

Yours respectfully,

K. Alexeyev

TO ALEXANDER BORODULIN

St. Petersburg, March 11, 1901

Dear Sir,

I did not write to you for so long, because I was very busy – rehearsals from 12 to 5 and make-up at 6.30, and then the performance until midnight. That is how I spend every day (don't think stage laurels are easy to get by).

I liked your first letter for its youthful sincerity, and, despite my big mail, I decided to reply, because I, too, have experienced and felt everything that you feel now. I know that I can give you good and sensible advice. Frankly, I did not like your second letter. There was something of a provincial's resentment in it. I mean such sentences as, "if I am not wanted, I won't impose", "I'll try and manage on my own somehow", etc. I would rather that I had not read those words. They indicated that you, still a very young man, have a somewhat touchy sensibility. If that is so, it is *very* dangerous for a would-be actor. I want to forget those words, which hinder me from speaking to you in comradely fashion.

Do you know why I gave up my personal affairs and devoted myself to the theatre? Because the theatre is the most powerful rostrum, still stronger in influence than the printed word and press. It has fallen prey to human riff-raff, and they have made it a seat of depravity. My task, so far as my capacity permits, is to purge the family of actors from ignoramuses, semi-literates and exploiters. My task, so far as my capacity permits, is to show the modern generation that the actor is a preacher of beauty and truth. For this reason, the actor should stand above the crowd, either in talent, in education, or some other virtue. Above all, the actor should be refined, and should appreciate and understand the geniuses of literature. This is why, to my mind, there are no actors. Out of a thousand nonentities, drunkards and semi-literates – the so-called actors – 999 should be purged, and one worthy of the calling picked out. My company consists of university people and technicians who have graduated secondary and higher educational establishments. Therein lies the force of our theatre.

Love of the stage has sprung up in you. Start by making sacrifices to it, because serving art means making selfless sacrifices. Learn... When you are a literate and developed man, come to me if my work will be to your liking then. Together with me and all my comrades, prepare yourself to follow a thorny, difficult and harrowing path, oblivious of glory and full of love for what you do. All this, to be sure, is feasible, provided you have talent... But talent alone is not enough, especially in the twentieth-century theatre. Ibsen squared in philosophical and social significance will monopolise the repertoire of the new theatre and only cultured people will be able to play such authors.

Provincial shouters and play-actors have reached the end of their road, and soon, God willing, a time will come when illiterate people will not be allowed by the law to serve on the stage. That is something the actors' congress is seeing to at present. To check my words, read Ibsen's plays, *The Master Builder* and *Hedda Gabler*, and decide for yourself how much more you have to learn to appreciate this universal genius. Those are just the sprouts. The fruit is still to come. To sum up, start learning, and I will then readily accept you as a helper. If you stay illiterate, I will consider you an enemy of the stage and will aim all my darts at you.

Your well-wisher,

K. Stanislavsky

Forgive me my poor handwriting and the slips of the pen, for I have no time to reread the letter. I am writing it between acts.

TO VERA KOTLYAREVSKAYA

April 18, 1901

My dear Vera Vasilyevna,

I have been conferred an excellent opportunity to write an exhaustive reply to your kind letter . . .

What should I say to you in consolation and encouragement? Perhaps it will relieve you to learn that, but for a few periods of my stage career, I *constantly* have the same feeling of dissatisfaction, anxiety and concern. To be sure, all expressions of sympathy we get from the public serve to encourage us, but not for long. For example, now that I have to pick a new repertoire for the coming season, I feel badly. Cumulatively, the dread of repetition, the dread of marking time, instead of progressing, makes me worry and suffer. I ask myself: what worries you? Do you fear that the public will not appreciate your labours? No, not at all. Such thoughts would be criminal for a settled man who works in art for the sake of art. I worry for myself, because of a dread to lose faith in my own ability and to become helpless in face of myself. Isn't that the very feeling that you are experiencing? But one is bound to admit that the good comes with the bad. There is an element of pleasure, of interesting things that fill everyday life, in these worries of the actor. Rob the actor of these worries, of this struggle, and he will ossify in his greatness and become "venerated". What could be more incongruous than a venerated actor, especially a Russian, fat actor . . . I prefer being pale, thin and nervous.

The search for new horizons, for new ways and means to express elaborate human emotions, and the worries that go with them, that is indeed the true atmosphere of the actor. One should not lay too much of an accent on that, lest one go under and become crazy, but God forbid that an actor should restrict his imagination to the academic framework and establish for oneself, once and for all, the laws of eternal (read banal) beauty and the rules for its reproduction. That is the kind of atmosphere in which one ossifies, and, naturally, grows fat.

You must believe that your worries are not in vain, and that they are designed to extend the horizon narrowed by conventionalities. To make the breach through which a human being with an as yet insufficiently developed imagination picks *from life* material for his creations, takes a lot of time, a whole lifetime, and making this breach bigger calls for great effort, labour and energy. What to do? If you lack the strength of Samson, you have to act like the prisoner who digs day in and day out to undermine the strong, age-old bars of the prison that keeps him from living people and God's light, without which he cannot exist. What is the outlook for this prisoner? New quest, new fetters, new prison bars. That is only too true. He will always long for people and for life... And so walk with a twisted gait, or with the bent back of an old woman, or with the majestic gait of a queen, but never in buskins, those senseless inventions of human conventionality. May your feet tread real earth – damp, moist, alive. If you step into mud, don't be afraid of it, for there too you will find a stone, perhaps a beautiful one, which you may use to step on without fear of soiling your feet. And the main thing – don't show this letter to my enemies, for then they will hate you, and will call me a symbolist, a decadent, etc.

I seem to have indulged myself and strayed into philosophy, and that is tolerable just so much and no more. Hence, I conclude with the following thoughts: God grant, that you find a way to bring all the truth and all the beauty of life to the stage. God grant, that in the search for this beauty you do not fear the mud with which people have smeared it. Bring to the stage, if necessary, beauty smeared with mud, and clean it of this mud for everybody to see.

Respectfully,

K. Alexeyev

If I don't mail the letter now, I'll tear it up tomorrow for it will seem too silly. I am sending it to you intact. Forgive me if you find parts of it unintelligible. I have absolutely spoilt my handwriting due to my haste in writing the *mise en scène*. But I cannot rewrite and correct the words that are unclear, for I have no time.

K. S. Stanislavsky and A. P. Chekhov. 1899

TO ANTON CHEKHOV

(a telegram)

Moscow, October 20, 1903

I have just read the play.* I am stunned, can't come to my senses. I am beside myself with delight. I consider the play the best among all the magnifi-

* See *Notes*, p. 291.

cent things you have written. Cordial congratulations to the brilliant author. I feel and appreciate every word. Thank you for the pleasure you have given me, and for the pleasure to come. Goodbye.

Alexeyev

(a telegram)

Moscow, October 21, 1903

The play has been read to the company. It is an exceptional and brilliant success. The audience was enraptured from the first act onwards. Each subtlety was appreciated. In the final act people wept. Like everybody else, my wife is delighted. No play has ever been received with such unanimous acclaim.

Alexeyev

Moscow, October 22, 1903

Dear Anton Pavlovich,

In my opinion, *The Cherry Orchard* is the best play you have written. I am fonder of it even than of the delightful *Sea-Gull*. It is not a comedy, nor a farce, as you wrote, but a tragedy, whatever outlet to a better life you may reveal in the closing act. The impression it gives is staggering, and is achieved by half-tones and delicate colours. There is more poesy and lyricism in it, and it is more theatrical. All the characters, the passer-by included, are brilliant. If I were offered to pick the part to my taste, I wouldn't know which I wanted most, so great is the attraction of every one of them. I am afraid the play is too subtle for the general public. The public will not soon appreciate all the subtleties. Alas, we shall have to read and hear a lot of stupidities about it. But the success will be enormous, because it is a captivating play. It is so very consummate that not a single word can be deleted. Perhaps I am biased, but I found no flaws at all. Just one: it calls for very great and subtle actors to reveal all its beauties. We won't be able to do it. At my first

To A. P. Chekhov with sincere affection and veneration. To the creator of the new theatre from the grateful stage director and actor K. S. Alexeyev (Stanislavsky).

Moscow, February 10, 1902

reading I was struck by the fact that I was at once enthralled and immersed in the play. This did not happen with *The Sea-Gull* or *The Three Sisters.* I have grown accustomed to the vague impressions I received during the first readings of your previous plays. I dreaded, therefore, that the play would not enthrall me in the second reading. But my fears were in vain. I wept like a girl. I wanted to restrain myself, but could not. I can hear you say: "But it is a farce"... No, for the ordinary man it is a tragedy. I have a special affection for it. There has been almost no criticism, although actors like to criticise. This time all of them seem to be toeing the line.

Whenever the voice of a critic arises, I smile and do not bother to reply. I feel sorry for him. Someone said: Act Four is the best, and Act Two is the weakest. That is laughable, but I do not argue. I begin to recount Act Two scene by scene, and the person is at once confused. Act Four is good precisely because Act Two is magnificent, and vice versa. I proclaim this play beyond all competition and criticism. Whoever fails to understand it, is a fool. That is my sincere conviction. I shall play every part in it with delight, and if it were only possible I would really like to play all the parts, the delightful Charlotte included. Thank you, dear Anton Pavlovich, for this great pleasure, the pleasure I have had and the pleasure I am still to get...

Let me shake your hand and please do not think I am off my head.

Fondly and faithfully,

K. Alexeyev

TO OLGA KNIPPER-CHEKHOVA

Contrexéville, July 13, 1904

My dear, kind Olga Leonardovna,

I have been wanting to write to you every day, but have restrained myself, because it is difficult to know from afar how you feel and how you are bearing up to your grief, and how fitting my letters would have been. Furthermore, I know nothing of what has happened and is now happening in Moscow, since I have no news and look in vain for Russian newspapers. I am in a great hurry to leave these French backwoods, because here, in solitude, it is harder to inure oneself to our common loss. I want to be and speak with those who have been struck by it. Here there is nobody except holidaymaking dolls. Fortunately, I took along two books of dear Anton Pavlovich's stories, and at present they are my best friends. I am reading them a second time and see between the lines what only a man who has known Chekhov, the best of all people, can understand. Where are you now, and when will I see you? Will you go to Yalta, or would that pain you? Will you change your Moscow home, or will you want to stay on in it?

My mother, thank God, has begun to relax and get better. Perhaps I shall soon be able to leave her here and hurry back to Moscow. There, I will get the answer to all my questions. God grant that I shall see you strong as I expect, knowing that you have graced the last days of a man who needed beauty more than anybody else. Having selflessly given him a portion of your life, you have kept him among us a few years longer, and we should be grateful to you.

I remain very faithfully and affectionately,

Yours,

K. Alexeyev

K. S. Stanislavsky and Z. S. Sokolova. 1900

TO ZINAIDA SOKOLOVA

Berlin, February-March 1906

Dear Zina,

. . . We are the heroes of the day. An unusual success. What the Russian papers print is only a fragment. The biggest success fell to *Uncle Vanya* . . . What reviews! We never had such reviews in Russia. What a sensitive appreciation of the Chekhov flavour! . . .

The most interesting and touching is the mutual affection that has sprung up between ourselves and the Hauptmanns. He is so captivated by us that the Germans no longer recognise him, whom they know as a taciturn man. There have been a few amusing episodes. During the intermission, at a showing of *Uncle Vanya,* he went out into the lobby (to everybody's amazement), collected a crowd and declared for everybody to hear (sic!):

"This is the most forceful of my theatrical impressions. Artistic gods, not humans are playing on that stage."

After Act IV of *Uncle Vanya* he sat still in his seat a long time, biting a handkerchief. Then he stood up, and wiped away his tears. Nemirovich-Danchenko came up to him, but all he said was:

"*Ich kann nicht sprechen.*"

Nemirovich told us he had the face of a Schiller or Goethe at that moment. After seeing *The Lower Depths* he said he had not slept all night, thinking about a play he intended to try and write specially for our theatre. In brief, Hauptmann has been conquered.

The next is Barnay. He is the director of the imperial theatres, but attends all our performances, presents us with flowers, and says for all to hear that he is learning from the Russians. Something quite unusual occurred today for Berlin. They have a critic here, by the name of Norden. He writes reviews in exceptional cases (the local Stasov*), always fulminating. He has never praised anyone yet. Today, in a short article, I read something like the following: "A big event has occurred in Berlin. Russians have come here. Each generation is destined to encounter six to eight big artists. In this company all are artists, all together. That is brilliant... All criticism is silenced. Let not only actors, but also diplomats, politicians, and those who say Russia is a lost land, go to the theatre and get acquainted with it. A nation that created such art and literature is a great nation. It has culture, but we do not know it. It is unlike ours, but it will do us good to learn more about it."

...Fond embraces to you and all. Send this letter on to all my brothers and sisters. However much I would like to, it is impossible to write the same thing to each one personally. The only time I have for letter-writing is the intermissions. The rest of my time is occupied.

* *Vladimir Stasov* (1824-1906) – distinguished Russian music and art critic.

TO VLADIMIR NEMIROVICH-DANCHENKO

Kislovodsk, November 16, 1910

Dear Vladimir Ivanovich,

I have received two of your letters; one is very moving, the other magnificent. One is somewhat shorter, the other immense.

In reply to the first I wish and have to express the best of my feelings for you, who is always in my heart (it is my affection that makes me sulk sometimes, and act angry – all from love).

I feel I am unable, at least this minute, to express my gratitude and the sentiment roused in me by your letter about our fraternal kinship, written to my wife during my illness.* Simply, I am not strong enough yet to give free rein to my emotions. When we meet again I shall embrace you all the more tightly. I am not even going to tell you that I believe and know, and have always known, of your kind feelings for me and I feel sure that you too believe and know of my feelings for you. I also believe that as the years go by our affection will grow stronger, because the former professional envy, vanity, intolerance, etc., will give place at a riper age to experience and wisdom. Once a man realises what success and popularity spring from, he feels like fleeing all men, as Tolstoi did.

To sum up, I am sending you brotherly thanks for your letter to my wife: I shall always treasure it in my heart. When we meet again, we shall embrace.

Now for the monster letter – I am staggered by its size, and ask myself: am I physically fit to reply to all the important questions you raise, for they cannot be answered off-hand and call for an exhaustive reply. To be sure, they deal essentially with the future of our theatre...

Let me touch lightly on what you say about my system. Before taking a part it has to be assessed in general from the literary, psychological, social

* See *Notes,* p. 292.

Vladimir Nemirovich-Danchenko. 1925

and living point of view. Only after that is done can one divide it, first into physiological units and then, on the strength of that, into psychological units or wishes. I know a few practical methods now (because it is my purpose to find a way of realising every theory. Theory without realisation is not my field, and I abandon it) to help the actor in his psychological, physiological, living, and even social analysis and appreciation of the play, and the role. But the literary analysis is up to you. You must make it not only as a writer and critic, but as a practical man. We want a theory backed by a practical and thoroughly tested method.

All I know so far is that before tackling my system we must: (a) induce the volitional process; (b) induce the process of searching – in a literary conversation (which is up to you), for I know how to sustain and develop the process of searching; (c) I know how to induce the emotional process; (d) I do not yet exactly know how to help the process of *embodiment*, but I have explored the ground and seem to be on the point of finding the way; (e) the processes of *synthesis* and *influence* are clear.

It is up to me now to find a practical way of exciting the actors' imagination in all these processes. This aspect is very poorly developed in psychology – especially the creative imagination of actors and artists. As for the rest, I think all of it is not only developed, but also quite thoroughly checked. A few odds and ends are down on paper. I believe you will agree with me in all respects. At the moment much of what you are told by third persons has reached their reason, but, perhaps, not their senses. In that lies the main difficulty. It is not hard to understand and remember. It is hard to feel and to believe. And that is what I want to talk about, but where to find the time (I mean you, for I am idle now), and where to find the energy?

Affectionately,

K. Alexeyev

TO VSEVOLOD MEYERHOLD

Moscow, February 10, 1912

My dear Vsevolod Emilyevich,

I am deeply touched by your good letter, which was prompted by fine sentiments, and I am very grateful to you and Mr. A. Golovin.* Wherever there is work and search, there is struggle. We struggle, but I do not dare complain about our adversaries. On the contrary, I respect them. The greatest suffering comes from the "theatre" itself.

Goodness, what a crude institution and art it is! I have lost faith in everything that serves the eye and ear on the stage. All I believe in is emotion and, chiefly, nature itself. It is more clever and subtle than all of us, but... !!?

Yours, until we meet again,

K. Stanislavsky

* See *Notes*, p. 292.

TO SERGEI BALUKHATY

Moscow, February 14, 1925

I am very grateful to you for your attention and treatment, and wish sincerely that I could help you in your interesting work. Bear in mind that the *mises en scène* of *The Sea-Gull* were made by the old, now completely rejected methods of imposing one's personal emotions on the actor, and not by the new method of studying the actor beforehand – his capacities, the material of his part, before creating the appropriate and desired *mise en scène.* In other words, the method of the old *mises en scène* belongs to the despotic director, against whom I now battle, while the new *mises en scène* are made by directors who depend on the actor.

In view of this I would appreciate it greatly if before speaking in the book about my *mises en scène,* you would give a foreword clarifying what I have just said.

With sincere wishes of success,

K. Stanislavsky

TO FIRMIN GÉMIER

Moscow, April, 1926

I, too, thought of the idea of uniting the actors of all nations during my two-year voyage with the Art Theatre to all the countries of Europe and America. I saw at first hand that the theatre is in a dangerous crisis everywhere.

Weakened at first by the cinema, and later beaten by the war, the theatre is compelled to serve the very bad taste of the newly-arisen elements who possess capital, a special class of profiteers who inundate the capitals of all countries and set the tune. The modern repertoire and modern productions adapt themselves mostly to their taste. Extravagant productions and the tinselly wealth of breath-taking hokum with nude women and sordid plots, much like the cinema's, are staged for them.

I am surprised that people who rule the countries and are concerned with the ethical, moral and aesthetic development of the peoples under their rule have, like everybody else, forgotten the lofty purpose of the theatre and, as it were, stricken it off the list of educational and improving media of mass influence, leaving to it the sole purpose of entertaining in order to distract people from politics.

A highly-placed person of the ruling class, whose name I am not at liberty to reveal because our conversation was private, said to me candidly: "I warn you, I hate the theatre." "Which theatre?" I asked. "The depraved and lowly theatre that I hate more than you do, or the lofty and noble theatre that should serve in the hands of every government as one of the best weapons for promoting friendship and mutual understanding between nations?" After that we had a long and tedious conversation about the theatre as a means of winning universal peace, of which so much is spoken in all parts of the world now that the war is over.

In nearly all the countries where I had to play in a language unfamiliar to a foreign public, totally unfamiliar to us, seeing an unfamiliar repertoire of a far-away eastern country entirely unfamiliar to them, we heard the following: "One such performance tells us much more than all the conferences, expeditions, congresses, lectures and scientific treatises that strive to define the soul of a nation in order to understand it better."

This capacity of the theatre is quite understandable. If the national genius describes the most typical and profound features of its people's soul in an exhaustive work of art, and if the most gifted actors of a country, combined with the best directors, artists and other masters of our collective theatrical art, who convey by common effort the work of this genius, the soul of the people and the details of its life, influencing its psychology – if these living interpreters appear in person in foreign countries and speak heart to heart about the things that comprise their spiritual nature, it is not at all surprising that such art and such productions convey more of the unseen and imperceptible, supra-conscious human emotions that are more necessary than anything else to know and understand another people and another country. Neither a scientific report, nor a lecture, a treatise, a conference, a dead book or newspaper, can do this.

They have their own sphere, conveyed by word of mouth and the printed word. While the field inhabited by the actor radiates invisibly from soul to soul.

I told this anonymous person that it is their responsibility to encourage that sort of theatre, a theatre of the human race, a theatre of mutual understanding.

TO THE MOSCOW ART THEATRE COMPANY

Moscow, June 26, 1926

My fond and dear friends,

We have had a difficult, but encouraging season this year, which I would describe in the life of our theatre as a second "Pushkino".*

In the last few years people have tried to bury the Art Theatre and its founders, saying that they were outmoded and backward. They tried to divide the "fathers" and the "children", that is, the basic Art Theatre, the "veterans", and the young people. But this season, thanks to a great common effort, the fathers got to know the children better, and the children got to know the fathers better, and we again have the close-knit Art Theatre family. The young people realise that intuition and inner emotion are not enough for a real actor, and that there is no art without consummate technique, without traditions built up through the centuries and that this was something they could get from none but the "veterans". As for us "veterans", we understood the enthusiasm of the young people, appreciated their talent and diligence, and this has created the desire to share with them everything we know.

The close-knit effort of actors, directors, musicians and vocalists, all the technical and working staff, the administration and the attendants, have yielded rich results – *six* complete productions and *two* prepared by the actors.

All of us have worked conscientiously, unstinting of our strength. We have commanded everybody's attention, that of the government and the new viewer. They are getting to know us. Now people look at us in a new way.

In parting with you until autumn, I should like to embrace every one of you and to congratulate you on a brilliantly completed season, and to express the hope that our future work will be still more close-knit and joyful.

Very affectionately yours,

K. Stanislavsky

* See *Notes*, p. 292.

TO HENRI BARBUSSE

Moscow, September 26 (?), 1927

I was very upset that I could not welcome you personally during your first visit to our country.

I trust that a genuine International of Art is growing stronger in these days of great upheaval. We are accustomed to seeing a kindred element in you and in all that you do, so strongly expressed in your novels and short stories. Art cannot now be narrowly exclusive, and we need the friendly support of the finest men of Western art. I beg you to believe in my deep respect for your activities, and in my sincere pleasure at seeing you in our midst.

K. Stanislavsky

TO HERBERT GRAF

Moscow, October 11, 1927

Doctor Herbert Graf,

I hasten to apologise for my delay in replying to your letter. It waited for me in Moscow, until I came back from my summer treatment. Due to my illness I came home later than expected. I thank you very much for the confidence you show in our Art Theatre. But before we come down to the business which interests you, I feel I must explain that the Art Theatre is purely a drama theatre. Its artistic principles are based entirely and chiefly not on the stage director of the Meyerhold and Tairov type, but on the stage director who is the actor's teacher. Our theatre develops chiefly the intrinsic technique of creation, and has achieved singular results in this realm after long and painstaking effort. It is on these results that the theatre draws, progressing in the said direction. We employ external resources only inasmuch as they are required for the actor's intrinsic creation.

Meyerhold and Tairov have other principles. While the stage director at the Art Theatre is a midwife for the actor, who receives the new creature born by the actor, my comrades-in-art, Meyerhold and Tairov, consider the director to be the head of everything, who must create single-handedly, while the actor is no more than putty in the hands of the chief creator. We consider the external approach to art, prominent in our country in the last few years, to be outmoded.

This essential difference between the two schools of thought compels a newcomer to our theatre to study all the principles of the intrinsic creative laws developed by us. We consider them the only vehicle of future art, of its development and progress.

The two opera studios, one bearing my name, and the other bearing the name of Nemirovich-Danchenko (the latter has toured Europe and America) are also based on the Art Theatre principles of intrinsic creation. There is also a slight difference between my studio and Nemirovich-Danchenko's.

Mine gravitates towards almost entirely intrinsic work with the singer. In Nemirovich-Danchenko's studio this trend merges with the newest external forms of production. The two studios are in the formative period. Their financial resources are extremely limited.

They are not able, therefore, to pay the people concerned as much as they deserve. Unfortunately, this deprives us of the opportunity to approach men of Russian and foreign art who have earned recognition.

I have written everything that could be written in a letter on the matter you have raised. It grieves me that our terms are not likely to be acceptable for you. But if I were wrong, and you would wish to work with us in the said circumstances, I shall be only too pleased.

Thank you again for your attention.

Best wishes, and I ask you to give my greetings to all the actors of the German stage that still remember us.

TO THE COMPANY
OF THE STANISLAVSKY OPERA THEATRE

Nice, January 14, 1930

My dear friends and studio members,

To begin with, let me confess that I miss all of you very much. The last time I saw you was at the jubilee, nearly 14 months ago.

I begin by thanking you for your two collective letters.

I am writing to you to support you from afar. I know that you are having difficulties, but that is nothing; it is beneficial even. It is high time you learned to be independent, because I am getting old. My illness is the first warning, and so long as I can still help you, I want you to develop leaders. Send them to me for instruction and instil discipline, because your future depends on your unity and energy.

Answer me, do you believe that the groundwork and the principle of our theatre are right? Do you want to work along other principles? If so, our ways must part, for we will never achieve anything together. Do you believe that it is the creation of the singer and actor, based upon the organic laws of nature, truth and artistic beauty that produce the theatre needed by the people and by Russian art, rather than production, the fancies of the director and the observance of transient and fleeting fashions in our art? If you so believe, than cherish, strengthen, love, and protect the principles of your art.

Will our theatre have any meaning without them? Will it be needed? If not, then you will realise yourselves that its salvation lies in the principles upon which it is based.

If you believe in the principles of our art, if you consider them correct and do not want to work in any other way; if you have learned the methods of achieving your goal and if you do your work so as to be able to say: I have done everything I could, the rest is beyond my powers – if all this is so, then what makes you despair? Is it because you doubt success? I want you to remember that if you have put much love, integrity, knowledge and

Konstantin Stanislavsky and Vladimir Nemirovich-Danchenko with actors of the Moscow Art Theatre company. 1928

nature-given ability into your new productions, success is sure to come sooner or later. Therefore, cast all doubt away and advance directly towards your goal without hesitation.

Let me ask you one more question: are you sure luck has spoilt you? You have no reason to complain about us. Your theatre is in its fourth year, yet you have been noticed in Moscow and abroad. Many of you are already known actors. The theatre has good proceeds. No concert passes without someone from our company taking part. Is that not enough? Do not frighten fortune away, and be satisfied with the big things that it is giving you in these hard times for all mankind. You are lucky. You were born with a silver spoon in your mouth, compared to others. You have no right to lose heart, to be depressed.

Possibly, you are troubled by the future of our theatre. But let me tell you, in our age every person who wishes to live must, to some extent, be a hero. If you are strong, firm, united heroes, then you can rest assured that you are viable, will surmount all obstacles, that you will survive. If a boat is smashed by the first wave, instead of cutting that wave in order to advance, it is not seaworthy. You should realise that if your company is not strong enough and is smashed by the first wave, your cause is foredoomed.

So let mutual artistic and comradely contacts grow stronger. This is so very important that one should not shrink from sacrificing one's pride, one's whims, one's temper, one's particular friendships and all other things that cut the collective intelligence, will and dignity like a wedge, splitting them apart, demoralising them, and killing the whole. The main thing for you is to organise yourselves well, in which effort I shall help you with my advice.

I am tired now, and can dictate no more. But I will note down every day how I could be useful to you from afar to knit your company together and to develop an intrinsically conscious discipline in it.

With fond embraces and love,

K. Stanislavsky

TO LEONID LEONIDOV

Nice, February 10, 1930

My dear and kind Leonid Mironovich,

Forgive me for not writing myself, but dictating. This is because I have to write a lot these days – the *mise en scène* for *Othello,* on the one hand, and the book which I must complete at all costs before I leave, on the other. Furthermore, I have a big mail. All in all, I would never cope with all of it if I were to write it myself, bent over my desk. That is why I dictate lying down. That is quite an achievement, because in the past I could not even as much as think about the theatre or the productions, or to write letters without getting excited. That sort of work ended very quickly in heart palpitation, and in spastic strokes. You are absolutely right. I have received all your four letters. All of them are very interesting. Two of them I will use in the book. Yet I have not even thanked you and not even confirmed their receipt, let alone replied to them. That is not right, and I ask for forgiveness, for I deserve leniency. The fact is that, as I do the *mise en scène* for *Othello* I feel a constant contact with you, because in thinking about the play I keep thinking of you too. It was probably this feeling of association that produced my sense of serenity.

Thank you for your remarks concerning the impressions created by my *mise en scène.* I have taken them to heart and consider them important, because they not only encourage me and give me strength for further work (it is very difficult to *write* a *mise en scène* so far away from everybody, without seeing, and only imagining what it will be like). I am very glad that the young people and the directors are interested in my work. I have nothing against its being read to them, if you think it useful . . .

I am eager to arrive at the scene in which you think you have failed, but which, as far as I remember, pleased me during the trial run of *Othello.* There was no reciting then. I shall try and help you with advice.

Let us look into Othello's state of mind. He was indescribably happy with Desdemona. His honeymoon was a dream, the supreme rung of amorous passion. It is this supreme rung that is poorly conveyed in the interpretation of Othello. The author, too, has devoted little attention to it, and too little space. Yet it is important, because it has to show what Othello is losing, what he takes leave of in the scene you consider to be a failure. By its nature, the scene is a borderline scene. In it, and after it, Othello descends lower and lower. May we abandon the pleasure which he has derived and which he has taken to his heart? Is it easy to understand one's loss? Whenever a man survives the thing he lives for, he is stunned at first, losing his balance, and then begins a harrowing search. There was pleasure at first, but how to live on without it? In the sleepless nights the man in his crisis reviews all his life. He weeps over what he has lost, valuing it more highly still, and at once compares it with the future in store for him, a future moulded by his imagination.

What does a man need to perform this immense inner work? He must retire into himself in order to review the past or see his future. It is a moment of tremendous self-penetration, and it is not surprising, therefore, that a man in such a state does not notice what is going on around him, that he becomes absent-minded, somewhat strange, and that when he returns to normal he is gripped by terror and looks for a pretext to pour forth the bitterness and pain accumulated in the time of his self-absorption.

That, I believe, is the essence, approximately, of Othello's state in this scene. That, too, is the source for the sets. That is why Othello runs up to the top of the tower in this scene, and then races down to a cellar littered with arms and household utensils, hiding there from people to conceal his condition.

That is why the line in this scene, as I see it, should be as follows: he climbs the tower to brood on the words, "she deceived me!" I object to the words, "Aha, so she deceived me!" because there is a threatening undertone in them, while there is no threat at all in Othello's state. If I remember rightly, when I played this scene I replaced "Aha" with "How? How? She deceived me?" What does that mean? What does it mean if the word "me" is accentuated? It means: considering our love, considering the fact that I abandoned myself entirely to her, that I am prepared to make every sacrifice, she could have spoken those three words to me: "I love Cassio", and I would have done everything in my power to fulfil her wish, I would either have gone or I would have stayed beside her to protect her; but how could she repay this loyalty, this complete abandon by deceiving me on the sly, and doing it with such devilish cunning? She is the devil in the guise of an angel.

I claim that Othello was not a jealous man, though usually portrayed as such. It was Iago, not Othello, who was a petty jealous man. It develops – I see it now – that Iago is jealous of Emelia in a small and sordid way. Othello is unusually noble. He cannot live with the notion that people do each other injustice, that they ridicule and smear a noble love with impunity! And this is the guise of a perfect beauty, a near goddess or divine purity and virtue, of unearthly kindness and delicacy! All these qualities are so artfully imitated that they are not distinguishable from the real thing!

Going back to the scene, I claim that it is not jealousy, but a morbid disillusionment in an ideal woman and human being never before seen on earth. It is a supreme pain, an insufferable torture. Othello sits for hours, motionless, his eyes fixed in space, brooding, trying to understand this unutterable lie. This is why, when Iago creeps out cautiously from below, like a snake, unnoticed, and says, as a doctor would to his patient, with unusual tenderness: "Well, General, enough of that", Othello trembles from an anticipation of the pain this torturer can cause him.

When the doctor approaches with a big bougie to plunge it into the aching wound, the patient groans from the thought of the coming torture. Usually, the performers of Othello fly into a rage at this point. But in reality we are still dealing with harrowing pain. It is so painful that past deceits and past illusions of happiness seem happiness in this pre-operational minute. He compares this illusion of happiness with what has arrived, and begins to take leave of life. There are two passions in him – Desdemona and warcraft. He is like a great actor who shares his life between the woman he loves and his art.

Hence, "Farewell serenity, farewell", etc., is a parting, a lament, a lament of his second passion. It is not at all a scene in which he extols the soldiers' life, as it is usually played. I will applaude you most heartily when

Konstantin Stanislavsky and Leonid Leonidov. 1932

you assume a pose, motionless, oblivious of everything around you, and observe in your mind's eye the picture that is so endlessly dear to a true exponent of the art of war. Stop, wipe away the tears that roll down your cheeks, fight down your sobs, and speak in a barely audible whisper, as people speak about the things they cherish, that are important to them.

The monologue may be interrupted by pauses, during which he stands embattled, silent, seeing the picture of what he is going to lose. During other pauses he may bend over the stone and sob soundlessly, shaking, moving his head, as though taking farewell. That is not the trance of a war-like man, but a lament, a farewell to life. After this farewell breaks his heart, he feels he must take out his torment on someone. That is where he takes it out on Iago. After he seizes him and almost pushes him down the tower, he takes fright at what he has nearly done, and runs back to the big space of the flat stone, and drops upon it, shaken by soundless sobs. We see him higher up, like a child, in a child's pose, on the rock, begging forgiveness, pouring out his pain to Iago, who stands below him, and at the end of the scene, when it is almost dark, the moon rises and the stars twinkle. Standing on the upper platform of the rock, Othello calls to Iago, and there, high up, between the sky and the sea, insulted in his finest feelings, calling upon the rising moon and the stars to be his witnesses, he performs a frightening rite, swearing revenge...

Fond embraces, thank you, remember me in the future.

Yours,

K. Stanislavsky

TO MAX REINHARDT

Nice, May 24, 1930

Dear Friend,

How gladly would I participate in the celebration of the twenty-fifth anniversary of the Deutsches Theater and your brilliant guidance! But to my great chagrin, I am too ill to shake your hand in person. I can do no more than join the countless admirers of your genius in this modest letter, and applaud you from afar.

We often hear these days that Reinhardt has created a life's work – one of the finest theatres in the world. But it is probably still more important that he has brought to life a whole generation of spectators, of gifted and consummate actors and stage directors. You have given your contemporaries an endless number of unforgettable stage creations. You have developed excellent traditions. You have founded a great school, a veritable culture. Your extraordinary intuition enables you to discover new talent, new strength so essential for the stage.

You are an actor with a rare gift, who regrettably almost never appears before the delighted audience on the boards. You possess an absolutely exclusive gift for organisation, which has enabled you to create a great number of theatres.

One of your prime achievements is that during a world disaster you managed to preserve the culture you have created, and to pass it down to the succeeding younger generations.

You are a leader of genius who has done an invaluable service to the world theatre. I should like to add a few more words about the role that lies in store for you in the future. It was great in the past, and the future will make it still grander. The time is near when only excellent theatres will survive in the world. All the others, the insignificant and mediocre, will be crushed by the cinema, the cinema which, moreover, has recently begun to speak. But the perfect theatre requires brilliant leadership. That is a rarity.

K. S. Stanislavsky and Max Reinhardt. 1928

For this reason your importance in the future will continue to grow. I wish you, my dear Reinhardt, from the bottom of my heart, that the second half of your life yields you still greater successes than the first.

Your creative genius will help you to preserve the eternal traditions that feed genuine art, to discover and justify new laws that will in the immediate and the remote future stimulate a further development of our art.

I turn to your kind mediation, in order to convey the best of wishes to all the actors, directors and members of the Deutsches Theater.

In conclusion, I beg you to forgive the mistakes you will encounter in this letter. Unfortunately, my command of the German language is incomplete.

I embrace you with deep-felt friendliness,

K. Stanislavsky

TO MAXIM GORKY

Badenweiler, September 29, 1932

Dear Alexei Maximovich,

Forgive me for my belated congratulations on your fortieth anniversary as a writer.

The delay is due to the fact that I live in the backwoods and do not read the papers, while the Theatre informed me about it after the jubilee was over.

Please accept my sincerest congratulations.

I rejoice over the fact that our theatre, always an intimate witness of your brilliant 40-year-old literary career, will bear your name, crowning and cementing our friendship.

From now on we will work hand in hand to develop the Soviet theatre, which alone can support the theatre that is going under in the world.

I regret deeply that I was not with you in those festive days celebrated in Moscow. May distance not dampen the warmth of my greeting.

Shaking your hand, I beg you to convey my congratulations to all your family from the deeply faithful

K. Stanislavsky

A. M. Gorky. 1934

TO THE PEOPLE
AT THE BIRTHDAY CELEBRATION

Moscow, mid-January 1933

My illness prevents me today from joining all the people who wish to honour me on my seventieth birthday. I appreciate the honour and the kind feelings all the more, because I know from experience how difficult and bothersome it is to arrange celebrations. One of the reasons why I declined an official celebration was that I did not want to fatigue actors, already much harrassed by new public performances. But since you wished to gather today in spite of this, the celebration touches me still more deeply and doubles my gratitude to all the organisers and performers, to all its participants without exception, and to all the guests.

My first deep bow goes to them as a sign of profound, sincere and heartfelt gratitude.

One cannot in a short letter say everything one would wish to say to friends and colleagues in a personal conversation on this auspicious day of one's artistic career. So I will say no more than fits into the pages of a letter.

At this time, with heart and mind perturbed by historical developments, it is difficult to unite a large group of people with one common idea. We artists are lucky that way, because we are brought together by our art, which, at all times, grows ever more necessary for men's spiritual life. There is no other field with so many different opinions, viewpoints, ways, "systems", discoveries, differences, enmities and quarrels as there are in art. Yet those divide people. In spite of this, we are bound to each other. It may be said that at today's gathering my friends and colleagues, my pupils and people of like mind – all of us – are united by *Stanislavsky's "system"*. What system?

At present, this system has developed into an entirely different, new, often diametrically opposite system in each of the theatres that have grown out of the Art Theatre, and yet, in spite of this, we are not strangers and are brought together by a common element that unites and guides everybody in the realm of art.

What sort of link is it? It is a link that stems from a system, but not Stanislavsky's system – from a system of the greatest of artists, the "creative nature of man".

This nature and all its creative laws are the same for all men, all trends, for all schools of genuine art. With regard to these creative laws we are all kith and kin. Whenever we deal with a departure from nature into the domain of countless conventionalities, we become strangers and stop understanding each other.

I write all this to make our connection clearer, more lucid and definite. I did not devote my artistic career to creating a new art of my own invention. I devoted it, purely and simply, to a most thorough and painstaking investigation of the creative nature of actors in myself and in other actors, in my pupils, in amateurs, musicians and singers. My labours were not those of an inventor, but of an investigator. They have not been in vain. This gathering of my friends, colleagues, collaborators and pupils, united by a common faith in the "system" of the greatest of artists, man's creative nature, proves it. This creative nature is eternal, understood, and necessary for everybody who approaches art.

My second bow goes to my friends and to people of like mind as a mark of recognition for the idea in art common to all of us, and that unites us.

The theatre is in the throes of a crisis throughout the world. In our country, too, all is not well with art, but nevertheless, thanks to the concern shown by our government, art is advancing and not dying. When we think of the future and of our dangerous rival, the cinema, we perceive the unhappy fate that lies in store for all the bad theatres in the world. They will have to give up their place to the cinema, which has begun to speak too loudly.

For all this, I see a rosy future for the theatre. There will be fewer theatres, but those that survive will be splendid, imbued with genuine art, and genuine art springs from the laws of creative nature.

Those who study and follow these laws may rest assured that nothing imperils them, and that the flower of renewal awaits them. But those who have departed from nature should lose no time and return to it.

Human nature is infinite in its diversity, and therefore an endless number of trends and schools of art will burgeon upon its laws. So much the better. It is something we should welcome, because if all types of art would resemble each other like two drops of water, they would be boring, and there is nothing worse in the world than boring art.

So let everybody create as they wish, as well as they can, let them do what they want to do, let them draw rows of eyebrows and circles on their faces, provided everything they do is inwardly justified by the eternal and obligatory law of creative nature.

My third bow goes to those of our colleagues who are destined to perform the immense task of salvaging the art of the actor through a return to the eternally young and unwilting art of nature, that greatest of artists.

TO THE ART THEATRE CLOAK-ROOM ATTENDANTS

Moscow, January 23, 1933

Dear Friends,

You thought of me on the day of my seventieth birthday and sent me greetings that are so very dear to me. I was deeply and sincerely moved by them. You are our helpers in creating productions. Our Art Theatre differs from many other theatres in that its performance begins the very moment people enter the theatre building. You are the first to meet the entering spectators. You can prepare them in a favourable or unfavourable way for the impressions coming from the stage. If the spectator is annoyed he is unable to abandon himself to the impressions emanating from the stage. He becomes absent-minded and unreceptive. If, on the other hand, he at once feels that he is respected the moment he enters the theatre, he receives the performance quite differently.

That is why I consider your work extremely important, and I greet and thank you for your congratulations as collaborators in the production of plays.

Please accept my most sincere and heartfelt gratitude.

K. Stanislavsky

TO MAXIM GORKY

Moscow, February 10, 1933

Dear Alexei Maximovich,

I am bed-ridden as I write to you. After my jubilee (its celebration came as a surprise to me) I fell ill and could not reply to your splendid and wonderful letter until now.

I do not know how to reply to such wonderful letters. I have no words in my vocabulary to suit the occasion and I fear that my reply will appear colourless beside the address.

I would be excessively self-assured if I imputed the flattering, betimes exalted opinion you have of me to my own merits. Whatever is placed at my door should in all justice be shared with Vladimir Nemirovich-Danchenko and my friends, the "veterans", who have always worked by my side. One half of what goes to my share should be ascribed to your kind sentiments and to the transports typical of a great writer. It is these kind sentiments and these transports that I accept with gratitude and joy as the most valuable of all my birthday presents.

I have been lucky. My life arranged itself. I was a tool in its hands. But this luck obliges me to pass down what life has given me before I die. Yet it is very difficult to impart one's experience to others in so complex a process as the art of an actor. In one's personal intercourse with a pupil one can show, play, present things that are difficult to put into words. Presentation is the realm of the actor. But when I take up the pen words fail me to define emotions. Since we last saw each other in Capri, where you took the trouble to read my opening lines, my trials of the pen in writing something of a "grammar of dramatic art", I have been straining my intelligence to convey on paper in the clearest and most lucid way what a stage novice should know. A book like that is sorely needed, if only to silence all the misconceptions concerning the so-called "system", which, as it is now being taught, only warps young actors. Order must be put into the matter.

But apart from that, theatrical art, or more precisely, the art of acting, is fast going under. The giants of the stage, the craftsmen, are departing one by one, leaving behind nothing but the recollections of their contemporaries and a few second-rate photographs in Bakhrushin's Museum. That is the reason why I decided to put my experience on paper, and why I fear the task so. It is a job for a real writer. Yet writing about art "scientifically", as lawyers and legal advisers did once at the Literature and Art Group, is boring and pointless.

Help me in this work (thrice done already) with your wise advice and experience.

I am carried away and busy with matters related to the inauguration of the Academy.* Everything has to be built up from scratch, from the staff of instructors, of which there are none, to the general structure and the teaching methods. If I could only fling off about a dozen years and get rid of my continuous ailments. I need a warm climate to regain my health, but to live in a warm climate means giving up my work, and if one has to give up work there is no point in living.

Those are the questions that bother me now.

I embrace you and thank you once more sincerely from the bottom of my heart for your indulgence and encouragement. Hope we shall meet soon. Hearty greetings to all your family.

Fondly faithful,

K. Stanislavsky

* The reference is to a project which Stanislavsky did not realise.

TO THE MOSCOW ART THEATRE COMPANY

Nice, October 20, 1933

Congratulations on the thirty-fifth anniversary of the by no means simple, hard-fighting life of our dear theatre. In this life hours count for days, and days for years.

Events of world impact, wars and revolutions unknown heretofore in history, have taken place. The pillars of states, society, morals, religion, science and art were pulled down and built anew. Crowds of people of different generations, ages, nationalities, walks of life and cultures have come and gone. We toured the cities of our own country, of Europe and of America. We worked at factories, in villages, and in the front lines. There have been successes, ovations, defeats, recognition, attacks, triumphs, crises, and revivals. We sought, found, lost, and created anew. Some of us died, new faces appeared, studios and theatres were brought to life.

Through all these years and events the Art Theatre has steadfastly borne its credo and struggled for the eternal in art.

Today, the day of its thirty-fifth anniversary, the Moscow Art Theatre is alive, recognised and solicitously protected by the government.

Such, in brief, is the Art Theatre's history.

Let us rejoice, let us recall those who created, supported, helped and encouraged the theatre in its darkest hours. Let us thank those who recognised it, who saved it and who protect it today. Let us honour the memory of the dear people who have departed from us. Let us show concern for the old men who created the theatre, with Vladimir Nemirovich-Danchenko heading the list. Let us show our affection and concern for the middle-aged, for the young, for all the men and women associated with our theatre, for all who contribute to its prosperity and life, for all without exception.

Long live the Art Theatre. May it never grow old, may it always renew itself, may it always cherish its credo and seek the eternal in art!

Stanislavsky

TO ROMAIN ROLLAND

Moscow, June 29, 1935

To dear Romain Rolland, the wonderful writer, the outstanding humanitarian of our great epoch, the champion of mankind, heartfelt and joyous greetings.

People's Artiste of the R.S.F.S.R.

K. Stanislavsky

M. I. Kalinin presents an Order to K. S. Stanislavsky. 1933

TO MIKHAIL KALININ,

Chairman of the Presidium of the Supreme Soviet of the U.S.S.R.

Moscow, February 8, 1938

Dear Mikhail Ivanovich,

I am deeply touched and moved by the special solicitude heaped upon me by the Party and the Government, who commended my public activities so highly in connection with my 75th birthday.

I have received a tremendous number of congratulations, letters and telegrams from all parts of our boundless socialist country, the far-away austere North and the wonderful sunny South.

I attribute this large number of letters to just one thing: our people's great fondness for art. Is that not a miracle? Nowhere, in no other country in the world do people prize and treat man so solicitously as in our country, the U.S.S.R. Nowhere else does art enjoy as much attention as it does in our country. Where else will you find this thirst for knowledge, for real culture? Only in our country.

Life is thriving, art blooming richly in places where wasteland, impassable tundra and wilderness lay in tsarist Russia. They are also studying my system in all those places.

That is why I love my country. That is why I am proud of my country, the country where genuine theatrical art is studied not only by big stage directors and actors, but also by workers, collective farmers and schoolchildren, who beg and seek my advice.

Only embittered enemies and blind men do not see how much has been done in our country in these twenty years.

I want to live, to live and to create for the good of my great country. I want to shake off my 75 years and be young again.

I bow to you respectfully, and thank you heartily for everything.

NOTES

MAN AND ACTOR

P. 25

GORKY, Maxim (Alexei Maximovich Peshkov, 1868-1937)

Konstantin Stanislavsky and Maxim Gorky were friends of long standing. The Moscow Art Theatre produced many of Gorky's plays, *The Philistines, The Lower Depths, Children of the Sun, Enemies,* etc.

Extracts from Gorky's letters are taken from his *Complete Works,* in Russian (Vols. 28, 29 and 30).

P. 31

LUNACHARSKY, Anatoly (1875-1933)

Prominent public and political leader, writer, playwright, the First People's Commissar for Education of the R.S.F.S.R. His article, "Stanislavsky, the Theatre and the Revolution", appeared in *Izvestia* on January 18, 1933. Reproduced here from the book, *Lunacharsky on the Theatre,* Vol. 1, Iskustvo Publishers, Moscow, 1958; the first section is somewhat abridged.

P. 47

NEMIROVICH-DANCHENKO, Vladimir (1958-1943)

Man of the theatre, playwright, stage director, People's Artiste of the U.S.S.R. Founded the Moscow Art Theatre jointly with Konstantin Stanislavsky. Passages from his book, *Of the Past,* are taken from the Akademia Publishers edition, 1936. Passages from articles and letters are taken from V. I. Nemirovich-Danchenko, *Stage Legacy,* Vol. 1 (Articles, Speeches, Talks, Letters) and Vol. 2 (Selected Correspondence), Iskustvo Publishers, 1952 and 1954. His speech at Stanislavsky's funeral is reproduced from a transcript kept at the Moscow Art Theatre Museum.

P. 70

VAKHTANGOV, Yevgeny (1883-1922)

Moscow Art Theatre actor from 1911, actor and director of the Art Theatre's First Studio from 1913. The studio he established (now the Vakhtangov Theatre) was named the Art Theatre's Third Studio by permission of Stanislavsky and Nemirovich-Danchenko in 1920. Vakhtangov's letter is reprinted from *Yevgeny Vakhtangov,* (Materials and Articles), VTO Publishers, Moscow, 1959.

P. 74

MEYERHOLD, Vsevolod (1874-1940)

Actor, stage director, man of the theatre, People's Artiste of the R.S.F.S.R. Moscow Art Theatre actor from 1898 to 1902. In 1905 he headed the Studio in Povarskaya, founded by Stanislavsky. From 1938 director of the Stanislavsky Opera Theatre.

His letter to Stanislavsky is a reproduction of the original, kept in the Moscow Art Theatre Museum.

P. 76

EISENSTEIN, Sergei (1898-1948)

Film director, Merited Art Worker of the R.S.F.S.R., producer of the well-known films *Battleship Potemkin, Alexander Nevsky, Ivan the Terrible,* and others. Passages from his *Autobiographical Notes* are taken from the magazine *Iskustvo Kino,* No. 1, 1962.

P. 79

TAIROV, Alexander (1885-1950)

Stage director, People's Artiste of the R.S.F.S.R. Founder of the Moscow Kamerny Theatre, which he headed from 1913 to 1948.

The article, "Wherein His Genius?", appeared in the newspaper *Vechernaya Moskva,* January 17, 1933. Here reprinted from the newspaper.

P. 82

KNIPPER-CHEKHOVA, Olga (1870-1959)

Moscow Art Theatre actress from 1898, People's Artiste of the U.S.S.R. Her article is reprinted from the collection, *About Stanislavsky,* VTO Publishers, Moscow, 1948.

P. 93

KACHALOV, Vasily (1875-1948)

Moscow Art Theatre actor from 1900, People's Artiste of the U.S.S.R. The article, "Not a Single Grey Hair", appeared in the newspaper *Sovietskoye Iskustvo,* January 14, 1933. Reprinted from the book *V. I. Kachalov,* Iskustvo Publishers, Moscow, 1954.

P. 96

VERBITSKY, Vsevolod (1896-1951)

Moscow Art Theatre actor from 1916. People's Artiste of the R.S.F.S.R. His recollections are reprinted from the collection, *About Stanislavsky,* VTO Publishers, Moscow, 1948.

P. 100

TOPORKOV, Vasily (b. 1889)

Actor, teacher, People's Artiste of the U.S.S.R. Moscow Art Theatre actor from 1927.

His recollections are reprinted from the collection, *About Stanislavsky,* VTO Publishers, Moscow, 1948.

P. 109

KHMELYOV, Nikolai (1901-1945)

Actor, stage director, teacher, People's Artiste of the U.S.S.R., actor of the Art Theatre's Second Studio from 1919 to 1924 and of the Moscow Art Theatre from 1924. His letter is reprinted from the *Art Theatre Annual.*

P. 110

SAKHNOVSKY, Vasily (1886-1945)

Stage director, teacher, People's Artiste of the R.S.F.S.R., Moscow Art Theatre stage director from 1926.

His recollections are reprinted from *About Stanislavsky,* VTO Publishers, Moscow, 1948.

P. 118

KEDROV, Mikhail (b. 1893)

Actor, stage director, teacher, People's Artiste of the U.S.S.R. Actor of the Art Theatre's Second Studio from 1922 to 1924 and of the Moscow Art Theatre from 1924. His articles appeared as a brochure published by the Art Theatre Museum in 1940.

P. 126

OLESHA, Yuri (1899-1960)

Soviet writer and playwright. The Moscow Art Theatre produced his play, *Three Fat Men* (1930-61). His article, "A Great Man of the Theatre", appeared in the Leningrad journal *Iskustvo i Zhizn,* No. 9, 1938, and is a reprint from that journal.

P. 134

POPOV, Alexei (1892-1961)

Actor, stage director, teacher, People's Artiste of the U.S.S.R., Moscow Art Theatre actor from 1912 to 1918, actor and stage director of the Art Theatre's First Studio from

1913 to 1918. His memoirs, *Recollections and Ruminations,* appeared in instalments in the journal *Teatr* (Nos. 10, 11 and 12, 1959; Nos. 2, 3, 5, 6, 9, 10, 1960). Reproduced here is the chapter, "Stanislavsky's Demise. More About the Teacher".

P. 145

OBRAZTSOV, Sergei (b. 1901)

Actor of the Art Theatre's Musical Studio from 1922 to 1930. Founder and stage director of the Moscow Puppet Theatre. People's Artiste of the U.S.S.R. Reproduced here are passages from his book, *My Profession,* Iskustvo Publishers, Moscow, 1950.

P. 149

OKHLOPKOV, Nikolai (b. 1900)

Chief director of the Moscow Mayakovsky Theatre. People's Artiste of the U.S.S.R. Reproduced here are passages from his book, *To All the Young,* 1961.

STANISLAVSKY AND THE WORLD THEATRE

(ALL LETTERS ARE REPRODUCED
FROM ORIGINALS KEPT
AT THE MOSCOW ART THEATRE MUSEUM)

P. 157

ROSSI, Ernesto (1829-1896)

Italian tragedian, toured Russia many times.

P. 158

BARNAY, Ludwig (1842-1924)

German tragedian and man of the theatre, founder and head of the Berlin Theatre; toured Russia in 1896 and attended performances of the Art and Literature Society.

P. 160

AALBERG, Ida Emilie (1858-1915)

Finnish dramatic actress, toured Russia frequently. Attended a guest performance of Anton Chekhov's *Three Sisters* in Petersburg, in which Stanislavsky was cast as Vershinin and Knipper-Chekhova as Masha.

P. 161

DUSE, Eleonora (1858-1924)

Italian tragedienne, toured Russia frequently; she wrote the letter while in Moscow in 1908.

P. 162

KVAPIL, Jaroslav (1868-1950)

Czech writer, playwright, stage director of the Prague National Theatre; met Stanislavsky during the Art Theatre's foreign tour in 1906 and 1922.

Reprinted from Kvapil's memoirs, *Of What I Know,* Prague, 1932.

P. 165

DUNCAN, Isadora (1878-1927)

American dancer, creator of dances to music by Gluck, Beethoven, Tchaikovsky, etc.

For Stanislavsky on Duncan see *My Life in Art,* chapter titled "Duncan and Craig".

P. 166

CRAIG, Edward Gordon (b. 1872)

English stage director, designer and theorist; produced Shakespeare's *Hamlet* at the Moscow Art Theatre in collaboration with Stanislavsky in 1911.

Reproduced here is a fragment from Craig's letter to Stanislavsky.

P. 167

MAETERLINCK, Maurice (1862-1949)

Belgian symbolist writer and playwright. His plays, *The Blind, The Intruder, Interior* and *The Blue Bird* were produced by Stanislavsky at the Moscow Art Theatre. Stanislavsky tells of his meeting Maeterlinck in summer 1908 in his *My Life in Art* (chapter "A Visit to Maeterlinck"). In the postscript Maeterlinck thanks Stanislavsky for his permission to copy the sets of *The Blue Bird.* This relates to the Parisian production of *The Blue Bird* at the Théâtre Réjane on March 2, 1911.

P. 168

VERHAERN, Emile (1855-1916)

Belgian poet, playwright and critic. At the close of 1913 Verhaern visited Moscow and saw some of the Art Theatre performances.

The letters in this book are from Verhaern to Stanislavsky, reproduced from originals in French kept at the Moscow Art Theatre Museum. Also reproduced are fragments from Verhaern's article, "Memories of Moscow", which appeared in the newspaper *Ruskiye Vedomosti,* January 14, 1914.

P. 170

COPEAU, Jacques (1879-1949)

French stage director, actor, founder of the Vieux-Colombier Théâtre, 1913-24.

Presented in this book is Copeau's introduction to the first French edition of Stanislavsky's *My Life in Art,* 1934, abridged.

P. 174

ANTOINE, André (1858-1943)

French stage director, actor, theorist, founder of the Théâtre Libre (1887) and the Théâtre Antoine (1893). Head of the Théâtre de l'Odéon in Paris, 1906-14.

His article appeared first in Boris Grigorieff's *Visages de Russie,* Paris, 1923. Here abridged.

P. 179

BELASCO, David (1859-1931)

American stage director and playwright. Founded a theatre in New York in 1902, which still bears his name.

Stanislavsky met Belasco during the Moscow Art Theatre tour of the United States, 1923-24.

P. 181

REINHARDT, Max (1873-1943)

German actor, director, stage reformer; head of the Deutsches Theater in Berlin.

Here presented are Reinhardt's letter informing Stanislavsky that he was elected honorary member of the Deutsches Theater, 1928, and a telegram of congratulation on Stanislavsky's 70th birthday, January 17, 1933. The document referred to in the letter is a diploma conferring on Stanislavsky the title of Honorary Member of the Deutsches Theater, signed by Reinhardt.

P. 183

GÉMIER, Firmin (1865-1933)

French actor, director, man of the theatre, headed the Théâtre de l'Odéon. One of the founders of the International Union of Stage Workers.

Visited the U.S.S.R. in 1928 to study the Soviet theatre. While in Moscow, speaking about the modern theatre, Gémier said: "I must pay tribute to Stanislavsky's genius. A genius such as he knows neither grey hair, nor old age. Ardent greetings to the great artist." (*Rabis,* No. 15, 1928.)

P. 185

CLURMAN, Harold Edgar (b. 1901)

U.S. stage director, teacher, a leader of the Group Theatre in New York.

The extracts are from Clurman's books *The Fervent Years,* New York, 1947, and *Lies Like Truth,* New York, 1958.

P. 189

MEI LAN-FANG (1894-1961)

Chinese actor, public leader. His article appeared in the Chinese journal, *Wenhui pao*, here reprinted from the journal *Teatr*, No. 9, 1953.

P. 191

ROLLAND, Romain (1866-1944)

French writer, music critic, public leader. His letter is a reply to Stanislavsky's address on Rolland's 70th birthday.

P. 192

INTERNATIONAL PEACE CAMPAIGN

An early international peace organisation of a considerable number of national peace groups.

On the back of his letter Stanislavsky wrote:

"It is essential that the peoples of the world, by concerted efforts, create a great new human culture that should make war, which is hated by all, unnecessary, and for ever silence the guns."

P. 193

BRECHT, Bertolt (1898-1956)

German playwright, poet, publicist, stage director and theorist, founder and head of the Berliner Ensemble, winner of the Lenin International Peace Prize. His article is a reprint from *Theaterarbeit. 6 Aufführungen des Berliner Ensembles*, Dresden, 1952.

P. 195

WYSOCKA, Stanislawa (1878-1941)

Polish actress, stage director and teacher. Wysocka's memoirs appeared in the journal *Scena Polska*, Warsaw, Nos. 2 and 3, 1938. Here abridged.

P. 201

ZELWEROWICZ, Aleksander (1877-1955)

Polish actor and stage director; twice winner of the State Prize.

Zelwerowicz's memoirs appeared in the journal *Scena Polska*, Warsaw, Nos. 2 and 3, 1938.

P. 205

VILAR, Jean (b. 1912)

French actor and stage director; since 1951 head, director and actor of the National Popular Theatre in Paris.

Toured the Soviet Union twice. The excerpt is from Vilar's introduction to the French edition of Stanislavsky's *An Actor Prepares*, Paris, 1958.

P. 209

CHAPLIN, Charles Spencer (b. 1889)

Actor and film director. In 1954 he was conferred the International Peace Prize.

P. 210

DE SICA, Vittorio (b. 1901)

Screen and stage actor, film director, a leading exponent of Italian neo-realism. The excerpt is from de Sica's interview given in 1956.

P. 211

DE FILIPPO, Eduardo (b. 1900)

Italian playwright, stage director and actor, many years head of a theatre in Naples. In 1962 de Filippo's theatre toured the Soviet Union.

P. 212

STRASBERG, Lee (b. 1901)

U.S. stage director, theorist, teacher, a founder of New York's Group Theatre; founder and head of the Actors' Studio in New York.

The excerpts from Strasberg's article are from the anthology, *Actors on Acting,* New York, 1949, and from the *Saturday Review,* New York, No. 38, 1955.

P. 214

REDGRAVE, Sir Michael Soudamore (b. 1908)

English actor, stage director, created many Shakespearean characters, associated with Old Vic since 1936. The excerpts from Redgrave's article, "The Stanislavsky Myth", are from the anthology, *Actors on Acting*, New York, 1949.

P. 220

GIELGUD, Arthur John (b. 1904)

English actor, stage director, distinguished interpreter of Shakespearean and Chekhovian characters.

P. 226

LEWIS, Robert (b. 1909)

U.S. actor, stage director and teacher, a head of the Actors' Studio in New York, author of *Method or Madness?*, New York, 1958, on Stanislavsky's system and its application in the American theatre.

The fragments are from Lewis's introduction to Stanislavsky's book, *Creating a Role.* published in New York in 1961.

LETTERS

(REPRODUCED WITH ABRIDGEMENTS FROM THE 7TH AND 8TH VOLUMES OF STANISLAVSKY'S *COLLECTED WORKS*, ISKUSTVO PUBLISHERS, 1961)

P. 231

Lucien Besnard, French theatrical critic and playwright. In 1896 Besnard attended performances by the Art and Literature Society of A. Pisemsky's *Autocrats* and Shakespeare's *Othello* with Stanislavsky in the title role. Besnard wrote to Stanislavsky about the *Autocrats:*

"I was delighted by your play of yesterday. To begin with, my heart goes out to your big personal gift. Finally, the ensemble, the consummate skill of your interpretation, are deserving of the highest of praise for you and your friends."

In his comment on *Othello* Besnard found fault with Stanislavsky's partners, and rebuked Stanislavsky for departing from generally accepted tradition:

"The play is produced excellently, with perfection, superior to anything I have ever seen in France and Germany. But although you have grasped Othello's innermost emotions, you did not play him in the Shakespearean tradition... Scores of times, as the play proceeded, your very interesting discoveries gave me joy, and yet I was grieved to see the nervous, much too present-day, much too 'untraditional' image of your character. I am sure that if you worked a bit with Irving or Salvini you would create an excellent Othello."

P. 236

Alexander Borodulin, a school-leaver who asked Stanislavsky in his letters to admit him to the Art Theatre company.

P. 238

Vera Kotlyarevskaya (Pushkareva) (died 1942). Actress of the Petersburg Alexandrinsky Theatre from 1898 to 1918.

P. 240

The reference is to Anton Chekhov's play, *The Cherry Orchard,* written specially for the Art Theatre. Stanislavsky received word of Chekhov's death while at Badenweiler on July 15, 1904, shortly before his departure with his sick mother to Contrexéville.

On July 7 Stanislavsky wrote to Maria Lilina:

"I am haunted by thoughts of Chekhov. I did not think that I was so deeply attached to him and that this would leave an aching void."

In his *My Life in Art* Stanislavsky wrote: "Chekhov died, but after his death he became even more beloved at home, in Europe and America... Chekhov is a landmark along the way paved in our art by Shakespeare, Molière, Luigi Riccoboni, the great Schröder, Pushkin, Gogol, Shchepkin, Griboyedov, Ostrovsky and Turgenev."

P. 245

Zinaida Sokolova (Alexeyeva) (1865-1950), Merited Artiste of the R.S.F.S.R., Stanislavsky's elder sister who started on her stage career with her brother in the amateur performances at the Alexeyev home. After 1919 she helped Stanislavsky in teaching his system and directing at his opera and opera-drama studios.

P. 247

"It seems to me that the way I deal with the *Karamazovs* (the reference is to Fyodor Dostoyevsky's *Karamazov Brothers*) will bring the actors closer to Stanislavsky's theory," Nemirovich-Danchenko wrote to Maria Lilina on September 9, 1916. "All the scenes and roles are first divided into units, or *wishes,* then translated into emotions, after which the circles are found. At first they memorise the units ("brackets"), then the words, etc.

"I believe that after this work very many will at once *come closer* to Stanislavsky. As for me, I am doing it sincerely and with conviction. Since I have probably failed to grasp everything, and still *do not accept* many things, though I understand them, I naturally do not conduct the rehearsal as precisely as Stanislavsky would, but trust that I am closer and *add* a few things of my own." *(Selected Correspondence.)*

P. 250

Stanislavsky was replying to a letter dated January 1, 1912, written in Meyerhold's hand and signed by Meyerhold and A. Golovin. "The rumour has spread here in Petersburg," the letter said, "that you are bearing the full weight of the agonising crisis in the struggle between two trends in the Moscow Art Theatre: the old, represented by a group of adherents of the naturalistic theatre, and the new, represented by yourself and the young people, who are looking for new ways in stage art. In your struggle we are with you."

P. 251

Sergei Balukhaty (1893-1946), literary critic, professor, Corresponding Member of the Academy of Sciences. While studying Chekhov and Gorky, Balukhaty showed an interest in Stanislavsky's direction and asked him for permission to use his book of *The Sea-Gull* for a comparative analysis of the productions by the Alexandrinsky and Art theatres.

P. 252

On April 8, 1926, Firmin Gémier sent Stanislavsky a copy of *Cahiérs du Théâtre,* published by the International Theatrical Society, and asked him to write an article for it, recalling that when they met in Paris Stanislavsky was favourably inclined towards the idea of an international union of art workers.

P. 254

From June 14, 1898, onward, the pupils of Stanislavsky and Nemirovich-Danchenko prepared with fiery enthusiasm in Pushkino, near Moscow, for the opening of the Moscow Art Theatre.

P. 255

Henri Barbusse (1873-1935). A festive function was held in Moscow on September 26, 1927, to honour the visiting French writer.

P. 256

Herbert Graf, senior director of the Breslau Opera House. In informing Stanislavsky how he produced operas, Graf wrote that he was deeply impressed by the performances of the theatre companies under A. Tairov and V. Meyerhold during their Vienna and Berlin tours, that he had undertaken new opera productions in the new style and would like to work at the Art Theatre "on the stage of the progressive artistic school".

P. 258

Eager to revive the opera, Stanislavsky headed first the Bolshoi Theatre Opera Studio and then the State Studio-Theatre and the State Opera Theatre (which now bears his name) from 1919 to the end of his life.

In 1941 the Stanislavsky Opera Theatre was incorporated with the Nemirovich-Danchenko Musical Theatre. The new company was named the Stanislavsky and Nemirovich-Danchenko Musical Theatre. Its repertoire features to this day two big productions by Stanislavsky – P. Tchaikovsky's *Yevgeny Onegin* (1922) and Rossini's *Barber of Seville* (1933).

P. 260

Leonid Leonidov (1873-1941). Moscow Art Theatre actor from 1903, People's Artiste of the U.S.S.R. Leonidov played Othello at the Art Theatre on March 14, 1930, according to Stanislavsky's plan.

In a letter to Golovin, the artist who designed the sets, Leonidov wrote: "Stanislavsky sent us his *mise en scène* from abroad. I think his work a masterpiece of directing."

P. 265

Max Reinhardt headed the finest drama theatre of Berlin, the Deutsches Theater, from 1905. The theatre was founded by Adolf L'Arronge (1883) and subsequently headed by Otto Brahm (1894-1904).

In 1905 Reinhardt founded a school to train young actors.

While an actor of the Deutsches Theater under Otto Brahm, Reinhardt tried his strength as a director at Berlin's artistic cabaret Schall und Rauch, which was reorganised in 1902 under his guidance into the Kleines Theater, with a new repertoire.

Reinhardt also headed the Kammerspiele, and, after 1903, the Neues Theater.

P. 268

In celebration of Maxim Gorky's 40th anniversary as writer and public leader the Presidium of the Central Executive Committee of the U.S.S.R. conferred his name on the Moscow Art Theatre on September 17, 1932.

P. 270

The celebration at the Moscow Theatrical Club of Stanislavsky's 70th birthday was one of many such functions held by theatrical groups throughout the Soviet Union. Stanislavsky listened to the broadcast of the Moscow Club celebration over the radio in his study.

P. 273

This letter chimes in with Stanislavsky's well-known phrase from *My Life in Art:* "The theatre begins in the cloak-room". These words illustrate Stanislavsky's sincere and profound respect for all people, even those with the most humble functions, associated with the theatre.

P. 274

This is a reply by Stanislavsky to Maxim Gorky's message of congratulation, of January 10, 1933. (See p. 28.) Stanislavsky saw Gorky on Capri in February 1911, and read to him the original notes for his book on the art of acting.

P. 276

Stanislavsky's address on the 35th anniversary of the Moscow Art Theatre was read at a jubilee gathering at the theatre on October 27, 1933, by Ivan Moskvin, People's Artiste of the U.S.S.R.

P. 277

Stanislavsky's message to Romain Rolland was published in *Sovietskoye Iskustvo,* June 29, 1935, on the French writer's arrival in Moscow.

P. 278

Stanislavsky was one of the first Soviet actors to be conferred the title of People's Artiste of the R.S.F.S.R. This was in 1923. In 1933 he was awarded the Order of the Red Banner, in 1936 the title of People's Artiste of the U.S.S.R. and in 1937 the Order of Lenin. On his 75th birthday Leontyevsky Lane, in Moscow, where Stanislavsky resided, was renamed Stanislavsky Street. A few republican theatres in the country took his name.

BIBLIOGRAPHY

THE WORKS OF KONSTANTIN STANISLAVSKY, VOLS. 1-8,
Iskustvo Publishers, Moscow,
1954-61 (in Russian).

Volume 1, *My Life in Art* (also Foreign Languages Publishing House, Moscow, in English).

Volume 2, *An Actor Prepares,* Part I, "The Creative Process of Emotion. The Diary of a Pupil", 1954.

Volume 3, *An Actor Prepares,* Part II, "The Creative Process of Impersonation. The Diary of a Pupil", 1955.

Volume 4, *Creating a Role. Materials for a Book,* 1957.

Volume 5, *Articles, Speeches, Notes, Diaries, Recollections, 1877-1917,* 1958.

Volume 6, *Articles, Speeches, Reviews, Notes, Recollections, 1917-1938,* 1959.

Volume 7, *Correspondence, 1886-1917,* 1960.

Volume 8, *Correspondence, 1918-1938,* 1961.

SINGLE PUBLICATIONS

My Life in Art, Iskustvo Publishers, Moscow, 1962 (9th edition), in Russian.

"The Sea-Gull" as produced by the Moscow Art Theatre. Stanislavsky's Directorial Script, Iskustvo Publishers, Leningrad–Moscow, 1938, in Russian.

Artistic Notes, 1877-1892, Moscow–Leningrad, 1938, in Russian.

Transcript of Talks at the Bolshoi Theatre Studio, 1918-1922, recorded by K. Antarova (3rd revised edition), Iskustvo Publishers, Moscow, 1952, in Russian.

Directorial Playbook of "Othello", Iskustvo Publishers, Moscow–Leningrad, 1945, in Russian.

Anton Chekhov at the Moscow Art Theatre, Art Theatre Museum publication, Moscow, 1947 (Library of the Moscow Art Theatre Annual), in Russian.

Ethics, Art Theatre Museum publication, Moscow, 1947 (Library of the Moscow Art Theatre Annual), Moscow, Iskustvo Publishers, 1962 (3rd edition), in Russian.

Director's Script of Maxim Gorky's *The Lower Depths,* Moscow Art Theatre Annual, Vol. 1, 1945, Iskustvo Publishers, Moscow, 1938, in Russian.

Articles, Speeches, Conversations and Letters, Iskustvo Publishers, 1953, in Russian.

Director's Script of the Mass Scene from Alexei Tolstoi's Tragedy, *The Death of Ivan the Terrible,* as produced by the Art Theatre. From *Stanislavsky. Materials, Letters, Investigations,* Moscow, 1955, in Russian.

Director's Script of Erckmann-Chatrian's Drama, *The Polish Jew.* From *Stanislavsky. Materials, Letters, Investigations,* Moscow, 1955, in Russian.

TO THE READER

Progress Publishers would be glad to have your opinion of this book, its translation and design and any suggestions you may have for future publications.

Please send them to 21, Zubovsky Boulevard, Moscow, U.S.S.R.

КОНСТАНТИН СТАНИСЛАВСКИЙ
1863—1963
(Воспоминания и письма)
На английском языке

Printed in the Union of Soviet Socialist Republics